Everyone wants a taste of the many connections the rich have to offer. Now with the know-how of Ginie Sayles, you can meet and greet the ones who have tasted success—and can bring you closer to your own dreams of wealth, security and love.

- Penetrate the "rich mystique"

- Increase your "market value" to rich clients

- How to dress and how to shop

- Social conversation techniques

- The six different kinds of rich

- Dating and relating

- Finding a "marriage-prone" relationship

Berkley Books by Ginie Sayles

HOW TO MARRY THE RICH
HOW TO MEET THE RICH

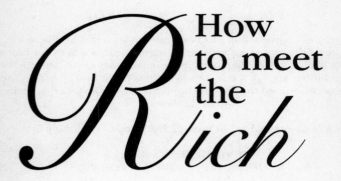

How to meet the *Rich*

*For Business,
Friendship, or
Romance*

GINIE SAYLES

BERKLEY BOOKS, NEW YORK

This book is an original publication of The Berkley Publishing Group.

HOW TO MEET THE RICH:
FOR BUSINESS, FRIENDSHIP, OR ROMANCE

A Berkley Book / published by arrangement with
the author

PRINTING HISTORY
Berkley trade paperback edition / April 1999

The Penguin Putnam Inc. World Wide Web site address is
http://www.penguinputnam.com

ISBN: 0-425-16685-6

BERKLEY®
Berkley Books are published by The Berkley Publishing Group,
a member of Penguin Putnam Inc.,
375 Hudson Street, New York, New York 10014.
BERKLEY and the "B" design
are trademarks belonging to Berkley Publishing Corporation.

PRINTED IN THE UNITED STATES OF AMERICA

10 9 8 7 6 5 4 3 2 1

I dedicate this book to our daughter,
Audrei—
Your life has been a gift to us.
We love you.

In Memory
During the time I worked on this book, I lost dear
and precious loved ones:
    My beloved father, T. R. Blackie Morris
    My dear aunt, Mertie Jane Barker Moncrief
    My good friend, Morris Cannan

And to my brother, Charles Edward Lefty Morris,
Atty., whose valiant struggle to hold on to life has
been heroic. You have made life better for so many,
Lefty, and in doing so, you have made your own life
outstanding. You have always been my hero.

$\mathcal{A}$cknowledgments

Thank you to God, and to my loving husband, Reed Sayles, and my mother, Vera Barker Morris, for their supportiveness, and to everyone who said prayers on behalf of my efforts.

VERY SPECIAL THANKS TO: My editor, Denise Silvestro. Your kindness and helpfulness have meant more than you can possibly know.

Additional thanks to: Harvey Klinger for your talent, to Judy Margolin for your intelligent legal mind and your caring manner, to Martha Bushko for a lot of sweet help, and to Neisha Cohen for remembering me and for your encouraging words.

Love to Austin Scott, Grant Scott, and Brent Scott; to my sister-in-law, Judy Morris, nephew Mark Morris, and niece Manda Morris; and to special friends, Pat and Robin Merendino from the former Mayfair Hotel and Pietro Romani at the Michelangelo Hotel.

For kind words and deeds regarding my work, thanks to Vessa Rhinehart, Louis Alvarez, Andy Kohler, Toby Berlin, Ira Strait, Alexis Quinlan, Sam Bickley, Lucy Broadbent, Kerry McKenna, Belinda Jones, and Earnest Winborne.

Additional acknowledgments to Liz Perl and the publicity staff at Berkley Books, including Hillary Schupf; the terrific sales staff and distributors; and Maureen Raspa in accounting. And to public libraries around the country, *The American*

Heritage Dictionary, Reflections, Quotes of Great Women, USA Today, A&E's *Biography,* PBS biographical productions, *Town & Country* magazine, Zig Ziglar, Conrad Hilton, John Paul Getty, Helen Gurley Brown, Thomas J. Stanley, William D. Danko, Letitia Baldridge, Susan Sommers, Teri Seidman, Sherry Suib Cohen, Alan Flusser, John T. Malloy, and Arnold S. Goldstein, all of whose multiple works have been great resources. Also, certain chapters from my own books, *How to Win Pageants, The Seduction Mystique,* and *How to Marry the Rich,* have provided resource material for this book.

Contents

Part 3
SOCIALIZING WITH THE RICH

Part 4
ROMANCING THE RICH

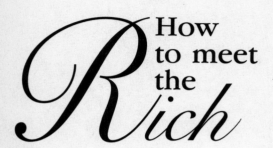

How
to meet
the
Rich

Part 1

The Rich Mystique

$\mathcal{Y}$ou and the Rich

"Richness rubs off on you."

—Ginie Sayles

Chances are, if you are reading this book, you are either already Rich, or you have a better than average chance of becoming Rich. In my thirteen years as a consultant about the Rich, the majority of my clients have had money. The Rich it seems, have an infinite interest in other Rich people—in doing business with them, in socializing with them, and in marrying them.

But why, you may ask, would the Rich need a book that tells how to meet other Rich? Wouldn't they have this information, already?

Not really. They have certain advantages, yes; but they are just as mystified by the Rich, and because there are so many different types of Rich (as you'll learn later in the book), they are often just as unsure of how to dress, talk, and behave around other Rich.

If you are not yet Rich, I say you are on your way. You are obviously fascinated by the Rich and are making an effort to meet them. Once you do, it's only a matter of time before you have money yourself. **Richness rubs off**.

REASONS TO GET INVOLVED WITH THE RICH

When you associate with the Rich—whether for business, friendship, or romance—you make contact with the very people most able to help you attain your dreams.

Business Reasons

• You may be looking for backers for an invention or for a business of your own.

• You may work on commission and would benefit from having Rich clients who can pay sizable sums.

• You may offer products or services that are best suited for Rich clients.

Social Reasons

• You want your children to have upper-class educational and social opportunities you never had. This is your chance to open doors for your children.

• You are making more money now and your old friends can not keep up with you. Although you want to keep your old friends, you also want new ones who can afford activities you can now afford.

• You grew up Rich but are new to a community. You have some contacts from your family and friends back home, but you want to develop additional ones.

• You are the "wind-beneath-the-wings" support system to your spouse and want to create business opportunities for both of you through advantageous friendships.

Romantic Reasons

• You are newly Rich and want to marry someone in the same financial bracket.

• You associate with the Rich—for business or social reasons—and find yourself attracted to the Rich lifestyle and want to become a part of it.

The Rich Can Make You Rich

There are lawyers, accountants, plastic surgeons, physicians, and dentists whose talents came to the attention of the Rich; these professionals cultivated the silk stocking trade, and went from having Rich clients to being Rich themselves. There are chauffeurs of the Rich who eventually went into the transportation industry—developing a fleet of limousine services, shuttle services, bus lines, hotel-to-airline services, etc. There are maids to the Rich whose work was so diligent and efficient that they now have their own maid services that were financed by their former Rich employers.

During the depression, Conrad Hilton had to borrow money from one of his bellboys. The bellboy also took a cut in pay and worked hard to help Hilton through the crisis. Afterward, Hilton made him a manager, then gave him ownership in certain profitable Hilton hotels.

James is a hairdresser whose talent, hard work, and personality thrilled his affluent clientele. Word got out and he ended up with salon chains and became famous as a stylist to the Rich and famous. Michael, a chef who started working as a cook in the home of a wealthy business executive ended up with restaurants, television cooking shows, and glossy full-color cookbooks and cooking videos.

There are artists, singers, dancers, even psychics who have attained a place in the world because of a Rich benefactor. And there are playwrights and authors who could never have made it without the support of a Rich spouse.

Even actors and politicians have been sponsored to fame and fortune by admirers who were Rich. Movie star Clark Gable supposedly had a wealthy, older wife who helped him become a star. Prime minister of England Benjamin Disraeli married a wealthy, older widow who had the political connections to help him achieve his ambitions.

Tyrone is a tailor who ended up with his own line of clothing because the Rich noticed his eye for style and perfection with a

needle. Jeff is a stockbroker who ended up with his own brokerage firm because of his success in handling investments for a
specific Rich client, who got his Rich friends to put up money,
too. Sarah, an architect, socialized her way to the top of society
in a major city and cultivated the clientele for her unique building designs. Betsy is a waitress who—on a dare—became involved in society activities and met a Rich man who married her.

What did all these people have in common? They *associated*
with the Rich.

• They deliberately put themselves in positions to meet the
Rich.

• They kept their talents exposed to the Rich.

• They made sure the Rich were aware of their stability and
dependable and honest character.

• The Rich made these people Rich, too.

$\mathcal{T}$he Fourteen Layers of Class

> *"Money and Class are not the same thing."*
>
> —*Ginie Sayles*

People are grouped together in a social class according to many things they have in common, including money. Typically, the three classifications are upper class, middle class, and lower class. The middle class is a working class, which includes white collar professionals to many types of blue collar workers—all of whom support our country with the broadest tax base and a good standard of living. The lower class is made up of transient workers, welfare recipients, and those whose poverty keeps them below a decent standard of living.

But in this book, when I use the word "Class," I'm referring to behaviors and traits associated with the upper class—an accumulation of qualities, a layering of experiences, habits, and traits that create the "texture" of a Rich lifestyle. Throughout the book, I capitalize Class and Rich to represent those behaviors and traits.

Most people think all the Rich are basically the same. They lump "the Rich" into one generic mass, and think all Rich people know one another and socialize together. But, out of six Rich people in the same neighborhood, each having seventy-five million dollars, only two of them might socialize with each other. They may have only a nodding acquaintance or no acquaintance with the other four. And they may look down their noses on some of them.

The truth is, two people can have the same amount of money and not be in the same Class. Relationships among the Rich are based on how many traits—what I call "layers of Class"—people have in common. And having certain layers of Class in common can even override differences in wealth.

It may sound a bit confusing, but the best thing about this is that most layers of Class can be *learned*.

$\mathscr{T}$HE 14 LAYERS OF CLASS

There are fourteen layers of Class and just knowing the layers will be invaluable as you associate with the Rich. When you meet people with money, you will understand their modes and codes of life according to the layers of Class they project and you can apply your business goals or social goals in ways they understand.

The first three layers of Class listed require money. But if you don't have money, you can still have Class if you acquire at least ten layers out of the fourteen.

Class Layer One—Wealth

Many people use the terms "affluence" and "Rich" interchangeably, but there is a difference. According to the U.S. Census statistics, affluence begins with seventy-five thousand dollars. But in the real world of money, affluence begins with a quarter of a million dollars, while Rich begins with one million dollars. And in the world of billionaires, a millionaire is merely affluent. It depends somewhat on your financial perspective.

But, whether you are affluent or Rich, *money and Class are not the same thing*. You could win the lottery today and change financial class, but you would not automatically have acquired Class.

Money only gives you one out of fourteen layers of Class. If you meet someone who is a billionaire but who has none of the other layers of Class, and if you have all the other layers of class but no money, then *you* have more Class than the billionaire.

How You Can Develop the Money Layer of Class. You could win the lottery, come into a huge inheritance, marry well, or employ various questionable methods, but I think the most acceptable way to get money is to earn it.

Class Layer Two—Lineage

"Old money" means a family has been Rich for more than a hundred years. Since a generation is forty years, it takes three generations—which adds up to one hundred twenty years—for a family fortune to be considered old money. Real lineage, however, begins with fourth-generation old money, because the founder of the fortune passed away before the current generation was born (or while they were young).

If money had been in your family for four generations but ended with you, you still have lineage (but it will end with you, unless you restore the fortune).

If you have little money, but you are blood-related to current, reigning royalty (certifiably), you have a degree of lineage.

If you are closely related to a past or recent celebrity, you have a touch of lineage called "reflected glory."

How You Can Develop the Lineage Layer of Class. Unless you are fourth generation, there are only two ways to get lineage: being adopted by vintage money or marrying into it.

Class Layer Three—Memberships

Memberships are the most Class-conscious layer of all. And memberships can be very exclusive, because they are created as a social domain of equals—people who are alike in their layers of Class. Money cannot help you here if you do not have the other Class layers in common with the members.

Money is required, yes, because the memberships are expensive; but just as often, you must also have a similar educational background or level of community standing. Some memberships even require your father, brother, sister, mother, or a grandparent to have been a member, but those clubs are, thankfully, rare.

Exclusive memberships can include everything from country clubs to yacht clubs or hobby clubs or school clubs.

Some clubs retain their exclusivity by requiring you to be

sponsored for membership by one or more existing members
and a vote of approval by the board.

How You Can Develop the Membership Layer of Class.
Connections are the key to most memberships, and connections
are friendships you develop with the Rich through business, education, or social situations. When you become a member of one
prestigious club, you will find opportunities to join others.

There are some memberships you may never attain, but your
best shot for breaking through the barriers of exclusive memberships is to acquire the other layers of Class that follow.

Class Layer Four—Education

The quickest way to cut across Class lines is through education. If you went to school on academic scholarships, you have
a strong layer of Class, with or without money. This can be com-
pounded if you have studied abroad or have been awarded fel-
lowships, such as a Fulbright or Rhodes Scholarship.

Academic achievement is respected and rewarded among the
upper classes, so the layer of education is more important than
money when the Rich evaluate you. However, there are individuals who have acquired so many of the other layers of Class that
the lack of this particular layer is not even considered. One no-
table figure who did not have a college education was the late
and much loved Princess of Wales, Diana Spencer. However,
Princess Diana had all the other Class layers, including the layers
of lineage and money.

Most upper-class high schools, colleges, and universities
stress a liberal arts curriculum. A liberal arts education gives a
broad understanding of many subjects, emphasizing the human-
ities.

Private schools are usually considered the best source of education—and Ivy League schools are the most elite of private
schools. A person makes contacts and connections through Rich
private schools that can be valuable for life.

I know a Rich man who was terribly poor when he was a
child.

"Ginie," he said, "the day I was graduated from Harvard Law
School, I knew I had it made. Not from the education itself,

because I never practiced law, but I made my fortune from the connections I made at Harvard."

There are a few public schools with just as much clout for making the "right connections" as private schools. Beverly Hills High School in Los Angeles and Highland Park High School in Dallas, Texas, are two public schools on the high school level that equal a private school in prestige.

Most state universities (that bear the name of the state—such as University of Georgia, University of Wisconsin) have a nice crop of students from the upper classes mixed into their majority of regular coeds. Such state universities develop reputations for outstanding "departments"—the music department, say, or the journalism department—that attract Rich students.

How You Can Develop the Education Layer of Class. You may not have an equal bank account or an equal lineage or equal access to exclusive memberships, but you *can* have equal knowledge.

Oh, some may think an education from a public school is inferior to one from an expensive private institution, but this is not necessarily true. After all, if you read the same books and study the same information, and if you apply your own intelligence rather than rely solely on the credentials of professors, then your education is within the same realm.

Education is something you have control over. If you do not have a lot of the other layers of Class, the educational layer adds immeasurably to you. And you can pursue an education no matter what your age.

Class Layer Five—Arts

One of the perks of being involved in the arts is that it provides an excuse to socialize with others. Through fund-raising events or opening night galas, you have a reason to dress up in your finest, don your best jewels (faux or fine), and move through a roomful of donors with a drink in your hand and make light, breezy chitchat about the arts.

There are basically three types of people involved in the arts: patrons, artists, and appreciators. Patrons are usually Rich and they are the backbone of the arts. They are the ones who donate large sums of money to keep the arts alive for present and future generations. They do this by underwriting a production (paying for it) and by becoming financial donors. And, yes, they do benefit from it with recognition—and also with a tax write-off.

Artists, themselves, have a certain cachet with the Rich, as well. Anyone with exceptional talent will fascinate Rich patrons. Often the Rich will invite them for weekends in their country home or to parties and dinners. Sometimes the artist is invited as a "breath of fresh air" personality to parties; but just as often, true and lasting friendships develop, based on the love of the art.

Even minor artists or performers in a production can meet the Rich through opening night or cast parties hosted by a patron.

You may not be an artist or a patron, but you can discuss and enjoy the arts as an equal with patrons if you are an authentic appreciator. Opera, theater, dance, literature, music, sculpture, painting, historical architecture and archaeology are just some of the arts you can learn to enjoy.

How You Can Develop the Arts Layer of Class.   Like all of us, you most appreciate what is *familiar* to you. If you grew up in the French Quarter of New Orleans, your soul moves to the rhythm of Dixieland jazz. If you grew up listening to bagpipes, you are stirred to tears by their beauty. If you grew up dancing at country-western hoedowns, you love every toe-tapping beat of C-W. If you grew up studying classical piano, you pause when you hear distant strains of a Chopin étude.

In order to cultivate a genuine appreciation of new art forms, you must create a *new familiarity* with them. You do that if you buy a CD or tape of, say, the great operatic arias, and play it over and over as soft background in your car and at home.

At first, it may sound strange, even ugly, but keep playing the same music every day, for three or more weeks. Then, one day, the magic happens. You are brushing your teeth or waiting at a red light and suddenly the very sounds that were alien to you weeks ago now thrill your soul.

At that moment, a composer who may have died two hundred years ago, or longer, has *communicated* with you. You feel it, you hear it, you understand it . . . and for the first time, you love it.

Why? Because you have become familiar with it.

Class Layer Six—Social Savvy

The Social Rich are those who get involved in life on a grand scale, cultivating many friendships along the way—for they know that socializing is about people. They experience many people in a variety of social settings. You can see many of the Social Rich in pictures splashed across the society page each day.

And the Social Rich work hard at helping others in the process. They believe that extravagant parties are justified if a charity benefits from it. They have a term for it: *noblesse oblige*, which means "nobility has an obligation" to help the less privileged. I am afraid they take the liberty of defining nobility as the financial elite.

Still, I have to admit, those who have this layer of Class know how to act appropriately in practically every situation. They are gracious, personable, and when they converse with you, they make you feel as if what you have to say is the most important thing in the world. They throw the best parties and are the guests everyone wants to invite. They've got social savvy.

How You Can Develop the Social Layer of Class. You will be okay socially if you learn how to introduce yourself and others; not to hang back by yourself or to linger too long in one group of conversation; to limit your drinking at any social; and never to be the first to arrive or the last to leave. You can learn the specifics of these behaviors from a wealth of wonderful etiquette books on the market, or from the chapter "How to Have Class and Good Manners" from my book *How to Marry the Rich,* which deals specifically with occasions when you socialize with the Rich.

Be sure to learn society's "debt" system. If you accept an invitation, you are indebted to return the courtesy by hosting an event. For all its smiles and glitter and lighthearted banter, socializing is not free.

The only exception to this are "goodwill" parties given by a company to clients or by the CEO to the office en masse. You have no obligation to reciprocate these.

But if the CEO and spouse invite you to a non-business private dinner and you accept (which you had better do), you incur a social debt. Such an invitation implies that you have been accepted socially, and you are expected to reciprocate.

Learn to reciprocate with ease and simplicity. Give a brunch, an afternoon tea, a cocktail party, and a formal dinner and you will have the basic social skills that you need in order to shine (See Chapter 23).

Class Layer Seven—Political Clout

Those who have this layer of Class have influence on policy makers. They may be involved in everything from local offices, such as mayor or council seats, to state and national elections. They may occasionally run for office, but mostly they serve on important committees and are known as "the powers behind the throne."

People with political clout can make things happen. Sometimes it's their money that gives them clout; other times it's their influence over others—power begets power. However they attain their political clout, these people are great allies to have. They can be invaluable in helping you obtain your goals.

One year, I worked on a Kennedy Memorial publicity committee in Dallas. The committee was made up of a future gubernatorial candidate, a bright woman scientist, and an owner of television stations and newspapers. The president of a major publicity firm chaired our group. Two of these people later became valuable contacts for my own goals.

How You Can Develop the Political Layer of Class. If you want to cultivate political clout and you have no money, do the following:

   • Rent from a mail service a *street address*—not a box number—in an affluent neighborhood. This gives you access to membership in the more affluent chapters of political organizations.

• Telephone your political party of choice and ask for the chapter in that area. Give your new address for the mailing list.

• Go to the meetings of your new Rich neighborhood chapter. If you are willing to work hard as a political volunteer on committees, you can meet people who can be advantageous to your goals.

The debt system applies here, too. If you call upon the Rich for a political favor and they do it, it is automatically expected that if they later call upon you, you are obligated to return the favor. If you do not do so, you can expect nothing further from them. If you say you will do something and then don't follow through, you are persona non grata and will be politely ignored and left out.

Class Layer Eight—Travel Sophistication

Ease among many cultures is the trademark of this Class layer. The credo of sophisticated travelers is that your home is wherever you are. This means that you can easily adapt to the customs of the land you are visiting, without comparing them negatively to the way you do things "back home."

Rich Hot Spots

Rich hot spots are often in primitive cultures, unspoiled by tourism. Quaint fishing villages with native marketplaces are popular with the Rich.

As word gets out that the Rich vacation there, people who are not Rich begin flocking there—simply because the Rich do. As these quaint and primitive places experience a boom, big business comes in with real estate development, and an economy of tourism destroys the originality of the culture. *When that happens, the Rich change destinations.*

Not all Rich retreats are primitive. Country villages in the south of France and northern Italy are not primitive but they offer charm in simple, natural beauty less touched by tourism, and unique regional foods.

Some Rich hot spots are very touristy, such as Paris or Amsterdam, Monte Carlo or Hong Kong—cities that provide first-class amenities, glamorous nightlife, top-flight entertainment, and lavish cuisine.

Chic travel spots change about every three years, but if you have a travel agent from an organization that deals with upper-class clients, you will be able to keep up with such changes.

How You Can Develop the Travel Layer of Class. If you are under thirty-five, try a brief stint in jobs abroad. If you are in your teens or early twenties, exchange student programs can be a great way to attain this layer of Class.

If you are entrenched in a career, however, or have marriage or family obligations that keep you near the home fires, you still can add this layer of Class by making travel a priority in your budgeting.

To develop the travel layer of Class, your first foreign trips should be to the "classics"—London, Paris, Monte Carlo, Venice, Rome, and Amsterdam. Subsequent trips should expand your European grasp. Choose at least two of the following:

Edinburgh, Scotland
    Dublin, Ireland
Munich, Germany
    Vienna and Salzburg,
    Austria
Florence, Italy
    Athens, Corfu and
    Mykonos, Greece

Lisbon, Portugal and
    Madrid, Spain
Geneva, Gstaad, St.
    Moritz and Zurich,
    Switzerland

After the European enrichment, you can add the Pacific continents of Australia, New Zealand, Hong Kong, Tokyo, and our Hawaiian Islands. Visit Old Quebec City in Quebec, Canada, for French culture on our continent; and Nova Scotia for peaceful beauty and Scottish culture. British Columbia and Banff are also in beautiful Canada, which is magical in the summer months—especially June.

To follow the Rich in the United States, New York City is a must. If you can, try to experience the East Coast in autumn at least once; Charleston, South Carolina, in April; Scottsdale, Arizona, or the Florida Keys in January; coastal California and Napa Valley anytime.

Finally, short Caribbean cruises are affordable, today; but go on a major cruise line with a first-rate reputation. The Rich also like Mexico, Argentina, Brazil, and Costa Rica, which are full of colorful history, culture, and natural beauty. Bali, Viet Nam and Thailand are immensely popular with the Rich.

Although travel does cost money, there are ways to see the world without breaking the bank. Airlines offer some very good deals—check newspapers and the Internet for bargains. Perhaps you can't afford to fly first class or stay in a suite at the Ritz, but that's okay. What's important is experiencing new cultures, acquiring knowledge about other places, and developing travel sophistication.

Class Layer Nine—Sports

Sports is the one layer of Class where perspiration is worn with pride. It is believed that sports build character, therefore, the more difficult the sport, the better the character development.

Sports of Class include snow skiing, crew (rowing), tennis, squash, racquetball, lacrosse, polo, sailing regattas, soccer, rugby, field hockey, and mountain climbs. The more "social" sports of Class include equestrian competition, foxhunting, skeet shooting, golf, badminton, and croquet.

How You Can Develop the Sports Layer of Class. You only need to master one sport and to be a spectator of two other sports in order to genuinely acquire the sports layer of Class. As a spectator, learn enough to discuss what is happening intelligently or to place a few bets. Save money so you can enjoy first-class seating at events.

Sports of Class are expensive to play, but there are ways to get around heavy costs. Scour newspaper classified ads for used equipment in the brands you want. Shop for expensive sports equipment in discount athletic stores, wholesale shops, or during "after-season" sales. Practice the sport in a less expensive way—say playing tennis at the public courts—before showing off your stuff at a private club.

It's a smart idea to invest in some private lessons. Learning how to do something right the first time is better than having to correct the wrong methods you learn by trial and error or from an amateur. Lessons can often be taken at country clubs or private sports clubs where you are not a member. Call and ask to speak to the Pro. Lessons are usually reasonably priced.

However, to play sports with Class requires more than merely learning the skills of the game. The real distinguishing line of Class is if you follow these rules:

- Play hard—fully concentrate

- Don't complain

- Don't cheat

- Be modest when you win

- Give no excuses when you fail

- Shake hands with winning opponents: congratulate them and compliment their skill

- Never play a game you are not qualified to play

Class Layer Ten—Values

"People first" is the operative value of true Class. Human life is more important than money, and a person's feelings mean more than possessions.

You may have just broken a priceless Ming vase, but you won't know it when you are around the Rich with this layer of Class. They consider your feelings more valuable so they will quickly assure you that they had tired of the old thing and had been on the verge of replacing it, anyway, and you have simply done them a favor.

This layer of Class has another telltale value: appreciation for someone's time. "Time is the most valuable thing a person can give" is one of the mottos for this Class layer. If you give them a hand-wrapped gift, they will marvel at the beauty of your gift-wrapping. Having gingerly unwrapped the gift, in a show of respect for your labor, they lay the wrapping aside, carefully. When they see you have also given them a gift you made yourself, they will gasp and gaze at it in wonder, speaking first about the *time* you gave—making it clear that they value *your time* as the most important quality in the beauty of the work. Then, they will compliment the details of your workmanship, pointing out three or four specific details as being superb.

How You Can Develop the Value Layer of Class   Deep, deep reverence for human life is the wellspring for this considerate treatment of other people. I once met a Rich man from the Middle East whose gentleness fairly shone in his face. I asked why he left his country, and his words have stayed with me. "My countrymen were going to war against each other because of religious differences." He shook his head sadly and added, "To kill a man because he does not think the way I do, is insane. I could not stay."

Tolerance for differences, respect for life—values show in a person's unwillingness to hurt people, whether it is with a gun or a barbed comment or a haughty look of contempt at someone who has less money.

It is a matter of values for human life and human feelings, first.

Class Layer Eleven—Achievement

"If I were rich, I'd spend all my time in a Jacuzzi while one person gave me a manicure and another gave me a pedicure," one young woman said to me a few years ago.

I smiled, knowing she probably spoke from feeling a bit tired; but then I asked her, "How long would you do that?"

"Forever," she said and sighed.

I patted her on the arm, saying, "You would tire of it after a few hours. . . certainly after a day. And I really don't think you could keep doing it more than a week."

Her view that the Rich do nothing but indulge in luxurious personal attention is fairly common.

Yes, there are some people with money who have pursued ongoing sybaritic pleasures, and they ended up feeling purposeless and, lost, as if something were missing and they didn't have the foggiest notion what it was. This compounds into self-pitying misery, alleviated by prescription drugs, alcohol, and tragic death.

If you have not witnessed it yourself, view the video of *Reversal of Fortune*. It is a true story of a woman's life that was wasted in wealth. Fortunately, most of the Rich are not that way.

Just as philanthropy justifies having money, so achievement justifies existence. I call this the quest for relevance. The achievements of a parent or grandparent are not enough. The gifts you inherit from their achievements are only a launching pad for your own abilities.

How to Achieve the Achievement Layer of Class. To become an achiever, take inventory of the following:

- Your talents
- Your curiosities
- How you would like to be remembered

Talent is an ability that comes naturally to you and is easier for you than most people. It is a genetic inclination that can be developed into an outstanding achievement. Gloria Vanderbilt is a perfect example of an heiress who refused to limit herself only to a social role. She became a high achiever in art and business.

If you do not know what your talents are—and may even fear you have none—then make a list of your natural *curiosities*. What catches your interest? What sparks your imagination? Prioritize your list, then set about taking lessons and developing this area of interest on a regular basis for a minimum of two years. Commit to it. Do it. You can find a latent talent emerge.

Write the epitaph you would like inscribed on the hearts of people about your life—and the epitaph you would like inscribed on your family history for your achievement—*how you would like to be remembered.*

Review both every day as you work on developing your talents and you will discover yourself becoming a high achiever.

Class Layer Twelve—Hobbies

Hobbies are taken more seriously by the Rich than by any other social class, perhaps because hobbies are leisure interests and the Rich take leisure seriously.

Gardening is an all-time favorite hobby of the Rich. It can be a restful pastime or a true passion. It may be as simple as planting flowers for each season, or it may extend to having small or large hothouses constructed for special varieties. It can extend to the cultivation of a rare plant or include traveling to remote regions of the world to study a certain species.

Collecting is also a common pastime. Popular collectibles among the Rich include first edition hard-bound books, signed by the author (if possible); old maps; old linen; coins; stamps; porcelain (Chinese or Japanese or fifteenth-century Palissy); metalwork, such as pewter or brass; or the precious metals of silver (Revere Silver, for example), gold, or platinum.

Hobbies are even built around the preservation of "antique skills"—methods no longer used in a craft that will be lost if not handed down. If the Rich do not learn the skills themselves, they support those who do. Quilting; pottery; needlepoint; basketry; bead designs; and glass or stone designs to make lamps, windows, walkways, and such are highly regarded, as are native skills and arts. The Nantucket basket purse made by natives of Nantucket Island is a status symbol among Rich women on America's east coast.

There may be some overlap between collecting as a hobby and collecting as an investment. Similarly, there may be some overlap in refurbishing antique cars as a hobby and also as an investment.

You may become confused when you hear someone talk about boating as a "hobby." Instantly, you think of it as a sport. However, to the Rich, sports create physical and character fitness, whereas hobbies create intellectual and skill fitness. An activity is only a sport if it is intended as an athletic pursuit or if it is vigorously competitive. If it is a mere interest, approached with leisure, it is a hobby and not a sport. Fishing, target shooting, and skeet shooting can be considered hobbies or sports.

Painting and sculpture are also popular hobbies of the Rich, as are astronomy, playing a musical instrument, bird-watching, and floristry, which is a pastime that is altogether separate from gardening.

Many times, the hobbies of the Rich are helpful to science or government groups. For instance, bird-watchers may provide important data to scientific and government agencies.

How You Can Develop the Hobby Layer of Class. Study several pastimes that pique your curiosity, and choose one. Then, learn everything you can about it. Subscribe to at least one publication about it. Look up your new hobby interest in the *Directory of Associations* and write or call the various associations to get on their mailing lists. If you can afford to join an upscale chapter, do. If not, at least ask if you can visit a meeting with the possibility of joining.

Pursue, pursue, pursue your own personal development in this layer of Class. It creates friendships with many interesting, worthwhile people.

Class Layer Thirteen—Philanthropy

Giving is the way the Rich judge each other. It may be true that they are judged not by how much they have, but by how much they give; but I think they judge how much they have *by* how much they give.

And giving absolves guilt for being so Rich when so many people are not. So it is a nice system: the Rich justify their riches and get a tax deduction to boot (not to mention the recognition they get for it). And the "causes" do, indeed, benefit. Just as the Rich perpetuate the arts, they also expand the sciences through generous donations.

How You Can Develop the Philanthropy Layer of Class. There are two ways to give: anonymously and publicly. Try to do both.

You practically feel your soul grow when you give and absolutely nobody knows about it. Nobody. Not a family member, not someone at an organization. Nobody.

And, oddly, I find that when I help someone who does not like me, and that person never knows it and I never tell anyone,

I not only feel the growth of my own soul, but I literally see obstacles in my life melt away. It is as if this act of anonymously giving to a person who begrudges me something dissolves that person's power to hurt me, and it dissolves my resistance to that person, which in turn opens my heart to solutions. Try anonymous giving for yourself and see what happens.

However, in some cases, it can be beneficial for people to know about your philanthropic efforts. When I assigned my author's royalty on *How to Marry the Rich* to a scholarship for single parents, I wanted people to know I wouldn't make any money at all from the book. I wanted them to know that they become partners with me to help single parents get an education every time they buy a copy of the book.

It is my hope people will give the book to friends (even if just for fun) and make it a stocking stuffer during the holidays. In doing so, they will help single parents get a college education.

Where should you give money? Try to recall a period in your life when you needed help, find people who are in that position now, and give to a cause that benefits them. Because I had been a single mother who went through college on welfare and a student loan, I wanted very much to help other single parents— especially since my education has been so beneficial to me.

If you have not had a period of financial need in your life, consider giving to organizations that fight diseases that took the life of a family member.

Helping children, animals, or senior citizens can warm your spirit. Look through a directory of philanthropies in the public library and see if anything tugs at your heart.

Class Layer Fourteen—Manners and Self-Care

Self-care is really the fifteenth layer of Class, but I include it here with manners because the Rich with this layer of Class consider self-care to be an act of good manners. To them, it is rude to subject anyone to having to look at you if you are not clean, neat, and well groomed. Some people with this layer of Class would not dream of coming down to the breakfast table until fully dressed and perfectly groomed. It is considered the height of rudeness and disrespectful to others if you do so.

Self-care includes absolute, daily cleanliness, including bath, shampoo, skin care, nail care, elbows, knuckles, teeth, and breath, as well as spotlessly fresh clothing, well-fitted and properly worn.

And when we talk about manners, don't confuse them with mere etiquette. They are not the same thing, at all. Class manners embrace a whole attitude toward people that shows up in conversation, in behavior, in relationships. The way the Rich handle crisis or frustration, the way they employ snobbery as a protective device to distance people who are trying to use them, the way they handle service and sales people tells you the quality of Class manners a person has.

Manners are so important that a son's or daughter's marriage prospects come under close manners scrutiny by Rich parents. That a suitor has no money is not as important as whether or not his or her upbringing was coarse—with trashy fights at home, loud neighborhood brawls, screaming in the front yard, kicking in the wall in a fit of anger, abusive language, bragging, hitting children, neglected civic or social responsibilities, or wasteful spending—and the degree to which the suitor is still influenced by this background. The son or daughter may not mind some of the "manner-less" behaviors, may even be intrigued by them, but the parents will discourage a marriage if they know such tendencies exist.

The most definitive layer of Class is manners.

How You Can Develop the Manners Layer of Class. The basis of all good manners is to make other people comfortable, yet never to treat them as better than you or as less than you.

When you see people who speak in the same tone to the janitor of a building as they do to an executive in the same building, you see good manners. What they say to the executive may be on a different subject, but their tone and manner of talking to the executive is no different than it is for the janitor.

If you do not like the way a person behaves, you never correct them and you are never rude. You resort to a "distant friendliness."

You are not haughty at all to a person you dislike. In fact you speak and smile at the same level you would with your friends, but it does not quite reach your eyes. The person senses it but can't quite put a finger on it.

In all other respects, you have a simple, unaffected thoughtfulness of others. This is manners. And this is simply Class.

*Y*OU MAY BE RICHER THAN YOU THINK

Each layer of Class is like a layer of wealth. So how rich are you when it comes to Class? Tally it up—you may be richer than you think!

Adding Class in layers adds richness to you and therefore increases your "market value" to potential Rich clients, Rich friendships, and Rich mates. It is a personal Richness that is the equivalent of money, and it is a personal Richness that you can control.

Twenty Ways to Lose Class—Fast!

1. Flaunt large-vocabulary words (very second-rate)

2. Have trinkets dangling from your rearview mirror

3. Have strongly opinionated bumper stickers or T-shirts

4. Have chipped nail polish or uneven nail lengths

5. Chew gum or use a toothpick in public

6. Tell off someone in front of others

7. Slurp coffee or other drinks

8. Don't bathe daily

9. Wear terribly unmatched or wrinkled clothes

10. Constantly voice your opinions without reserve (twice a day is enough)

11. Wear clothes with shoddy buttonholes

12. Wear scuffed shoes

13. Have dirty fingernails, knuckles, or elbows

14. Talk loudly enough for people at the next table to hear you (on purpose)

15. Make a scene in public

16. Try to impress anyone!

17. Ridicule someone poorer than you

18. Act superior

19. Act inferior

20. Be antagonistic or rude to workers

Now that we've explored the Fourteen Layers of Class, you can see that the Rich are not a homogenous group. Different people have different layers of Class, which show up in different values, habits, and traits.

But you still may be asking, What are the Rich really like? What do their daily lives consist of? What do they wear around the house?

Come with me! I'm going to take you inside the estates, mansions and homes of six Rich families—and give you a rare glimpse into their external lives with six profiles of the Rich. You'll be meeting the *Old Money Pedigrees*, the *Flamboyant Old Money*, the *Status New Rich*, the *Practical New Rich*, the *Celebrity Rich*, and the *Roller-Coaster Rich*, I'll tell you about their careers, their marriages, their jewelry, and even their pets.

You'll see that although each is certifiably *Rich*, they're all quite different. And nowhere are the differences among the Rich more obvious than in the view each has about designer-label clothing. For this reason, I have begun each chapter with a quote that expresses how each type of Rich feels about designer clothes.

$\mathcal{O}$ld Money Pedigrees

"If it takes a designer's label on the front of my garments to let people know my clothes are expensive, then the quality is not good enough."

—Jonathan and Virginia Pedigree

Jonathan Pedigree IV grew up on his family estate, which was built by his grandfather, near Charlottesville, Virginia.

Every summer, his family spent two months in the mountains of France near Switzerland, where his father took him on vigorous mountain climbing expeditions (to build character), and one month sailing in Nova Scotia, on the Bay of Fundy. On winter holidays, the family went skiing in the Canadian Rockies.

As for social sport, Jonathan IV learned the tradition of riding to the hounds (foxhunting), and his father completed his training as a Virginia gentleman by teaching him, in depth, about thoroughbred horses and Southern politics.

His mother, on the other hand, oversaw his schoolwork, and exposed him to theater and charity obligations. She insisted he learn golf, and as he grew older, she involved him in investment art. On his own, Jonathan IV enjoyed history and tinkering with mechanical equipment.

Jonathan IV was taught that his family name was sacred and that guardianship of family money and family heritage was his first duty, above all else.

Preserving the traditions of his social Class was instilled in him—temperance in indulgence, sportsmanship in competition, discretion in relationships, honesty in business, and fairness to those dependent upon him. And from his parents, he absorbed the subtle manners that identify him as being from the Pedigree Class.

Education

After attending a private boarding school for boys, located in Woodberry, Virginia, Jonathan IV—like his father and grandfather before him—went to the prestigious University of the South, known as Sewanee, because it is located in Sewanee, Tennessee. There, he made average grades as he earned a degree in history.

During the summers, Jonathan IV and some of his fraternity brothers took jobs in Europe, working in luxury resorts and mastering the language of that country.

Marriage

After college, Jonathan IV married Virginia Lee Belle, a Richmond debutante, and enjoyed a two-month honeymoon abroad. They have two children, Jonathan V and Jenny. Over the years, their married life has evolved into an amiable sharing of some activities as well as democratic pursuits of separate interests.

Career

Jonathan IV's financial business is transacted each weekday morning between 5 and 10 A.M., when he consults with his wife and their investment advisors on commodity and stock investments. He keeps very close tabs on the international market and analyzes all important trends.

Every morning, he quickly scans three newspapers, including *The Wall Street Journal, The New York Times,* and *The Washington Post.* Once a week, he reads *Barron's* and the *Investment Times.* He may go on-line on his computer for market updates and stays available to his financial advisors by cell phone.

The rest of his day is given over to a casual and comfortable lifestyle and the enjoyment of his two great passions: philanthropy and refurbishing antique cars.

Once or twice a month, he attends board of directors meetings for a bank in Charlottesville and one in D.C., where he is a large stockholder.

Virginia has been a devotee of ballet since her own childhood ballet lessons. Because she sometimes underwrites entire ballet productions, a D.C. ballet company allows Virginia to live out her dream of working out with the ballet dancers twice a week.

She also spends a great deal of time interviewing the dancers for upcoming books, and in fact, Virginia has two books to her credit, and both are biographies of famous ballet dancers. Visiting ballet stars are frequent weekend guests at the Charlottesville house.

As demanding as her lifestyle is, Virginia schedules a weekly lunch with her daughter, Jenny, and also rides horses with her once a week.

PHILANTHROPY

Jonathan IV chairs the boards of two art societies and he is on the board of regents for Sewanee, where he also founded a sizable scholarship. In Charlottesville, he added a wing to a hospital and named it after his father; and he donates regularly to scientific research in heart disease, the disease that claimed his mother's life.

Virginia never misses opening night of the ballet company she helps sponsor. Virginia's charitable interests also include women's shelters, education programs for older women, and paying the costs of families who cannot afford to be close to a dying child.

HOBBIES

Gardening is Virginia's hobby. She plants flowers for each season, working alongside the yard person during planting and then carefully watching over her fledgling plants. She subscribes to gardening journals and belongs to a garden club to exchange tips.

Jonathan IV is a regular on the antique car show circuit for antique Bentleys. He scours the country, and when he finds an old Bentley, he enjoys dickering to get the best deal he possibly can. He then finds it relaxing to come home from a board meeting and crawl under the old car, taking it apart and rebuilding it with parts he orders. Once he has it in good running condition, Jonathan IV sets about reupholstering the interior and, finally, repainting it. Then, he sells it for thousands of dollars more than it cost him. He does not need the money; he simply enjoys the hobby of refurbishing the cars while the businessman in him enjoys the investment profit he makes.

Not driving a Bentley himself, Jonathan IV nevertheless keeps the one that started his hobby, the one his favorite grandmother owned and left to him when she died.

$\mathcal{H}$OMES

Jonathan and Virginia Pedigree refer to his ancestral house (28 rooms, 320 acres) outside of Charlottesville as their official residence. That is where they are registered to vote, and they have it listed on their driver's licenses and passports.

However, they spend considerable time in their four bedroom town house in Georgetown, due to their active business and social life in Washington, D.C.

Virginia donated her family's ancestral house in Richmond to the Virginia Historical Society, complete with family memorabilia, to avoid paying unnecessary taxes and upkeep on the old mansion.

Furnishings. Mahogany furniture, original art, and hardwood floors with well-worn Kirman rugs from the second half of the nineteenth century grace the rambling ancestral home in Charlottesville.

Tied-back silk draperies fall into a puddle of fabric on the floor that shows no need to economize on material. Current draperies are a new version of the original ones, even in identical fabric that had to be ordered from a shop in London, England, that specializes in out-of-date cloth.

White roses from Virginia's hothouse are cut daily, and fill blue and white Chinese porcelain vases throughout the house.

The Pedigrees shun the formality of French Louis XIV, XV, or XVI furniture styles, which they consider to be gaudy and slightly pretentious, preferring instead a casual elegance of well-loved family pieces.

Though some of their furniture is museum-quality, it is arranged semiformally and lived in comfortably. Their possessions are kept in good repair, but they use everything they have, even walking their rare rugs to the last valuable thread.

The four-bedroom town house in Georgetown is furnished entirely in Mahogany reproductions from Charleston, South Carolina.

Staff. The Pedigrees hired a husband-wife team as cook and housekeeper, respectively, to live in. The housekeeper brings in outside workers from Charlottesville once a week to help with certain household chores.

A driver was hired to drive Jonathan IV and Virginia between D.C. and Charlottesville two days a week, while they work out of their briefcases and cell phones in the backseat. The driver also doubles as a handyman around the house.

Quarters for the driver-handyman are over the six-car garage. Opposite him are the quarters of the married cook and housekeeper.

A British-trained nanny used to have a room on the third floor of the main house, next to the children, but when the children went away to school, she moved to Boston. Jenny and Jonathan V send her pictures every Christmas, along with a rum cake, and answer her letter that comes once a year.

In addition to the live-ins, Jonathan IV and Virginia hire people to look after their grounds, pool, horses, and two boats. They each have a secretary who coordinates daily life for Mr. or Ms. Pedigree.

The town house in Georgetown has no live-in help, only a housekeeper who comes by for several hours each day.

Pedigrees speak of their staff as "help" or "workers" or "staff" (or household staff, domestic staff, office staff), not as "servants" or "domestics." They say "driver" not "chauffeur." They say "car," not "limousine" or "limo." In fact, Pedigrees avoid using flashy-sounding vocabulary in general. They use a simple, direct, and unpretentious manner of speech.

$\mathcal{P}$ETS

In addition to their horses, the Pedigrees have a seven-year-old Saint Bernard named Bernie, who lounges near Virginia's favorite chair.

A large, saltwater aquarium with an array of exotic fish is built into the wall of young Jonathan V's room. He enjoys studying fish and grew up caring for them.

Jenny has a white Persian cat.

$\mathcal{A}$UTOMOBILES

Jonathan IV personally drives an eight-year-old Oldsmobile, which is his favorite car. As mentioned, he also owns an antique Bentley, which he works on as a hobby. The family has a three-year-old black Lincoln Towncar for the driver to take them places.

Virginia drives a white Ford Taurus Wagon around Charlottesville and keeps a Volvo in D.C. Until graduation from Sewanee, young Jonathan drove a secondhand BMW; then he traded it in for a new Jeep Grand Cherokee. Daughter Jenny drives a vintage Fiat.

All cars are kept clean and in top running condition by the live-in driver-handyman.

$\mathcal{S}$TYLE OF DRESS

The Pedigree family never wears designer labels that show anywhere on their clothes—and neither do their friends. Pedigrees consider clothes with designer labels showing as equal to wearing a price tag still pinned to the sleeve of a garment in public. Even Jonathan IV's briefcase will not have a large designer emblem or large imprint of the designer's name on it.

The Pedigrees most often wear custom-tailored clothing, properly monogrammed with their initials in a small diamond shape. And they have several pairs of handmade shoes.

But Pedigrees also buy clothing they like, and because they *buy clothing for quality and not for price*, they have items from Orvis, Talbots, and even Ralph Lauren (without insignia).

Conspicuous consumption repels the true Pedigree. They spend a lot of money for fine clothing and possessions, but only if the quality warrants the expense. This is simply a way of life that they do not question—and would never dream of flaunting.

Jonathan's tie widths and lapels and Virginia's hemlines have changed very little—because people of the Pedigree Class do not follow fashion (and consider it déclassé to do so). Any change in style evolves very, very slowly.

They ignore sections of fashion magazines that tout "what's new" because they consider such clothes to be trendy fads for "attention-seekers."

And since the Pedigree Class does not change styles, Jonathan and Virginia wear favorite clothes for years. They add a few new items each season and discard a favorite only when it is beyond repair.

They do not dress for other Classes or to impress other people. This unchanging, classic style—with no designer labels showing—is the "feather" of the Pedigree Class and it is one of the ways they identify each other. And they wish only to be identified with their own Class.

Their clothes are made from pure fabrics, such as cashmere wool, 100 percent cotton, 100 percent silk, and 100 percent linen, which require more expensive care, such as dry cleaning or hand washing and hand finishing to retain their beauty.

Classic bright red is a staple among Pedigree women. This is worn with matching bright red nail polish (even on short nails) and bright red lipstick.

Sunny yellow, solid white, bright pinks, turquoise, and royal blue accentuate the fine texture of good fabrics. Virginia and Jenny also wear bright colors in shoes, belts, and handbags.

Around the house, and depending upon the season, any member of the Pedigree family may gad about in old Bermuda shorts with sandals, or sweatpants and a T-shirt with threadbare tennis shoes. But at all times, their personal cleanliness is intact.

Black clothing is primarily worn after five o'clock by Pedigree women and is considered too severe for day wear. Navy is their dark color for daytime. However, for impromptu after-five cocktail parties, there will be a black silk or knit dress (long-sleeved or sleeveless), worn with pearls and black, dressy, St. John slingback heels (not too high) and a small black silk or black leather purse. A black dress for after-five is a travel staple, as well.

When given a leopard-print panty and bra set as a holiday gift from a lingerie store she patronizes, Virginia politely sent a thank-you note and quietly had the gift given to charity. Even black underthings are considered too exotic and are only worn under dark clothes that white underwear might show through.

Jonathan IV and his son wear plain boxer shorts in white. Virginia and daughter Jenny wear plain white silk or cotton bras, panties, and slips.

Seasons are observed, religiously, in dress. After Labor Day, white is not worn; and on September 25, the first official day of autumn, all sandals, summer shorts, and summer clothes are packed away.

Even during warm autumn days, the Pedigree family will wear fall clothes, in lightweight fabrics such as a classic Madras plaid.

Fall coats are made of corduroy or of heavy wool for really cold days. Because a fur coat is considered a winter coat, it is not worn before December 22, which is the first, official day of winter.

For Christmas and New Year holidays, red, black, or green taffeta dresses are traditional evening wear, as are black velvet jackets with silk ascots, tweed pants, and low boots in black suede.

On March 20, the first official day of spring, the Pedigree family begins wearing light wool or knits, with lightweight spring coats for cool days. In the South, white shoes and accessories are worn by Pedigrees between Easter and Labor Day. Not before and not after. In cooler eastern and northern climates, white shoes and accessories are worn between Memorial Day and Labor Day.

Hairstyles. Jonathan senior and young Jonathan wear their hair in a traditional, side-parted style that is cut short in back and above the ears, with fullness at the top and sides.

Virginia's blunt-cut hair is above-collar, though she occasionally has it cut short (never skimpy) for summer. Jenny wears her blunt cut to her shoulders. Both females vary the style only with occasional bangs, a headband, clasps, a ponytail at the nape of the neck, or worn up for dressy occasions.

Cosmetics. Virginia wears a very sheer makeup base with sunscreen, a natural-color lip-liner and mascara for daily wear. She wears either eye shadow or eyeliner, but never both.

Jenny wears no makeup base. She wears a light brown eye shadow and pink lip gloss.

Neither female wears frosted lipstick or frosted nail polish, but both wear classic red lipstick and nail polish.

Manicures and pedicures take place at least once a week. The two men's nails are kept short and at even-lengths. Jenny and Virginia keep their nails fairly short and buffed to a shine or with clear nail polish or classic red. Those are primarily their only three choices.

Before a special event, a professional makeup artist from D.C. comes to their house and applies makeup for them.

Fragrance. When she wears a fragrance, Virginia wears Sisley eau de campagne or the fragrance blended exclusively for her. Jenny wears Jickey, the toilet water by Geurlain that her great-great-grandmother wore.

Jonathan IV wears Bel Ami by Hermes. His son wears Jockey Club, an old men's cologne by Caswell-Massey.

Jewelry. Pedigrees do not wear accessories that "brag" and shout "Look at me, I'm rich!" Virginia wears a slide bracelet, whose sliding gold and precious stone pieces were added, year by year, by her family, from her ninth birthday until she was sixteen—a tradition for many Southern Pedigree girls. She also wears small gold loop earrings and a thin, gold sculpture necklace of a ballet dancer that Jonathan IV had made for her a few years ago.

Whereas platinum is the metal of choice, Virginia has a collection of sterling silver jewelry that she wears in the summer with silver-tipped brown leather sandals, matching handbag, and a thick silver cuff bracelet and western silver earrings. There is an assortment, too, of Hermés enamel bangle bracelets and coral earrings.

Virginia wears diamonds only *at night*, though she more often wears a string of pearls and pearl stud earrings. She has a safe full of beautiful jewelry that was passed down to her, which she wears to very formal charity balls, but some pieces are kept as "investment quality" jewelry—part of the family assets. Other family heirlooms were donated to a museum, thus alleviating the family of their care and providing enjoyment of them to the public. Virginia has a few pieces of jewelry in good rhinestone and mock pearl for travel, when she would not jeopardize the security of real stones.

Jenny collects real tortoiseshell jewelry and hair accessories, and she wears round, tortoiseshell eyeglasses.

Jonathan IV does not wear a lot of jewelry; however, he frequently wears his grandfather's gold Bulova watch and he has several pairs of monogrammed gold cuff links. Those items and his wedding ring are the only jewelry he wears with much frequency. And Jonathan IV never wears diamonds.

Although Virginia and Jonathan IV consider body piercing and tattooing barbaric and uneducated, they would never be rude to someone with pierced nose and cheeks and fad tattoos. Virginia and Jenny, themselves, have pierced ears, although it is only one pierce per ear.

MANNERS

Several key behaviors distinguish Pedigree manners that you will see in Jonathan IV, Virginia, their children, and others of their Class.

• They are completely "present" when they listen to you. They do not glance at their watch or sigh and shift from one foot to the other as if hastening you along. If they have to be somewhere else, they apologize, sincerely, that they must go to an appointment, and say they would love to hear the rest of your fascinating tale . . . perhaps over drinks, soon (this may never happen, but it is a graceful exit that lets you feel cared for).

• They are polite to service people, but Pedigrees do not talk about their own lives to anyone but close friends and family—and they are not persuaded by service people to buy new styles or items that are not part of their Class traditions.

• They definitely know which fork to use. Etiquette is not slavishly followed, but they have the basics down. If, by chance, they do not know something, they are not embarrassed about it. They simply ask.

• They are "unrushed." They maintain a smooth leisure of movement and speech. This unrushed manner in Jonathan IV and Virginia is both graceful and elegant. The expression "grace under pressure" sums up their lack of panic when pressed.

• Body movements are contained. If they gesture, it is mostly from the elbow. Facial expressions are limited to a smile, a nod, a raised eyebrow.

• Their social conversation is perhaps the most telling trait of all. "Small talk" is the most identifying characteristic of the Pedigree Class, along with the following:

　　—Tone of voice is either a quiet confidential tone that no one can possibly overhear, or a clear, forthright tone.
　　—They do not introduce gory or disgusting topics.
　　—They do not talk much about themselves.
　　—They talk about "small matters"—such as the proper way to open a cellophane-wrapped package—as if they were important, and they talk about "big matters"—such as the value of their stock plummeting or other personal failure—as if they were small, dismissed with a wry smile and clever comment that downplays their significance (though they may be hurting inside from the event).
　　—They never "tell off" anyone. They may secretly feel the same disgust toward a person who is being told off, but they, themselves, will never do it.
　　—Tact is the hallmark of their conversation. Pedigrees understand the subtle difference between tact and lying and never confuse the two.

—They do not brag, and consider it tasteless to carry on about money, possessions or accomplishments. Their credo is that if their money or accomplishments are of any importance whatsoever, you will hear about it from others.
—They have perfected the art of the put-down for those who do brag. Instead of being rude or seeming impressed, they simply say "How nice for you" in a passive tone.
—They accept compliments. If you compliment them, they will respond with warm graciousness and then turn the conversation to something else (but they are pleased).
—They rarely apologize. Only a brief "Sorry" can be expected. They consider it perfectly natural to make mistakes without having to apologize for it.
—Likewise, they rarely explain themselves. Rumors and scandal can be swirling around them, they will not stoop to mention it, nor to explain themselves unless it is in a court of law or to their immediate family (and they may even decline to discuss it with family).

FAMILY LIFE

Family life is a loosely knit structure, with each person in the family pursuing his or her own life and interests. High expectations are implied but not harshly imposed or preached.

Lecturing and punishment are considered barbaric by both Jonathan IV and Virginia. Democracy rules supreme in the Pedigree family life. Disappointments in one another are rarely discussed, but are keenly felt.

Family activities are planned primarily around holidays together—and holidays are built around sport activities, such as ski trips from the day after Christmas through New Year's Day. They attend at least one art or theater event together each year—a Broadway play in New York, for example, or an exhibition in London.

SOCIAL LIFE

Jonathan IV and Virginia build their activities as a couple around a social season in late May. They first spend two weeks at the Spoletto Festival in Charleston, South Carolina, which they contribute to financially.

Immediately after Spoletto, Jonathan IV and Virginia enjoy their social season as a couple in London. From opera at Glyndebourne, to horse racing at the Derby and at Ascot, and cricket at Lord's, they enjoy a constant round of events, cocktail parties, and dinners.

They follow all required standards of dress—hat and gloves for Virginia, top hat and morning coat for Jonathan IV—and they look forward to seeing friends they may not see at any other time of the year.

UNDERSTANDING THE PEDIGREES

If there is one word that best defines the motivations of a Pedigree, it is "authentic." From who they are, to what they have, the Pedigree is authentic. And to a Pedigree, the nature of authenticity is simplicity. The more fluff, puff, and trimmings something has, the more pretentious it seems—whether in dress, furnishings, house, car, vocabulary, or personality.

Jonathan Pedigree IV and his breed are secure in who they are. They are responsible, comfortable, and conservative in behavior but liberal and tolerant in thought; and they respond best to people who exhibit similar values and behavior.

They will be favorable to someone outside their Class who presents himself or herself in a simple, authentic manner. They prefer an authentic country bumpkin to a pretentious personality.

Too, a Pedigree likes to have a full daily calendar. Whether filled with volunteer work, hobbies, sports, business, or social events, Pedigrees like to be busy (while appearing "unrushed").

If you target Pedigrees as clients, or want to socialize with them, or hope to court one of them, incorporate the methods and values of the Pedigree *that you sincerely wish to have* into your own life and make them a natural part of you. There is nothing more authentic than that.

four

$\mathcal{F}$lamboyant Old Money

"As far as designer labels go, if you have it, flaunt it!"

—*Cliff and Maggie Flamboyant*

As a child, James Clifton Flamboyant—who later dropped the III from his name and refers to himself now simply as Cliff—drove off more than one nanny and was responsible for the demise of more than one valuable antique.

Cliff's parents were in middle age when he was born, and they described his energy as "creative" rather than destructive. But although they enjoyed indulging his every whim, they were never able to form a close bond with their only child.

As Cliff grew up, his father often invited him to sail with him in regattas, but Cliff considered his parents too old and tired to be much fun, and declined. However, he enjoyed tennis with his friends at the Country Club.

Tradition is synonymous with boredom as far as Cliff Flamboyant is concerned. Not only does he not care about family history, he cannot even remember all the names of his ancestors. Furthermore, he thinks it unimaginative to do the same things over and over just because that's the way they have always been done.

And as far as the sanctity of his family name is concerned, Cliff thinks it is only as sacred as the bank thinks it is on a check.

EDUCATION

Suspended from three prep schools, Cliff disliked classrooms and school activities so much that private tutors became an extra appendage for his school years. To everyone's surprise, however, Cliff became more serious in college and was respectably graduated from Yale.

MARRIAGE

Somewhere between prep school and college graduation, Cliff discovered women outside of his social set and began showing up for family Christmas dinners with a nightclub singer or some girl he met in a drugstore the week before.

Not surprisingly, Cliff went through a succession of tabloid marriages, including one to a famous lingerie model and one to a movie star.

But by late middle age, Cliff married his third and final wife, a rather lackluster woman named Maggie Jones, from a nondescript background.

Out of place with Cliff's family, Maggie is nevertheless appreciated for the fact that she does not put their family name in the tabloids the way the other two wives did.

CAREER

Cliff relies on money managers of his inherited wealth instead of a career. When a news reporter asked Cliff if he could be a self-made genius like his grandfather, Cliff shook his head and proclaimed himself "a self-made spender."

Cliff dabbled in a few movie productions, though it was rumored he only did so to promote the career of one of his mistresses.

PHILANTHROPY

The idea of giving money without recognition is an alien concept to Cliff. He once offered to give a building to one of the prep schools that had suspended him . . . but only if a statue of himself be erected outside of it. The school declined, "with regrets."

Any donations Cliff and Maggie have made to organizations have been with instructions on how they wish to be recognized for it.

ℋOBBIES

Because of their love for the new and controversial, Cliff and Maggie like modern art. They like searching for pieces they believe will be valuable in the future. Mostly, they cultivate the friendship of an artist who is the latest rage and set up a round of showings and parties in the artist's honor.

ℋOMES

All ancestral homes were sold as soon as Cliff inherited them. He and Maggie have a fifteen-room New York penthouse on the upper Eastside that overlooks the East River. The penthouse is listed as their main residence, but they winter in a house they own in Palm Beach, Florida. And once a year, they lease a yacht in Monte Carlo during the Cannes Film Festival.

Furnishings. Declaring antiques to be nothing but "old furniture," Cliff had his parents' elegant collection auctioned at Christie's. Cliff and Maggie have new decor every three years.

Currently, Cliff's New York penthouse is ultramodern, with large, mirrored rooms and windowed walls that flood all the rooms with light. Accented with lush, imported trees, the floor is black marble and the furniture is Breuer S-shaped tubular steel.

The latest high-tech amenities are available, and televisions, VCRs, computers, and mini-bars are built-in and electronically controlled so that a gray wall moves back to reveal them or closes to conceal them.

A valuable Picasso dominates the dining room, and a black

fireplace that has the appearance of being suspended dominates the living room. There are no lamps, only recessed lighting.

Their house in Florida has a similar uncluttered, lean style.

Staff. A butler and a cook are permanent staff, who migrate with Cliff and Maggie to their Palm Beach house in the winter and take care of the New York penthouse the rest of the time. A houseboy in New York remains in the penthouse in their absence.

The Florida house does not have a permanent staff, except for a live-in caretaker. When the Flamboyants are in residence, the butler hires extra workers.

A full-time chauffeur shuttles them around New York in a white stretch limousine. A pilot and a copilot are on call for flights in their private Gulfstream jet.

Maggie has a personal assistant on staff, who also travels with her. Her personal assistant coordinates her wardrobe, lays it out, helps her dress, styles her hair and applies her makeup.

In conversations with others, Cliff refers to domestic workers as "staff" whereas Maggie speaks of them as "servants." Cliff sometimes says "car and driver" or other times he has picked up Maggie's habit of saying "limousine and chauffeur."

$\mathcal{P}$ETS

Two afghan hounds live year-round in New York and do not travel. The Flamboyants have no pets in Florida.

$\mathcal{A}$UTOMOBILES

In addition to their New York limousine, Cliff drives a Porsche and a Jaguar in Florida. When not being chauffeured, Maggie drives only the latest model Rolls-Royce.

$\mathcal{S}$TYLE OF DRESS

Maggie never wears an outfit more than twice. After the second wearing, her personal assistant automatically sends her clothes to be sold at a consignment store. Cliff wears his wardrobe for one season, only; and he and Maggie wear designer labels with obvious insignia. In fact, Maggie looks down her nose at anyone who does not wear an obvious designer label.

Like their Pedigree counterparts, the Flamboyants like quality that requires expensive upkeep. Silk is a favorite, as is cashmere, satin, leather, fur, and a synthetic fabric known as microfiber.

Cliff buys all his wife's lingerie for her, making sure she wears pure silk and fine lace. He wears various colors and styles of designer briefs.

When he wears a tie, Cliff likes the ones that make a statement with bold patterns or unusual color combinations.

Maggie favors brilliant colors and splashy patterns that are typical of Escada and Versace.

Hairstyles. Cliff has worn his hair long, below his shoulders, and sometimes tied back; or completely shaved. More recently, however, his silver-streaked hair is cut just below his collar.

Maggie's hairstyle is always current. Short, long, layered, blunt, swing, tousled, French twist, chignon—Maggie has worn them all, as a brunette, a blonde, and a redhead.

Cosmetics. By ten o'clock every morning, Maggie Flamboyant is perfectly groomed, including makeup base, blush, contour powder, highlighter, lipstick and complete eye makeup. She does not wear her nails long, but she does not wear them quite as short as a Pedigree, and always has her nail polish and lipstick coordinated with her clothes.

Fragrance. Maggie wears a different perfume for every occasion, but her favorite is Bulgari. Cliff wears a variety of men's colognes, preferring Kouros overall.

Jewelry. Society columns chronicle the social life of Maggie and Cliff Flamboyant, complete with descriptions of Maggie's latest jewelry.

Cliff likes jewelry, too. He wears a thick gold wedding band with a large diamond. On his right hand is a pinkie ring with two rubies in it. He has several pairs of diamond cuff links, along with his monogrammed gold ones.

Because of their active social life, the Flamboyants wear most of the jewelry they own.

ℳANNERS

You can identify Flamboyants by the following, distinctive behaviors:

• The Flamboyants do not waste their time talking to anyone they are not interested in; and they do not feign polite interest.

• Snobbery is the way they put you in your place. They ignore service people and never engage in conversation with them. If a service person greets them, they may not speak back.

They tend to impatiently order service and sales people about. They rarely ask a salesperson's opinion, and if it is offered when they did not ask for it, they either ignore it, stare briefly at the person, or tell them they did not ask their opinion.

• They follow etiquette casually.

• They are often in a hurry and are not patient with anyone who holds them up.

• Their social conversation is full of gossip. They chatter about who is in bed with whom and whatever someone has done that is outrageous. Talk dwells on the latest "in" spot, the hottest new media personality, and they talk a great deal about themselves.

—Tact and lying are the same thing to the Flamboyants and they do both, according to convenience.
—They throw their weight around to get what they want. If you do not know who they are or how important they are, they will gladly tell you.
—They never apologize. Like the Pedigree, they consider it natural to make mistakes without having to apologize for it.
—They only explain themselves to the media, so everyone can know their problems; and they are at their happiest when rumors and scandal swirl around them.

*F*AMILY LIFE

Like others of their Rich style, the Flamboyants provided a nanny to care for their two children, from infancy through age seven, while Cliff and Maggie were gone—often for months at a time. And at the age of eight, the children were sent to boarding school.

Cliff and Maggie may have seemed neglectful of their children, but the truth is that they did not want to discipline a child. On some level they felt they could ignore the parental duty of discipline by putting the child in the care of someone who had been trained for the job.

As their children reached college age, the Flamboyants became better parents, because the children could then participate in adult activities with them, which allowed Cliff and Maggie to be "friends" with their children. Cliff is a bit bossy, at times, but Maggie has become rather close and supportive of her adult children.

The Flamboyants have two family lives: their current family life with their own children, and their family life that was adjudicated by a divorce court for their children by previous spouses.

Divorce cut heavily into Cliff's finances with the combination of alimony to his two ex-wives and child support payments for four children he seldom sees.

Fortunately for the children of his first marriage, Cliff's father and mother—fearing his future marriages might usurp money from their grandchildren—set up sizable trust funds in the name of each child that would be available to them at the age of twenty-one.

*S*OCIAL LIFE

Every season is the social season for the Flamboyants. Spur-of-the moment trips to Amsterdam or Paris or to a friend's ranch in Argentina, the film festival in Cannes—Cliff and Maggie are in demand. They are on the party circuit during their winters in Florida and on the top guest list for Academy Award parties in the spring.

Nightlife is every night when they are back in Manhattan. As part of New York's café society, Cliff and Maggie dine out most evenings and dance at the hottest spots.

Fashion models and best-selling authors, Broadway actors, movie stars, artists, designers, ex-politicians, and "exes" of movie stars, along with a whole bevy of media personalities can be found there—drinking too much and dancing with Cliff or Maggie.

Understanding the Flamboyants

If there is one word that best defines the motivations of a Flamboyant, it is "excitement." From who they are to what they have, the Flamboyants follow excitement. And to a Flamboyant, the nature of excitement is "newness."

The more new, outrageous, glittery, shimmery, and expensive something is—whether in dress, furnishings, house, car, or personality—the better.

You will either love Cliff and Maggie or you will deplore them. There is no in-between. Their strengths are grand and their weaknesses are self-destructive. They are extremists and mostly self-centered; but they are where the action is. And what's more, they *are* the action.

Cliff Flamboyant and his breed define themselves by what they have. They will only have a favorable attitude toward someone outside their Class if that person has attained high-profile wealth or has been highly publicized.

If you target Flamboyants for clients, or want to socialize with them, or hope to court one of them, become a media favorite.

Flamboyants live for the moment and for the daring impression they are making.

$\mathcal{S}$tatus New Rich

*"Designer labels are trophies of suc-
cess. I worked hard for my success. You
bet I wear designer labels."*

—*Dr. Ed and Judith Status*

Dr. Edward Status is a self-made millionaire who has done
everything right. He made all the right moves, which brought
him the success he wanted. A pioneering oral surgeon, he is also
an inventor of dental devices as well as a wealthy real estate
developer who set up a string of cosmetic dental clinics across
the country.

Ed Status was born into a lower-class family in a small town
in Colorado. Since the public school was the only school in
town, Ed attended with children of all classes.

It was when Ed visited his friends who lived in the nice part
of town that he felt a growing shame for the shabby neighborhood and tiny house he lived in, and the powerlessness of his
parents in their world. The poor, he concluded, were at the
mercy of those with money.

$\mathcal{E}$DUCATION

During his final years of high school, as Ed's friends talked
about going to college, he noticed the richer boys were going to
private colleges.

When two of his best friends who were Rich told him they

were going to Tulane in New Orleans, Ed applied for and won a scholarship to Tulane.

Ed held part-time jobs in college so he could pledge a fraternity and have extra spending money. Then he examined careers with the potential to make good money and decided on dental school.

But four years later, when Ed was facing the high expense of dental school, he figured out how long it would take him to pay back his student loans and decided not to go into debt with a loan.

It was then that Ed became aware of married students whose spouses supported them by working and paying the bills; so Ed decided it was time to get married.

MARRIAGE

When Ed met Judith, she was a schoolteacher, painfully aware that all her girlfriends were married; so when Ed proposed marriage a few weeks after they met, Judith quickly said yes.

And though Ed and Judith had each married for practical reasons—Ed to finance dental school and Judith to have a husband of any kind—it was nevertheless a good marriage that worked extremely well.

CAREER

For the next six years, Judith was the primary breadwinner, putting Ed through dental school and supporting him while he got on his feet as an oral surgeon when he moved them back to Denver.

Throughout their financial struggle, they maintained a sincere relationship that grew in affection, respect, and most of all, mutual goals. When Ed's practice grew into a profit-making enterprise, he asked Judith to stop working so she could concentrate on building their social life.

He remembered his parents' social isolation and felt that much of it was due to their lacking so many layers of Class. It was Judith's task to cultivate social layers of Class for them through art and charity involvement. And she did. Judith worked diligently as a volunteer for the Denver Historical Society and other causes, until she became adept in her social-climbing role.

And during those years, the Status's had three children—two girls and a boy: Katy, Mindy, and Marcus.

PHILANTHROPY

Many of Ed's clients and even business partners respected him in business but seemed to have an inner clique socially that he and Judith could not fully penetrate. And the one thing Ed and Judith both wanted was true social acceptance.

Philanthropy became their ticket into society. Ed and Judith became patrons of the arts, and their large donations bought entré to society. And, eventually, they were invited to private parties in the homes of the city's social leaders.

HOBBIES

Most of Ed's hobbies made him wealthy. In his early career as a dentist, Ed would have an idea while he was working on a patient. Later that evening, he would work at home, trying to design and to develop equipment in his workshop that would make dental work easier.

In recent years, however, Ed became interested in flying. He took lessons and now flies his own plane, a single-engine Cessna.

Judith has no hobbies. Her time is given over to her social interests and the social interests of her children.

HOMES

The three-story, white marble-finished house of Ed and Judith Status looks like a small-scale French château. With thirty-two rooms, it sits on top of a hill in the richest neighborhood of Denver, Colorado. It is surrounded by rose gardens, and there is an outdoor swimming pool and a tennis court.

In addition to the Denver house, Ed and Judith own a two-story Tyrolean-style house in the mountains of Telluride, Colorado, where they go with their children every Thanksgiving and on frequent weekend jaunts.

The Status family also has a beach house in Costa Rica, where Ed has set up an office to expand his dental inventions into Central and South America.

Furnishings. Antique French Louis XV furniture lends a formal museum atmosphere to the Status mansion, and many of the rooms are used only when there are guests. The children are only allowed in the family den that adjoins the kitchen and in their own rooms upstairs.

An American flag is flown daily in front of the house. Ed Status is patriotic. He gratefully credits his country for the fact that he was able to move from one social class to another.

Staff. A two-story building behind the main house in Denver was built as servants quarters. There are six live-in workers: a butler, a chef, two upstairs maids, a downstairs maid, and a chauffeur.

A gardener, a personal trainer, and Judith's social secretary come to the house on a daily basis.

The house in Telluride has only a live-in housekeeper. The house in Costa Rica has a live-in housekeeper and her son, who is the gardener.

Ed and Judith are demanding employers, who, because of their extremely high standards, have difficulty keeping employees.

Status Rich speak of their staff as "servants" or "domestics." They say "chauffeur" and "limousine."

$\mathcal{P}$ETS

Judith believes that animals are not meant to live in the house with people. The idea of getting dog or cat hair on her clothes, even from a well-brushed pet, is abhorrent to her meticulous nature.

Automobiles

Dr. Ed Status buys only American cars for himself, saying "I made my money in America, and I spend my money in America."

His wife, however, owns a German-made Mercedes. One of his daughters drives a Japanese Lexus, the other has a Japanese Mazda Miata. His son, Eddy, drives an American Corvette.

Style of Dress

The Status family dresses in nothing but designer clothes with designer insignias in plain sight. Judith's shoes bear the double C of Chanel, which is also prominent on her handbags and suit buttons; and she wears them as proudly as a scout's merit badge.

Likewise, all her children are designer dressed with labels in clear view, for everybody to see.

Ed buys American designer Ralph Lauren suits and clothes, but he yields to wearing Armani suits when his wife buys them for him. Whatever suit he wears, Ed Status is always perfectly turned out, from his haircut and tailoring, to his manicure and shoeshine. No detail of dress is missed.

Even around the house, the Status family dresses nicely. They never lounge around in robes or old clothes or with no makeup for the women.

Ed and Judith wear the very latest of fashions. Ed's tie widths and lapels change accordingly; while Judith's hemlines rise and fall with the dictates of fashion magazines.

When they encounter Pedigrees, the Status class does not realize that the unchanging clothing style of a Pedigree is part of their Class; the Status family simply thinks the Pedigrees are people who have money but no taste or awareness.

The Status Rich wear clothes only one season and then give them to Good Will.

The Status Rich wear a lot of silk and cashmere because they are known as fabrics of quality; they consider cotton too humble and rarely wear it. They do wear the synthetic microfiber in expensive designer styles.

However, the Status Rich do want people to think they've had their money forever. They incorrectly believe that old money wears subdued colors in dull tones, and mostly grays and blacks. Therefore, Ed wears mostly gray and Judith has a closet full of black suits and dresses, beige pants, skirts, and blouses, and rust-colored outfits.

Hairstyles. Judith and her daughters have their hair shaped and colored regularly. Both Katy and Mindy wear their hair long, sometimes in ponytails perched high at the tops of their heads. Ed wears his hair very short. Marcus wears his hair to his collar.

Cosmetics. Judith and her daughters wear a lot of makeup and apply it themselves. For special occasions, they have it applied at a local salon.

Judith's nails are fairly long, with a French manicure; and she insists her daughters wears their nails the same way.

Fragrance. Judith wears Champs Élysée. Daughter Katy wears Angel, and Mindy uses Organza by Givenchy.

Ed wears Imperiale men's cologne by Guerlain. Young Marcus occasionally slaps some of his father's cologne on. Otherwise, he doesn't wear it.

Jewelry. Ed and Judith wear his-and-hers matching gold Rolex watches, each with a diamond bevel around the watch face. And they wear the watches at all times. They replaced their original wedding bands with diamond-and-gold wedding rings years ago.

Ed rarely wears cuff links, but he has a few pairs, in diamond, and gold. He wears no silver.

Judith has a large collection of gold necklaces, unusual gold bracelets, and a variety of gold earrings. And she has diamond necklaces, earrings, and bracelets. The only pearls she wears are in a three-tier choker with a ruby clasp and matching pearl-and-ruby ear drops.

Judith changes her jewelry with her clothing. Every item is coordinated with a particular outfit.

Manners

Ed and Judith Status are perfectionists. They expect a lot of themselves, and they expect a lot of other people. They want to do everything "right." You will see a lot of the following manners in the Status Rich:

• The Status's judge you by your car and clothing. If you look poor, they hope you won't speak to them. If you stop them to talk, they will glance about to see if anyone is seeing them talk to you. Then they will glance at their watches and make an excuse to leave.

If you are not an upper-income person—or not in society— they will speak, but their eyes will rake over you in a way that lets you know you have been evaluated and found lacking. Furthermore, their manner is condescending, or has the reserve of haughty disapproval.

• Oddly, they talk casually about the details of their lives with salespeople and workers. Although they voraciously read to keep up with whatever is in style, they are very insecure about knowing what is in vogue. For that reason, their purchases can be influenced by salespeople.

• Because they are self-conscious about manners, any sort of social error will make them feel humiliated. And they privately criticize others they see who do not do "the right thing."

• The Status Rich will throw their weight around to get what they want. Ed is hot-tempered and short on patience, instantly putting people in their place. Judith tries to intimidate by acting indignant.

• Both Ed and Judith are good conversationalists. Their social talk consists of interesting topics in the news—which is why they religiously read *Time, Newsweek, People,* and their local papers.

• They often say things to have an "effect" or to impress.

• They quickly apologize or explain themselves to people they consider important.

FAMILY LIFE

The Status Rich view their children as a social extension of themselves. High expectations are lectured to them, and punishment exacted if the child fails. Punishment might range from yelling at them or grounding them, to spanking them or ridiculing them.

However, Ed and Judith Status love their children deeply, and family life is fairly important to them. Family holidays revolve around school vacations, when the children are taken to different destinations in Europe, or to one of the Status houses, in Telluride or Costa Rica.

SOCIAL LIFE

Much of the Status's social life revolves around social climbing or the latest fad activity publicized in expensive glossy magazines. Ed and Judith Status make friends easily, but each friend is compartmentalized according to how socially influential the person is.

And because they kowtow to people with more social influence than they have, Ed and Judith expect kowtowing from anyone who has less social influence than they. Friendships are instantly disposable if a "friend" falls from social grace or has financial problems.

UNDERSTANDING THE STATUS RICH

If there is one word that best defines the motivations of a Status Rich, it is "prestige." From the clothes they wear to the cars they drive, it is only significant to them if it has prestige. And to a Status Rich, the nature of prestige is to make an expensive impression.

Ed and Judith Status are only secure in who they are according to what they have, and how much it impresses other people. They respond best to people who are "in the know" or who have prestige in their line of work or family background.

$\mathscr{P}$ractical New Rich

"P. T. Barnum said of circus-goers, 'There's a sucker born every minute.' If P. T. Barnum were alive today, he would be a fashion designer."

—Bob and Martha Practical

Bakery giants Bob and Martha Practical jointly created their fortune as a husband-wife team. From a single doughnut shop, this couple grew to stand as an American success story.

Bob Practical was born in Chicago to immigrant parents. His mother never learned much English, and his grandfather, who came to America later, never learned English at all. They lived together in a small house in a blue-collar suburb. His father worked as a cook in a diner, but his grandfather had poor health, so his mother stayed home and took care of him.

Martha grew up in a small, working-class town in Illinois, the only child of a single mother who worked as a supermarket manager.

$\mathscr{E}$DUCATION

Bob dropped out of high school to work when his father died, leaving Bob's mother and grandfather unable to support themselves.

Martha finished high school and, when her mother married, Martha moved to Chicago by herself to find a job.

MARRIAGE

Martha worked as a file clerk in a Chicago mortgage office. Her pay was so small, she found a weekend job as a cashier at a bakery. There, she met Bob, who was a baker.

The minute Bob Practical saw Martha, he knew she was the woman for him. When he introduced himself to her, he said, "I'm Bob. I spend all day baking pastries . . . and by the way, I intend to marry you."

Martha laughed and put his comment aside as teasing. But while working together, Bob and Martha often talked about improvements the bakery could make. And as they talked, an attraction grew between them and their ideas turned to ambition.

When they married six months later, Martha and Bob had one simple dream—of owning their own bakery. And they worked hard, economizing to save every cent they could for three years to capitalize their dream.

CAREER

Beginning with a tiny doughnut shop at a busy intersection, Martha and Bob baked and served their own doughnuts. After two years of steady growth, they opened another doughnut shop and a separate bakery specializing in fancy pastries. Within five years, their doughnut stores were franchised throughout the country.

During this time, Martha had two children, David and Ruth, but still worked with Bob, often with the children in tow. David and Ruth grew up working in the shops, and were expected to take over their parents' business someday.

The doughnut franchise mushroomed, and Bob and Martha, as always, poured the majority of their money back into the business. This time, they began packaging many of their products and selling them frozen or in mixes to supermarket chains.

Six years later, a major international food corporation took notice of their rapidly growing supermarket line and bought it for fifty million dollars.

Martha came out with a cookbook on pastries and landed

her own cooking show on cable, selling videos of each program. She presented herself as an average homemaker, which enabled her to wear simple clothes, despite her minor celebrity.

After David was graduated from the University of Illinois, he joined his dad in running the family business.

Ruth works in the family business, too, but she is a sophomore at the local junior college with her eye on law school.

PHILANTHROPY

From the day they opened their first doughnut shop, the Practicals have always sent a daily batch of doughnuts to a homeless shelter; and they generously give to their religious faith.

Sought out by charities and fund-raisers, the Practicals support only what they believe in. They are not enticed to give just so they can socialize with other Rich.

Indeed, the Practicals are a fairly self-contained satellite within themselves. They would rather be with each other than with anyone else.

HOBBIES

David and Bob like to shoot pool in the den, Ruth likes to read, and Martha collects pastry recipes.

HOMES

When they first married, Martha and Bob lived in a cheap one-bedroom apartment and stayed there until well after their business was thriving.

It was only after the children were born that they moved into their first real house, which was a modest stucco, in a lower-middle-income neighborhood.

Ten years later, when Bob and Martha were millionaires, they moved to a nice suburb so the children could attend a better public high school, and that is where they still live.

The Practicals' red brick house on Chicago's north side is an unpretentious four-bedroom, single-story house. When they became very wealthy, the Practicals saw no reason to move. They were happy there.

But they made a few renovations, adding two upstairs rooms over the garage, which gave them more space, plus they added a large, glassed-in sunroom with a heated swimming pool inside. The one-acre yard that surrounds the house has a wrought-iron fence, flower gardens, and large trees.

Because they like fishing and hunting in the mountains, the Practicals bought a small hunting and fishing cabin in Colorado for vacation getaways.

Furnishings. Oak is the wood of choice for the Practicals because it is light-colored and informal. Oak-washed furniture with over-stuffed sofas and chairs fill the gold-toned wall-to-wall carpeted house.

There is even an oak-paneled den, complete with a standard-sized pool table. Hanging over the brick fireplace is the first dollar bill the practicals earned, proudly framed. Above it hangs a mounted deer head from one of Bob's hunting trips.

The Colorado hunting cabin is rustic inside and out, with used furniture that cost very little.

Staff. The Practicals' household routine is so ingrained that they only have a housekeeper, who comes twice a week.

There is also a yard-care service that comes once a week in the summer, and only when needed the rest of the year. David and Bob alternate taking care of the swimming pool.

The Colorado cabin has no one looking after it. The Practicals lock up when they leave, and take care of it themselves while they are there.

$\mathcal{P}$ETS

Bob bought a bird dog for hunting, and it has become a part of the family.

$\mathcal{A}$UTOMOBILES

In the early years of their marriage, Martha and Bob drove one car—a used Chevy Impala. When the children were born, Martha bought another used car—a Chevrolet Caprice—and Bob drove the old Impala.

When David got his driver's license, he inherited the old Impala until he earned enough money to buy his own Chevy Blazer. Bob drives a Ford Bronco and Martha drives an Aurora by Oldsmobile.

Ruth drives a Ford Mustang convertible.

$\mathcal{S}$TYLE OF DRESS

Designer labels are frivolous to the Practicals. Bob and Martha consider their wealth so hard-won that they continue to shop frugally. Until their success, they shopped resale stores, Target, K-Mart, and Wal-Mart. Now, they buy off-the-rack clothes at J. C. Penney and Macy's department stores.

They still will not pay more than three hundred dollars for a suit or dress, or more than one hundred fifty dollars for a pair of shoes—and they complain about that.

However, Martha and her daughter keep up with styles. Their hemlines move up and down, according to fashion.

Bob has to be forced into new clothing styles by Martha, or he would wear the same thing all his life. But Martha is careful to stay away from anything too faddish, because she and Bob expect good wear from everything they buy. Usually, they wear clothes at least two years. Martha and Ruth both love fancy satin underwear, while Bob and David stick with no-nonsense cotton briefs.

Around the house, the family uniform is old jeans, plain shirts or T-shirts, and very worn, very comfortable tennis shoes (non-designer).

Permanent press, denim, and cotton are favorite clothing fabrics for the Practicals. They prefer silk-blends over pure silk, and, in fact, fabric blends and synthetics of any sort make more sense to them than impractical fabrics that are expensive to care for and easy to ruin.

The Practicals wear a lot of blue, tan, and white, although they add a few colorful pieces and a sprinkling of black from time to time.

Hairstyles. Martha and her daughter perm and straighten their hair according to the trend. They don't spend a lot of money on fancy salons or hair care products. They just want something stylish and easy to handle. Bob and David both wear their hair in very short military styles.

Cosmetics. For daily wear, Martha applies her own makeup, using only powder, lipstick, and mascara. For night or dressy occasions, she adds makeup base, blush, and a touch of eye shadow in the crease of her eyelids. And Martha still wears makeup she buys at the drugstore or at K-Mart.

Ruth wears whatever her friends at school are wearing and shops with them.

Fragrance. For their first Christmas, Martha gave Bob a bottle of Old Spice, and that is the scent he wears to this day. His children have given him different men's colognes over the years, but Bob gives them away.

Martha, too, still wears her favorite fragrance from their early days of marriage: Jean Naté.

Ruth wears Pleasures and David wears CK One.

Jewelry. Although he gave Martha a new set of diamond wedding rings on their thirteenth wedding anniversary, to replace the zircon rings she received when they married, Bob Practical is sentimental. He has never removed his plain gold wedding band and vows it will be buried with him.

His son and daughter bought him a stainless steel and gold Seiko watch for Father's Day, to replace his much-loved but very old Timex. Bob has only one pair of cuff links, in gold.

In addition to her diamond wedding rings, Martha has a pair of diamond stud earrings. She also has a gold watch and a gold band necklace to match her round earrings. She does not wear bracelets.

MANNERS

The Practicals are down-to-earth people. Most people who meet them would not guess they have money, because their way of life and their manners are simple and unassuming.

• They listen to you without expressing approval or disapproval, even if you brag.

• They treat service people as equals, but a Practical rarely discusses personal issues with anyone but family. And they are definitely not persuaded by service people to buy anything.

• Etiquette is not followed by the book. The Practicals have the belief that if you are basically considerate of other people, what you do shouldn't bother anybody. If they attend a dinner and don't know which fork to use, they are not embarrassed about it. They simply ask or use the one they want to use.

• They are busy, but they take the time to be polite if someone stops them to talk.

• They speak their minds in conversation and expect you to do the same. The Practicals are always "bottom line" in their dialogue with anyone, including each other.

—They do not throw their weight around; but they will definitely "tell off" anyone they think is rude or wrong.
—To them, tact and lying are the same thing, and they rarely use either one.
—They do not brag about anything and consider it "bigheaded" to carry on about money or possessions.
—If you compliment them, they will act as if it is nothing.
—They apologize only if they think they are wrong.
—They rarely explain themselves. They think whatever they did—good or bad—is none of your business. And they stick up for family, no matter what.

FAMILY LIFE

Family is everything to the Practicals. They enjoy a close family life with their children. They vacation together, fishing and hunting in the mountains of Colorado, sunning on the beaches of Maryland.

The family is not interested in going to Europe or taking cruises, but they took a trip to Australia, where they went deep-sea fishing.

Social Life

Outside of their family activities, the Practicals socialize with people they meet through their religion. Mostly, though, they are clannish and would rather be with each other than with anyone else.

Understanding the Practicals

If there is one word that best describes the Practicals, it is "thrifty." From who they are to what they have, the Practicals are thrifty people. And to the Practicals, thriftiness is expressed by not trying to impress anyone.

The Practicals are very secure in who they are. They do not feel a need to impress anyone, nor are they impressed by anyone.

$\mathcal{T}$he Celebrity Rich

*"My public wants expensive glamour—
and designer-label clothes are part of
media glamour."*

—*Jewel and Rocky Celebrity*

Celebrity Rich can be categorized as *primary* or *secondary* fortunes. If you were a celebrity first, and then became Rich, you are a primary celebrity. If you were Rich first, and then became a celebrity, you are a secondary celebrity: any money you make from being a celebrity is a secondary fortune.

In our profile, Rocky is a primary celebrity and Jewel is a secondary celebrity.

Rocky grew up in a series of foster homes. He made poor grades and was unpopular in school. Lonely, he spent a lot of time writing poetry and then setting it to music.

Jewel is the daughter of Cliff Flamboyant by his first wife. She grew up with privilege, but longed for the attention of her absent father. Her mother pointed out to her one day that her father never had time for her, but he always had time for celebrities.

Pictures of Cliff entertaining movie stars, fashion designers, and rock stars were frequently flashed on CNN and television magazines and scattered throughout pages of *People* and *US*.

$\mathcal{E}$DUCATION

Rocky left school in the ninth grade when he sold a song to a band who happened to be in town. They let him tour with them, in exchange for writing lyrics and taught him to play various instruments.

Jewel quietly attended the Chapin Day School in New York. There, she hid behind her round, tortoiseshell spectacles and made fair grades. Mostly, she thought about her father, who never called. In fact, Jewel's father was noticeably absent from her debut. He was in Paris on his honeymoon with Maggie.

When Jewel went to Brown University, she had no idea what she wanted to major in, so she signed up for the same courses as her college roommate, who was majoring in drama.

$\mathcal{C}$AREER

Once Rocky learned to play the band's musical instruments, he filled in whenever a band member was sick. One night the lead singer got in a fight with the drummer and stormed out just before curtain time, so Rocky stepped in and electrified the audience with a wide vocal range and a bold, sexy performance. After that, the job was his—and Rocky was only eighteen years old.

Performances soon became sold out wherever the band went. Two years later, they signed with a new agent who got them a recording contract. To promote their upcoming release, they were booked as the opening band for a major rock concert, and by the age of twenty-five, Rocky was a music superstar.

With a degree in drama and estate money from her grandparents, twenty-two-year-old Jewel exchanged her eyeglasses for contact lenses, had a makeover, and headed for Broadway.

To her disappointment, no one was interested in representing her. But word got out that Jewel was the daughter of celebrity-hound Cliff Flamboyant, so a movie producer who had fallen on hard times got in touch with her.

The producer said she would let Jewel star in a movie if Jewel would pay for the production of it. Jewel agreed to pay two-thirds of it, if the producer would reduce the film budget by half and come up with the rest of the money elsewhere. The producer did so, and two years later, the movie was released.

It would have received no attention whatsoever if Jewel's publicist had not badgered a film critic into seeing it, resulting in a grand review of Jewel's performance.

Instantly, agents were eager to sign her, reporters were eager to interview her, and plum supporting roles in good movies were being offered to her. And best of all, her father called and invited her to vacation with Maggie and him in the Mediterranean during the Cannes Film Festival.

MARRIAGE

Jewel and Rocky met on her father's rented yacht in Monte Carlo. Paparazzi photographs of the good-looking young couple laughing together appeared in several tabloids because they looked like the perfect celebrity couple of their generation.

When the media fell in love with them as a couple, their publicists encouraged them to date. A year and a half later, they married in a glitzy Hollywood wedding.

The marriage of Rocky and Jewel is an awkward blend of two careers that often means long separations. Rumors abound about a pending rift between them, but publicists for each star insist everything is all right.

PHILANTHROPY

Rocky works tirelessly for reform in foster homes. Jewel grew up involved in charities and continues to support her favorites.

As a couple, Jewel and Rocky participate in many benefits for AIDS as well as world hunger benefits. They also help the Make a Wish Foundation, an organization founded to make wishes come true for terminally ill children, the preeminent charity supported by Hollywood celebrities.

*H*OBBIES

Rocky's career was an outgrowth of his songwriting hobby, and he continues to consider it a hobby as much as a business.

Jewel took up sculpting, but after a discouraging six months, she switched to painting landscapes.

*H*OMES

Jewel, who is used to wealth and privilege, would just as soon live in a nice high-rise condominium, since they are seldom home; but Rocky grew up hearing that Beverly Hills was the home of the stars, so a sprawling Beverly Hills mansion is his proof that he has made it against the odds.

Rocky settled on a Beverly Hills mansion that was the home of a 1960s rock star. Jewel objected that it was too big, and too gaudy, but Jewel's publicist convinced her that Rocky was right. Their public image requires star grandeur—with bigger-than-life trappings.

Her consolation prize was to choose their house in Florida, where other stars have second homes.

Jewel chose an Italian villa-style mansion near the water that is modest in size compared to the ones surrounding it.

Furnishings. The Beverly Hills mansion was bought completely furnished in plush Middle Eastern fabrics and thick Persian rugs. Jewel sees it as overdone opulence. Instead of being grand, she says it is grandiose, tacky, and pompous.

The Florida house is furnished in Italian decor synchronous with the house design.

Staff. Each house has a live-in house manager, who employs a live-in housekeeper and three live-in maids. Additional employees are hired by the house manager from a service as needed.

There are groundskeepers in each location who come frequently to keep up the places. And there is a security guard for each house.

Rocky has his own bodyguard, but a chauffeur doubles as

Jewel's bodyguard. Both stars have personal assistants and fitness trainers.

Jewel refers to their staff as "help" but Rocky speaks of them as "servants." Sometimes either of them may say, "Our man who does the lawn" or "Our boy who tends the pool."

Pets

Rocky keeps a harnessed mastiff at his side most of the time. Jewel has no pets because she travels so much, but she loves cats.

Automobiles

When she is not being driven in the limousine, Jewel drives a white Excaliber. Rocky has a collection of cars, including an antique race car, a Rolls-Royce, and a utility vehicle by Lexus.

Style of Dress

Because they are constantly in the limelight of television and tabloid cameras, Jewel and Rocky wear an outfit only one time.

And because they receive so much publicity, famous designers send them an unending stream of clothes to wear—free—as long as the designer's name is publicized by the star wearing that outfit.

For public appearances, Rocky has a trademark silver earring that dangles to his left shoulder, but apart from that, Rocky and Jewel wear styles that can only be called avant-garde.

Sheer, see-through shirts with flowing sleeves and open to the waist for Rocky, and plunging necklines and skintight satin for Jewel are the Celebritys' stock-in-trade. Rhinestones, sequins, glitter, and patent leather are worn by both. Dramatic black and silver is Rocky's usual color scheme. Solid white is the color most seen on Jewel. Rocky wears the underwear he made famous for a designer on billboards, magazine and television ads. Jewel titillates her audience and the press because she wears no underwear at all.

Around the house, Jewel wears sweatpants, a T-shirt, and socks. Pinning her hair back, Jewel wears no makeup. She has permanent cosmetics on her eyebrows, eyeliner, and lips, so she looks good without makeup.

Rocky pads around barefoot, wearing just his underwear and an undershirt or no shirt at all. Since they are always dressed like stars when they go out, this very casual, half-dressed state is their only liberation.

Hairstyles. Both Rocky and Jewel wear their hair long, blond, and wild.

Cosmetics. When he goes out, Rocky wears heavy eyeliner completely around both eyes.

Jewel's makeup style is light and natural looking, but that is due to the makeup expertise of her personal assistant, who also styles her hair before Jewel goes in public.

On a daily basis, Jewel has an aromatherapy massage after she works out with her personal trainer and soaks in her Jacuzzi. Twice a year, she goes to an exclusive health spa for full body treatments and a week of pampering.

Fragrance. Recently, Jewel Celebrity was signed to promote a lower-priced line of fragrances in her name, so she now wears only those perfumes when she goes out. At home, she likes the lighter Vita-Spa spray cologne.

Rocky wears M—Pour Monsieur, a masculine French fragrance.

Jewelry. The jewelry that Rocky Celebrity buys for Jewel makes headlines. There was a million-dollar emerald collar necklace from a famous jeweler on Rodeo Drive, and an African diamond the price of which could only be rumored.

Unknown to the public, the jewels the Celebrities wear are mostly "loaners" that, like their designer clothes, are on loan from a jeweler just for the free publicity Rocky and Jewel can bring. The jewels go back to the store afterward.

MANNERS

Celebrity manners have been coached into them by their publicists and managers. They must always be aware of the public and the press and behave graciously while dressing outrageously to get media attention.

• With a bright smile and perhaps a hand wave, their eyes scan the crowds. Jewel sometimes blows a kiss to cheering groups.

• Jewel is polite to service people, but does not discuss her life to anyone but her publicist, manager, and a shrink.

• Etiquette is a source of anxiety to Rocky. He fears making a social mistake that could be leaked to the press and pounced on by tabloids. Before any event, Rocky has his manager find out the exact protocol expected and he practices it over and over before he goes.

• Jewel and Rocky have learned that their social talk with other people must serve a purpose for advancing their careers.

• They never "tell off" anyone, because of their public image, although they may stage a fight with each other in public to generate headlines.

• They rarely explain themselves. Rumors and scandal can be swirling around them, and they will be delighted. After all, that is what keeps them celebrities—being talked about, written about, and asked about.

FAMILY LIFE

Though publicity shots of Jewel and Rocky at home depict the couple swimming together in their pool, cuddling on a sofa in front of the fireplace, and cooking together in the kitchen, they do not really spend much time together at home. Their professional lives keep them away from each other for months at a time; and during their lengthy periods apart, each has been photographed with other lovers. When questioned by the press about the pictures, Jewel or Rocky always deny sexual misconduct, and neither ever questions the other about such reports.

When their schedules happen to find them at home at the same time, they are each absorbed in their own interests and have little in common to talk about, other than occasional career matters. Their ideas are so far apart that when they talk about anything else, it usually turns into a fight, with Rocky shouting and Jewel retreating into silence.

Still, Rocky and Jewel have a psychological symbiosis. For all the loneliness and lack of communication between them, their marriage is the closest either has ever had to a family life. Rocky thinks they would have a better family life if they have children, but Jewel has told him she has no intention of having a child and the subject is one of frequent speculation by the press.

Social Life

Unlike their sparse family life, Rocky and Jewel Celebrity have a packed social life, built primarily around career development: balls; galas; award ceremonies and related events; celebrity sport tournaments; charity socials; cast or band parties; high-powered dinners in the homes of top movie or recording producers; expensive restaurant dinners with other celebrities; cocktail parties; pool parties; gambling; and ski weekends abound. They try to attend these events together because they attract much more publicity as a couple than alone.

But the fine line between work and play blur in their social lives. Their best friends are managers and agents, lawyers, producers, publicists, media executives, and promoters—with whom neither Jewel nor Rocky can risk confiding truths that might damage the career of either of them.

Understanding The Celebrity Rich

Being "somebody" and having money are the driving forces behind the Celebrity Rich. And the way they know they are "somebody" is if they are recognized by the public and if they are the center of media attention.

Sometimes, a Celebrity Rich will mellow over time and seek Pedigree ways and interests. Even so, they are tied to their public persona and have to keep up media-hype appearances.

Other Celebrity Rich never mellow. In fact, their weak sense of self apart from their persona cannot bear to be unrecognized, and they struggle to maintain their hold on the public. They do outrageous things to gain media attention. Well into old age, they cannot gracefully let go of their media position, and grab any exposure they can.

$\mathcal{R}$oller-Coaster Rich

"When I have money, I buy designer watches for their hock value when I'm broke."

—*Tip Roller*

"$\mathbf{W}$hich fortune?" Tip Roller will ask if you inquire about the founding of his fortune. A risk-taker who thinks failure and success are flip sides of the same coin, Tip has been up and down, rich and poor, so many times he describes his life as a Theme Park experience.

Tip is a combination of old money and new money. He has the heritage of a Pedigree and the rebellion of a Flamboyant—but his spirit is that of a risk-taking entrepreneur. He grew up on the Double R (Roller Ranch) near Ardmore, Oklahoma, where his great-great-grandparents were among the first settlers in the area. Although the cattle ranch was successful, it was the discovery of oil that made the family rich.

$\mathcal{E}$DUCATION

Tip went to local schools and rode in the rodeo until he was college age. Then he attended Pepperdine, a private college in California, and learned to love the West Coast.

MARRIAGE AND CAREER

Tip's fortunes have been inextricably intertwined with both career and marriage. At his parent's urging, Tip worked for a time on the Double R. But ranch life was not for Tip. He liked talking to the oil operators who leased their land and found himself interested in getting into the oil business. With his family's initial financing, Tip formed an oil company and began drilling for oil.

That same year, Tip married a hometown girl and they eventually had two boys. But after five years, his wife discovered he had a mistress in Oklahoma City and she divorced him.

Unfortunately, his divorce happened at the same time Tip realized that his inexperience in the oil business had cost him. He filed for bankruptcy and left for California.

He thought he was finished with the oil industry, but a few years later, Tip went into drilling for oil and gas around Bakersfield, California. This time, he had learned from his Oklahoma mistakes and he struck oil—big time!

For six years his luck held and Tip Roller was wealthy man. He worked hard and played hard and was a regular in nearby Las Vegas where he gambled for big stakes and took his losses without a word.

It was in Las Vegas that Tip met a showgirl and dated her every weekend. Eventually he married her, but they divorced a year later.

Tip then married a Bakersfield woman and had two more children; but he still gambled a lot, drank a lot, and had a lot of other women. Not surprisingly, Tip's third marriage ended—and once again, his finances were at risk.

This time, the price of oil had plummeted and oil production loans were being called at the bank. Within a year, Tip lost everything he had—the luxury cars, fine homes, expensive furniture. Once again, Tip Roller was flat broke.

Knocking around from odd job to odd job, Tip spent a lot of time in the library, reading the *Oil & Gas Journal*. There, he met a librarian, and married her a short time later. Now he is back in the oil business and already has a solid asset base once more.

PHILANTHROPY

Always quick to give money to any of his friends who fall on hard times, Tip insists the money is a gift and not a loan, refusing ever to be paid back. Apart from that, Tip's philanthropy amounts to little more than dropping a few coins into the Salvation Army kettle at Christmas.

HOBBIES

Las Vegas dice tables are the closest thing to a hobby Tip ever had.

HOMES

From the family ranch, to a one-bedroom apartment, to a million-dollar mansion, and then to a trailer park, Tip Roller has lived up and down the scale of money. Currently, he and his librarian wife live in a modest town house that is nicely furnished. But since his fortunes have gotten better, Tip now has his eye on a million-dollar house in Santa Barbara.

Furnishings. When an interior decorator tried to interest Tip in antique furniture, he shook his head and chose brand-new Chinese black lacquer and fine Asian textiles, screens, and porcelain. "When my furniture becomes antique," he said to the decorator, "I want to be the first ancestor who used the stuff!"

Staff. During his prosperous years in the multimillion-dollar house, Tip Roller hired a ready-made staff from a domestic agency, which included a houseboy, a cook, and two maids. When speaking of his staff to others, he refers to them by their title: "our houseboy," "our cook," "our maids."

However, during hard times, Tip cleaned his own apartments, did his own laundry at laundromats and opted for fast-food burgers and fries rather than to cook, himself.

𝒫ᴇᴛѕ

Tip has no pets except when he is married, and has always let his wives and children choose them. Currently, he and his librarian wife have a red Irish setter.

𝒜ᴜᴛᴏᴍᴏʙɪʟᴇѕ

Over the span of his career, Tip has driven Mercedes and Cadillacs. He even had a Zimmer once; but his favorite transportation today is a Ford pickup.

Tip would never buy a limousine, so he hires a limousine service for special occasions.

𝒮ᴛʏʟᴇ ᴏꜰ Dʀᴇѕѕ

Levis' 501s, creased down the front, worn with a black T-shirt, a tan sport coat, Ostrich cowboy boots, a leather belt with "Tip" hand-tooled on the back, and a large silver monogrammed buckle is Tip's business attire. For casual wear, Tip takes off his sport coat.

He does not wear a suit, no matter who else does, and no matter where the meeting is being held. However, Tip does own a tuxedo that he wears to appropriate parties. Occasionally, he wears a cowboy hat.

Tip dresses the same around the house as he does for daily wear—jeans, T-shirt, and cowboy boots and belt.

Tip Roller likes to keep things simple and unprentious. He wears mostly cotton, and wash and wear, plus cold-weather wools and leather.

Hairstyle. Tip varies his hair length from above his ear to below his collar. When his hair is short, he wears a neat moustache. When long, Tip wears a neatly trimmed beard.

Fragrance. Tip smokes cigars and thinks that's enough.

Jewelry. Tip wears a Tag Heuer stainless steel and 18-carat-gold watch, his gold wedding band, and a silver bracelet. He has a wardrobe of silver belt buckles and diamond-stud cuff links.

MANNERS

Roller-Coaster Rich have an understanding of all levels of society. Tolerant and not easily impressed, the Roller-Coasters have a sociable manner.

• They interact with you while you talk, perhaps interrupting to add to your tale. If your story is troubling, they frown and shake their heads, smile when you tell the happy part, and laugh when you are trying to be funny. And then they pick right up and tell you a story, too.

• They are friendly to service people and may talk about their lives with them in much the same way they do with friends. They are a soft touch for being talked into buying things they do not need; but they never change clothing style, no matter what a salesperson says.

• They may or may not know etiquette, according to the way they were brought up, but they don't worry about it. If they pick up the wrong fork, they will continue to use it.

• They are always busy, but they do not behave or speak with panic. Their gambling nature keeps a cool, poker face.

• Body movements are robust. Everything in life is bigger to them than it is to everyone else. Gesturing and animated facial expression is a natural part of Roller-Coaster conversation.

• Like the Pedigrees, the Roller-Coaster Rich talk about "small matters" as if they were important, and talk about "big matters" as if they were small.

• They do not like to "tell off" anyone, but will if pushed. They do not back down to people.

• They understand the subtle difference between tact and lying and use both, if necessary.

• They do not brag, for the simple reason that they have lost everything they ever bragged about before. But they do tend to joke about their loses. They are not offended by those who do brag—and in some ways, they actually enjoy it.

• They apologize for the errors of their ways, but they do not change.

• They explain themselves, humorously.

UNDERSTANDING THE ROLLER-COASTER RICH

If there is one word that best describes the Roller-Coaster Rich it is "challenge."

It is almost as if Tip Roller enjoys the challenge of making money when the odds are against him, so that once he has the money and the challenge is gone, he sets himself up to lose it just so he can have the "odds-against-him" challenge all over again. Boredom is worse than death to Tip.

Tip Roller is a person you should never give up on, because he is the original "Comeback Kid." He has the talent to make money, yet he makes choices that keep him vulnerable to loss.

Part 2

Doing Business
with the Rich

nine

Business Styles That Succeed with the Rich

> *"Businessmen can achieve notable success by discerning the possibility of things which others consider impossible."*
>
> —*J. Paul Getty*

There are four basic business styles that succeed most with the Rich.

- Serendipity Style

- Goal-Intense Style

- Success-Oriented Style

- Progressive Style

These four business styles differ from one another in the ways they view time—past, present, and future—and in the ways they achieve goals.

One style is not better than another; all four of them are successful business styles. Study each style, discover which one most closely resembles how you do business, and learn how to optimize your business performance.

You can even develop a style. Well, except for the Serendipity Style. You are either born with it or not, and if you absolutely have it, you will never change. The Serendipity Style, like the other three, has some downsides, but also some great upsides.

SERENDIPITY STYLE

If you have a Serendipity Style in business, you operate purely from the heart and instinct. You do not understand the meaning of fixed goals and structured methods of achieving them. The idea of having a step-by-step plan is alien to you, and you change direction as easily as a weather vane.

Likable, easygoing, your goal-less Serendipity Style seems to stumble into success and riches. People think of you as "lucky" or "fated" and you see yourself that way, too.

But a closer look at the Serendipity Style shows that you have two strengths that create the success:

1. *You trust your instincts.* Call it a gut-level feeling or a hunch—you sense trends and opportunities. You may not have the slightest idea of where the trend or opportunity will ultimately lead, but you listen to your instinct and respond instantly.

Your thought process sounds something like this: "Hmmm, that sounds interesting. I'll try it and see how I like it." This offhand, roll-of-the-dice gambler's instinct is key to the Serendipity Style of business.

2. *You keep your word.* Most people are not aware of how responsible you are because of the casual manner of this style.

You do not necessarily go out seeking responsibilities, but you always do whatever you say you will do. And because your word is important to you, you are reluctant to commit yourself very far beyond the moment.

This hedging style drives a lot of people nuts. They accuse you of commitment phobia, but that is not true. You simply do not want to give your word if you are not sure you can keep it. If you do give your word, you can be counted on to keep it.

The Serendipity View of Time

Because you live entirely in the present, you get over disappointment faster than most people. You naturally feel pain at first, but not for long. Soon, it becomes the past, and the past has little hold on you. Eventually, you forget most of the unpleasantness of the disappointing venture, and always remember the pleasant.

The future does not have much hold on you, either. You cannot spend time worrying about the future, because you are too busy exploring now, sampling each and every second to see if you want more of what it has to offer. Your Serendipity Style defines "now" as an ongoing flux of change—and you live, totally, in it.

The life of a Serendipity is a timeless mosaic of one event interweaving into another event. You look at everything with openness, accepting change, and moving with that change.

The Serendipity View of Goals

You may listen and talk enthusiastically with friends about goals and great plans for the future because the liveliness of such talk is fun, but to you, it is merely fun talk for the moment. True to your Serendipity Style, you will forget such talk as soon as it is over, because you cannot seriously consider chaining yourself to a step-by-step plan for a long time. You cannot understand the gut-and-grind method of making a goal come to pass.

As a Serendipity, you live the charm of life, the luck of the draw, the hunch of the moment. Instinct and intuition are your guiding lights into the future.

Because you are so grounded in the present and not worried about the future, you're able to deal with whatever comes your way. Your style does not suffer great stress about expectations, because, somewhere in your heart, you believe that everything takes care of itself.

The Serendipity Response to Failure

Because failure only hurts a person according to how much ego is involved in an action, you do not feel failure often.

As a Serendipity, you have a healthy self-esteem that somehow lacks ego. And it is your very lack of ego involvement in what you do that makes your Serendipity Style take failure and losses in stride, even while feeling momentary disappointment.

A Serendipity is the ultimate good sport.

The Driving Force of a Serendipity Style

Curiosity and interest are the two driving forces of a Serendipity Style. Having a low threshold for boredom, you always follow your line of interest.

Serendipities are *not* persistent. Serendipities are not prudent. Serendipities are not disciplined. Serendipities are not structured. Serendipities have no drive, only curiosity.

If you are a real Serendipity Style, you will be involved in something only as long as it delights you—or only for as long as you have committed yourself.

You will not be disciplined, threatened, cajoled, or loved into doing something one day more than you committed to. As a Serendipity, you are responsible, not ambitious.

Your Serendipity Style does not take control and shape destiny to your desires. You respond to the opportunity of the moment, handle it responsibly, and enjoy it. This often makes you the right person in the right place at the right time.

All Serendipity Styles:

- Take risks that seem interesting to them

- Readily accept consequences

- Move enthusiastically to the next interesting risk

Serendipity Business with the Rich

Serendipity Styles work best with Status New Rich, Roller-Coaster Rich, and, interestingly enough, with Pedigrees.

Responsibility is your saving grace with Pedigrees. And because you are responsible, the ever-tolerant Pedigree will find your free-flowing style an interesting quirk in your likable ways.

Surprisingly, Flamboyants have a hard time with you. That is because their slightly unstable manner can only exist if they have a very stable, predictable, long-range support system.

However, if you have received a lot of publicity for your Serendipity Style, you will automatically attract Flamboyants. They may, however, always be a bit skeptical of you.

If you are a Rich person who also has this Serendipity business style, you will find yourself surrounded by opportunities who flatter your interests in something only to fatten their pocketbooks and deplete yours. Be very careful.

Serendipity Careers

A Serendipity Style is not at all suited for corporate life with the Rich. You can benefit from doing business with the Rich in areas that allow a great deal of freedom and change. Careers that cry out for Serendipity Styles are inventor, entrepreneur, and financial investor.

$\mathscr{G}$OAL-INTENSE STYLE

Quite different from the Serendipity Style is the Goal-Intense Style. Highly passionate about attaining a specific goal, you are "driven." With tunnel vision toward achieving any goal, you walk, talk, eat, sleep, and think of little else but attaining your goals.

You have two strengths:

1. You have the ability to spend large amounts of time alone, in dedicated effort toward a goal. And you are seldom aware of being alone because you are most fulfilled when working toward achievement.

2. "Long-term-commitment", is your middle name. You know exactly what you want out of life and you are willing to give whatever it takes to achieve it. Furthermore, you have a plan—a mental blueprint—that will get you there. No one and nothing will get in your way.

The Goal-Intense View of Time

Unlike Serendipties, who live totally in the now, Goal-Intense Styles move constantly into the future. In fact, the work you do now is your tool for manipulating the future—and you are impatient to get there. You are often accused of being a workaholic, and you are.

The Goal-Intense View of Goals

The goal is everything. All you do, all you think about, all you live for—it's all about the goal.

The Goal-Intense Response to Failure

The term "good loser" is impossible for you to understand. You hate failure and it eats at you. Your Goal-Intense Style will never accept failure; you will find a way to compensate for the failure in a stronger victory somewhere down the line.

Your style is very powerful, whether or not you realize it, because you control your destiny more than any other type of person.

The Driving Force of a Goal-Intense Style

Being the best, the top, the winner in anything is important to you. Your Goal-Intense Style simply cannot tolerate second-best from yourself.

A Goal-Intense Style

• Actively makes choices for his or her own life

• Easily sacrifice whatever is necessary in order to achieve a desired goal

• Welcomes competition

Goal-Intense Business with the Rich

Goal-Intense Styles work best with Status Rich, Celebrity Rich, Practical New Rich, and with Old Money Pedigrees.

Status Rich are goal-intense, themselves, and therefore they trust you. Hard-working Practicals want someone hard-working to handle their money and you fill the bill. Pedigrees always admire high achievers. Celebrities want their managers, agents, investment advisors, and publicists to be aggressive and successful in their behalf. They may butt heads with you, but they want a mover and shaker in their ball park.

Roller-Coaster Rich will want to do business with you, but

you would not touch a Roller-Coaster with a ten-foot pole. They are too financially unreliable for you.

Flamboyants will do business with you, because you are good at whatever you do. But Flamboyants may resent you because you are everything their families wanted them to be, and they did not become.

Goal-Intense Careers

A Goal-Intense Style is suited for any career choice. Corporate life, with its office politics, is a challenge to you. But you can also excel in any type of sales or as an entrepreneur.

SUCCESS-ORIENTED STYLE

If you have a Success-Oriented Style of doing business, then you have integrated the best of both the Serendipity and the Goal-Intense Styles.

You are a people person and you come across as a normal, balanced individual who simply achieves more than average and deserves it.

You have two strengths:

1. You like to make people happy.

2. You make realistic commitments.

The Success-Oriented View of Time

The future is real to you and so is the past, and both motivate you in the present.

The Success-Oriented View of Goals

As a Success-Oriented person, you do have goals and you are self-motivated and responsible in working to achieve them, but you are not dominated by your goals.

The Success-Oriented Response to Failure

When you do not achieve a goal, you will experience sadness or disappointment for a longer time than the Serendipity; you may even feel depressed about it for a while. But, failures and losses will not eat at you, as they do the Goal-Intense Style. And you will not feel compelled to compensate for them as the Goal-Intense Style does.

You will simply go back to your mental drawing board to revamp and restrategize, or you will set new goals that you will find equally as rewarding. Eventually, you may even consider your loss as having been for the best, although it may take some time to fully feel that way.

As a Success-Oriented Business Style, you give a pleasant impression of balance. You are easy to relate to and you do a good job of following through on your commitments to others.

The Driving Force of the Success-Oriented Style

You simply want to do well in life. You do not have grandiose goals and no dreams of splendor, but you want respectability, above all else. It is important for you to live on the right side of town, to go to the right places, to join the right clubs, to have the right friends, and to be accepted.

You are mildly competitive, but you will always stand up for your interests in business. Steady advancement in your chosen career is your idea of doing well.

All Success-Oriented Styles

- Are reliable
- Hardworking
- Give satisfactory results

Success-Oriented Business with the Rich

Success-Oriented Styles can work with anybody. Pedigrees love your innate good manners, which make you automatically think of how other people feel. Flamboyants adore your willingness to listen and to do things their way. You provide a very stable, predictable support system for them. Status New Rich like that you are impressed with them. Practicals relate to your simplicity of manner. Celebrities may not find you glitzy or gutsy enough, but they will be able to get along with you. And Mr. Roller-Coaster will like your nonjudgmental attitude to him.

Success-Oriented Careers

As a Success-Oriented Style, you are well suited for corporate life with the Rich. You are a natural when it comes to office politics, because you are subtle but smart when it comes to people. That, coupled with your hard work, keeps you moving steadily up the corporate ladder. You are good in sales, but could never be a high-pressure salesperson. "The customer is always right" is your motto. You sincerely try to find out a customer's true needs and offer products that will fit those needs. You do not oversell customers and they know it. Trusting you, they come back, and back, and back.

Public relations is also a good choice for this business style. If a company has unhappy customers, you know how to soothe them. If there is a nasty article in the paper, you know how to court the press so they will present your company's side, too. Your people skills are superb.

$\mathcal{P}$ROGRESSIVE STYLE

The Progressive Style of business is more of a process than an actual style. However, it is described here as a separate style to pinpoint the progression of personal change a businessperson may experience. It is also described here as a separate style because there are people who will never undergo strong progressions. For instance, if you are a true Serendipity Style, you cannot change.

The first stage of the Progressive Style actually resembles the Serendipity, but the similarities are surface only, and temporary. The noticeable difference between an early Progressive and a Serendipity is that the Progressive is nowhere near as responsible in his commitments as a Serendipity.

If you are a Progressive, at first you will seem just as live-for-today and non-ego-involved as the true Serendipity. You work without fused goals or a definite game plan. However, as an early-Progressive, your goallessness is actually a lack of confidence in your abilities. You hide behind the Serendipity behavior out of fear of failure. You may enter a business situation with the same "Hmmm, I'll try this" attitude of the Serendipity. You may have the same good-naturedness about losing as the Serendipity. But that is because you really did not think you could win anyway.

Then, to your surprise, you do better than you ever imagined. You slowly begin to realize that you have abilities you might be able to use repeatedly, that you may actually be able to achieve your goals. At this point, you begin a humble, cautious movement into recognizing that you might—just maybe—have some measure of control over your destiny. And at this point, you enter the Success-Oriented Stage of your Progressive Style.

The change into this style is very gradual, though, because you struggle with your self-confidence and your abilities as you shakily build your new self-perception. You are not even conscious of the change. You just feel a certain attraction to repeating the business experience, with a stronger interest in outcome and preparation for outcome. *You realize then that most success is learned through repeated effort—failure after failure—until a person puts it all together effectively.*

It is only with time and experience that you emerge as a confident player. Your ego needs surface and your sense of control over your time and your life strengthen. You develop a more powerful drive than before, perhaps progressing into a Goal-Intense Style, who is a formidable competitor and a very high achiever.

Many people who are successful in business with the Rich began in this Progressive Style.

The Progressive View of Time

At first, the Progressive shudders at the mere thought of time. The past is a collection of previous failures; the future is a frightening unknown; and the present is a time of hesitation and uncertainty because you don't think you can succeed at anything. Gradually as you enter the Success-Oriented stage, your perception shifts. The past becomes an education, the future is something you can control, and the present is a new opportunity to take responsibility and shape your destiny.

The Progressive View of Goals

As a Progressive, at first goals are something you don't set because deep down you feel you can't achieve them anyway. To avoid disappointment, you never attempt to achieve anything specific. However, once you begin experiencing success and slowly build up your confidence, you begin to realize that maybe goals are attainable, and see goal-setting as a means of controlling your future.

The Progressive Response to Failure

Early Progressives expect nothing more than failure. It is only after a surprising success and an eventual shift in perception, that the Progressive realizes that failures are stepping stones to success. The Progressive in the Success-Oriented stage fully understands that failures hold valuable lessons that can be incorporated in future endeavors.

The Driving Force of the Progressive Style

An early Progressive is motivated by one thing: the avoidance of disappointment. You don't get emotionally involved in your work, because you really don't think you're going to succeed anyway. You may work hard, but without any particular goal, and you never have a plan—if one avenue doesn't seem to be working, there is always another route to try.

Early Progressives:

• Set no specific goals, preferring to live for the moment

• Don't seem to respond at all to failure—it is the outcome they were expecting anyway

• Do not generally honor commitments or accept responsibility

As a Progressive Style, you move to the Success-Oriented Stage when you've had at least one taste of success—and found you like it. As you begin to entertain the idea that you can repeatedly succeed, you allow yourself to actively set goals and relish the thought of attaining them. In fact, success can become so desirable, that you become intensely driven and competitive.

Success-Oriented Progressives

• Begin to realize that their destiny is something they can control

• Begin to develop business plans based on the lessons learned from past failures

• May become so driven to experience success that they become Goal-Intense styles.

Progressive Business with the Rich

While your Progressive Style develops, you will have best results with Practical New Rich, because they understand what it is like to work your way up the ladder. You will also get along well with Roller-Coaster Rich because they are still learning, too. Pedigrees can be patient and nice, but they expect quality results.

During your early stages you could have difficulty with Status New Rich and Flamboyants because they are very demanding and have little patience.

Once you've moved on to the Success-Oriented Stage, you can begin to deal successfully with all types of Rich.

Progressive Careers

Your Progressive Style often has trouble in office politics because you are so unsure of yourself. Others sense this and take advantage of it, often running over you like a steamroller. Still, if you stay in a corporate setting, you are capable of success once you enter a Success-Oriented mode.

Progressives will succeed as long as they find the right career.

The most important key is whether or not you get excited about what you are doing. If so, you can progress more rapidly and succeed much sooner.

A real Progressive may not have much confidence, but does have two wonderful traits:

1. Desire. Progressives *want* success, they are just afraid.

2. Need. Progressives are needy. They need success.

Progressives discover their power and they deserve their success. This is as good a business style as any of the others.

ʃetting Rich Client Goals

"You've got to dream."

—Conrad Hilton

Apart from the rare Serendipity Style, the rest of us operate best in life if we anticipate a desired result—a goal. A goal is what *you want*. It can be an achievement, a style of life, relationships, or a desired possession. Attaining the goal proves that you have the power to provide fulfillment for yourself.

A goal is meant to serve you; you are not meant to serve the goal. Keep long-term goals flexible. A goal is most effective if you set it to be achieved in twelve to eighteen months, rather than three years, five years, or ten years. Like last year's outfit, last year's goal may not fit you this year. It may no longer be your style of expression. Alter or change your goal every year, according to your current needs.

After you have set an overall goal for the year, also set smaller, bite-sized goals that take you, step-by-step, to the attainment of your overall goal by the year's end—or sooner.

THE CONTROL FACTOR

Before you set your goals with a Rich client, distinguish between which business factors you have control over and which you do not. This step can save you from feeling like a failure if any of the uncontrollable factors block your success.

You do not have control over the morality of a Rich prospect, or others in the picture. You do not have control over how well your competitors may be prepared. You do not have control over what your Rich client likes or dislikes. You do not have control over what may have happened that day, or last week, or even last month, to the Rich client that affects his or her emotional coloration. It can be something as tiny as the person having trouble with someone who resembles you. These are things you cannot control.

Realize what you cannot control, then set goals around what you do control, such as grooming, timing your approach, product knowledge, communication skills, forethought as to what you will say in any business meeting with your Rich client, and the degree to which you will be prepared.

Fill out the following:

My eighteen-month financial goal: $ _____

It takes _____ Rich clients, investing $ _____ each for me to attain my financial goal.

(If you are in sales, it will read:)

It takes _____ Rich clients, purchasing _____ number of my products @ $ _____ each, for me to attain my financial goal.

What I *have* control over at this time: _____
_____

What I *don't* have control over at this time: _____
_____

Business ways I can meet Rich clients (after reading Chapter 11)
_____
_____

Social Ways I can meet Rich clients (after reading Chapter 18)
_____
_____

Now break the information down into how many potential Rich clients you will try to meet through business per month, and through social activities per month. These will be monthly sub-goals.

List how many business and social activities it will take per week to accomplish your monthly goals.

Finally, assign the business and social activities specific days in each week—and mark them on your calendar.

Now, you have laid a day-by-day foundation that builds into weekly accomplishments, which build into monthly completions and conclude in an eighteen-month success.

Success is a process. No one is a natural born success. By the same token, no one is born to lose. A desire is all you need to start with—a desire that is sincere enough to crystallize into a *decision* to attain goals you set for yourself.

*E*IGHT STEPS TO SUCCESSFUL GOAL-SETTING

Write a response to the following seven steps, stating your desired outcome in positive descriptions. Be specific.

1. Expectant Goal Statement
Write your goal, stated in the present tense, in positive words. To speak in the future tense postpones success; draw your desires into your present by speaking them into your present.
Example: It is December 20, and I am the top salesperson.

2. Behavioral Goals
Write down the behavior skills you will acquire to accomplish your goals.
Example: I can maintain eye contact and smoothly give an introductory spiel that tells

- How their business can benefit from what I have
- How much it costs
- How soon they get their investment back
- What kind of ultimate return they can anticipate

After that, I will answer their questions clearly and confidently because I will have thorough knowledge of my product or services.

3. Expectant Goal Experience

How will you feel the moment you achieve this goal? Fully describe it through all five senses. Describe the inner you and your perceptions at that moment, as if it is happening, now.

Example: I feel around me the congratulatory pride of my company/spouse/parent.

I see a flash of the camera as I receive the top award.

I hear a pop of the champagne cork and cheering voices of friends/staff.

I taste success, kisses, champagne.

I smell a savory celebration dinner.

Experience these sensations fully in your imagination.

4. Goal Schedule

Set a realistic time frame for achieving your goal. Give yourself margin for error. Set tiny, bite-sized sub-goals that you can successfully achieve every day—and congratulate yourself by keeping a running list of what you have achieved each day. It reinforces your success consciousness and keeps your expectations healthy.

1. Set a yearly goal.
2. Then break down the components of the yearly goal into monthly sub-goals.
3. Break each monthly sub-goal into smaller, weekly sub-goals.
4. Break each weekly sub-goal into daily tasks.

5. Desire

There are people who will tell you that in order to attain a goal, you must be persistent. But I am here to tell you that you do not have to be persistent to attain a goal.

There are people who will tell you that you must be dedicated in order to attain a goal. But I assure you that you do not have to be dedicated to attain a goal.

There are even those who will insist you must be disciplined in order to attain a goal. But this, too, is false. You do not have to be disciplined to attain a goal.

There is only one thing you must have in order to attain a

goal: Desire.

You see, if you desire something enough, you automatically persist. If you truly desire something, you automatically dedicate yourself to it. And if you intensely desire something, you automatically discipline yourself to attain it.

Desire is everything. Desire is the engine that runs the entire goal process. Desire creates the goal. And desire achieves the goal. You must *want it*.

6. Faith Statements

People can pooh-pooh affirmations all they want—I know they work! My life turned around in less than three weeks when I overcame my limitations with simple words. I call them "faith statements" because, by saying them daily, you can actually create faith. If you repeatedly hear that your goal is possible, you will come to believe it.

An appropriate faith statement for you, could be the following:

I, (your name), now express a Rich awareness and draw to me those who have a material wealth.

Write your own faith statement, according to what you want, and say it twenty-one times every day, for twenty-one days. It takes a human being about twenty-one repetitions to correct any in-grained error. By repeating your faith statement twenty-one times in a row, you are correcting the error of your belief system. It also takes a human being twenty-one days to develop a new habit, and you are developing the habit of faith.

7. Goal Faith/Goal Action

Do you have faith that you can achieve your goal? Most of us don't really know what faith is. We think it is a fuzzy hope in our minds. And yet all of us want faith. And we can have it.

Faith is an action of risk. If there is no risk, there is no need for faith. And if there is no action, there is no faith at all.

A farmer could say, "I believe wheat will grow in my field," and he or she could be absolutely right. But if the farmer does nothing, there will be no wheat growing in the field a year from now.

But, if the farmer says, "I believe wheat will grow in my field—and I believe it so much that I have bought a plow and seed and I am daily plowing and planting . . . then, a year from

now—even if pestilence or weather destroys the farmer's crops—
the farmer will have proven wheat will grow in his or her field.

Yes, faith entails risk. And, yes, you may stand in heartbreak,
like the farmer, whose work has been destroyed. You may feel
"what's the use?" rise in your throat and choke you with tears.

But you know that if you stop working and trying, you will
never reach your goal any more than the farmer will ever see
wheat waving in the field, ready for harvest, if he or she stops
taking the risk of plowing and planting.

Do you have faith that you can achieve your goal? Ask yourself this question every single day. You will know your answer
by whether or not you are valiantly taking action every day toward your goal.

Faith is action. And like the farmer, you know that the only
way you can ever achieve your harvest is if you continue to have
faith by taking actions of risk—and one day, you *will* succeed.

8. The Secret of Success

The secret of success is the word "secret." If you do not tell
anyone your goals, you won't be seen as a failure if you change
your mind about something. If you do not tell anyone your goals,
they cannot stop you, or impede you, or gloat if you do not
attain them.

But, most of all, if you do not tell anyone your goals, you
grow in power. Your goals do not need the approval of anyone.
Your goals do not need discussion with anyone (which is an
indirect form of seeking sanction, though you may think you are
only getting ideas).

Your goal is sacred. It is an indication of your potential. Do
not weaken it by telling anyone.

Again remember . . . the secret to success is the word "secret."

eleven

20 Ways to Find Rich Clients

"You must put the hours in."

—Helen Gurley Brown

You have identified your business style, and determined your goals. Maybe you want to climb the corporate ladder, or find a backer for your business. Maybe you're looking to sell high-ticket items to Rich clients or to manage financial investments for the Rich. Whatever your purpose, now you need to find the Rich to do business with.

1. RESEARCH

If you want to find Rich clients in a particular industry, find publications about companies in that industry in your public library.

Look up these books in the Reference Section of your public library:

• *Guide to Private Fortunes.* This book gives a thousand or more descriptive profiles of the wealthiest and most philanthropic individuals and families. It is published by the Taft Group.

• *Encyclopedia of Associations.* See if this directory has industry associations listed in your area of interest. If so, telephone those associations that are of interest and get them to send you information on their organization and the type of members involved. Then you can see if the association has potential clients for you and, if so, how to get access to their member information.

I love this publication and find it interesting to browse through, triggering all sorts of ideas for groups to approach.

• *Dun & Bradstreet Million Dollar Directory of America's Leading Public and Private Companies* provides information on more than 175,000 top businesses.

Keep in mind, not everybody who is active in an industry will be listed in a directory. A few will forgo being listed because they know that many people use *Dun & Bradstreet* as a solicitation tool. Still, there will be many who are listed, so use the *D&B* directories or services.

• *The Social Register* or *The Blue Book*. This is really not as reliable as it once was, but I think you should use every resource possible because it might turn up someone for you.

The annually published, two-volume *Social Register* is supposed to contain the names of women and men on society's A-list in the major cities. If your library does not have one for the city you want, contact The Social Registers Association, 381 Park Avenue South, New York, New York 10016. Not all people in the register are Rich, but if they have helped the Rich achieve their goals, they may be able to help you achieve yours.

• *Standard & Poor Register of Corporations* includes the company's name, address, and telephone numbers—plus names of key officers and the company's primary bank, accountants, law counsel, sales volume, and number of employees.

• *Industry Survey Reports* in specific professions are usually published as a book or as a report. Most industries have an industry report that provides basic information about companies in that industry.

• *The Reader's Guide* is helpful for national magazine articles over a number of years, whereas computers in the library may only list magazine and newspaper articles for the current year or past twelve months.

Newspaper microfiche can provide back copies of major newspapers. Once you have the names of several potential Rich clients, you can check the library index and see if there are any articles about them. As you read the articles, look for clues to their interests that will help you understand the person and build business rapport.

Some libraries offer a research service for a small fee. They might be able to provide you with information about certain industries that, in turn, can lead you to people you are seeking. Ask your librarian if there is a local or regional *Who's Who*. There are usually statewide or regional directories. See if your potential Rich clients are listed.

2. PUBLICITY

Wouldn't it be great to have the Rich seek you out? Well, publicity is the best way to attract the Rich to your business.

There are many great lawyers in this country, but the ones who are sought after by the Rich are the lawyers who get publicity. The same is true for physicians, chefs, investment brokers, fitness trainers, relationship consultants, memory trainers, and so forth. Sometimes the difference between a starlet and a movie star is made by publicity. The starlet may have more talent, but a star is made by publicity. The same is true of rock stars.

If you are an entrepreneur, the skill of attaining publicity is perhaps the most important part of your business. An entrepreneur should have press releases going out as frequently as possible.

• If you're not self-employed, know your company's policy about publicity before you seek it.

• A press release should be just one page, double-spaced, and typed on a clean white sheet of paper. If you represent a company, be sure the company logo is on top and include your business card.

• Be sure your telephone number is on the press release if you are not using company stationary and if you do not have a card to enclose.

• Connect your products or services to something currently hot in the news, such as global warming, or of seasonal interest, such as winter sports, the Fourth of July, or Christmas.

• Put the most important information in the first few sentences, answering the questions who, what, when, where, why, and how. Use the rest of the page to support that information.

• Type "FOR IMMEDIATE RELEASE" in all-caps at the top of the page. Sample:

FOR IMMEDIATE RELEASE

Arnold Ambitious   To: THE NEWS DESK
6864 South Mission Avenue
Bilby, Wisconsin 37611
(934) 888-3533

For Immediate Release

GLOBAL-WARMING SOFTWARE HEATS UP

"You can now monitor global-warming in your immediate area," says Arnold Ambitious [who], sales manager for EKO Electronics in downtown Bilby [where].

According to Mr. Ambitious, a new product called *Global-Warning at Home* [what] is the latest software to be introduced on the PC market today. The software is able to take information about your own area and, within seconds, provide you with current and predicted-future global-warming conditions [how].

This unique software is due to be in stores next month, [when]. Mr. Ambitious claims he is already taking orders from customers who are concerned about the environment.

"I've never seen anything like it," says Ambitious, whose company has sold PC software for the past ten years. "People really care. It looks

---

as if we will sell out this software almost as soon as we receive it in our store!"

Mr. Ambitious suggests interested customers should place orders, now.

• Mail or hand-deliver your press release to the news desk of your local newspapers and radio and television stations.

When I worked for a small Dallas stock brokerage house, we ended up with three brokers, and all of us were women. I typed up a press release titled "All-Woman Stockbrokerage Firm" and mailed it to every publication and television station in Dallas. A CNN affiliate came out with camera and crew and interviewed me, then took footage of our little office. *The Park Cities People,* a newspaper for the Richest community in Dallas at that time, did a story and sent a photographer out to get a picture of me and the staff. Many people—including wealthy ones who saw the TV show or read the news article—called me to inquire about investing.

3. BE AN OWNER

Yes, the Rich will occasionally do business with a junior executive from a large company, but they especially like to conduct business with business owners. Then, even if your business is small, you can reassure a Rich client that you are the owner and therefore the decision-maker who can negotiate special deals with them.

4. BE AN EXPERT

If you are not an owner, that's okay, as long as you become an expert. And being published in your profession establishes you as an authority in your field.

"But it takes so much time to write a book," you protest.

Not really. A two-hundred-page how-to book on a specialized subject can be written—and written well—in three weeks or less, once you have the information at your fingertips.

Because so many people asked me how to do it, I wrote a step-by-step manual, *Secrets of Writing a Book in Three Weeks, or Less*, which is available through Regis Distributing, Drawer 10007, Austin, Texas 78766.

You may or may not make a lot of money from book sales, but you will gain recognition as an expert in your field.

5. REFERRALS

Nothing beats a referral to get you in the door. It is always a plus if you can introduce yourself and add, "Your friend, Jill Andrews, president of Nationwide Bank, referred you to me. She thought you would be able to benefit from my services." However, never give a false reference. Your potential Rich client will most certainly call Jill later to see if she shares an unspoken obligation to you, or if there is in fact something Jill found special in you.

Likewise, be sure to ask a happy Rich client to refer others to you. Simply ask if the client knows someone who might benefit from your products or services. Any reference given by your respected Rich client is an excellent prospect.

Always ask for a referral, even if the Rich client declines your business. The person may want to soften the rejection by giving someone else's name.

6. MAILING LISTS

Order mailing lists of individuals in the income range and area that your business targets, and mail information about your products or services. Never buy an entire mailing list until you have tested it. Ask the mailing list company to let you buy a test number at a cheaper price. If the list is no good, you haven't wasted too much money.

Include some or all of the following in your mail-out:

• A typed sales letter, possibly having pictures of your product in it

• A brochure—or a sheet that spotlights a product

• An order form (preferably with an expiration date)

- A response envelope or a toll-free 800 number
- A large, full-color fold-out sheet
- Testimonials
- A "special offer" or "limited time offer"
- A discount coupon
- A list of any publicity about your products or services

Be sure your mailing piece does not look like junk mail. Postcards, either regular-sized or extra large (get size guidelines from the post office before you order any), can be very effective. People can instantly scan a postcard before deciding to toss it, whereas a sealed envelope can be tossed without bothering to open it.

Your sales piece is you, therefore, you want it to look like the quality of service you provide. Furthermore, all sales pieces should tell the Rich buyer

- What your product or service can do for the Rich—without mentioning "the Rich." Use words such as "exclusive" or "only those who understand the finer things . . ."

- Why the Rich should do business with *you* instead of anyone else (without bashing your competitors)

7. COLD CALLS

It's a numbers game. Only six out of a hundred people you cold call might be interested in your product or service. And out of those six, only two stand a fifty-fifty chance of buying.

Still, if you stand to make a large sum of money when you sell your services or just one of your products, then finding those six Rich people who are interested is worth the rejection of the other ninety-four people.

A goal of making fifty cold calls a day is pretty stiff, but there are a lot of successful people who do exactly that. For those of you who feel overwhelmed, take a compassionate approach with yourself. If you make only three cold calls a day, that is better than none. You have to start somewhere. Try to work your way up to five, then ten, then twenty, then fifty.

For a call to count, you must actually talk to the CEO or owner or executive in charge of buying your service. Talking to the receptionist does not count in your goal of fifty calls.

Your cold calls are only as good as your target audience. If you are targeting the general audience, you could use the telephone directory; but since you are targeting the Rich and their companies, buy prospect cards.

These cards are issued by mailing list companies, such as Dun & Bradstreet and ABI American Business Lists, but there are many others. Look them all up in your Yellow Pages, under Mailing Lists, and get them to send you information so you can compare them.

Good prospect cards provide company name, telephone numbers, regional offices, contact name, employee size, sales volume, business products and services, credit rating codes, and so on. Prospect cards of individuals give name, age, income, and telephone number. Some may include marital status.

Best Times to Call. The best days and hours to call Rich clients are Tuesday through Thursday, between 8 A.M. and 6 P.M. They often leave early on Fridays for the weekend or they are busy wrapping up things for the week, so you may not get the full attention you deserve. Mondays are generally hectic, catch-up days, and, again, they may not have quality time for your spiel.

Even so, I think that anyone you were unable to reach Tuesday through Thursday, you should try to call on Mondays and Fridays. Saturdays can be good days to catch someone in the office. These individuals often get their real work done on Saturdays, when the office is closed.

Getting Past the Secretary. When a secretary answers, give your name and a company name that sounds related to the Rich prospect's industry.

"This is John Doe with Smith, Brown, and Jones Properties. I am calling Ms. X about her South Padre properties."

You have bypassed the chess game of who, what, and why.

"Does she know you?" may be the next question.

"No, but she will probably want to discuss her South Padre properties with me."

Stay nice. Always, always nice. If the Rich client does not talk to you, ask when Ms. X might be available for another follow-up call. Leave your name and number if you like, but also call back if you do not hear from the Rich client. Every time you try to reach Ms. X, be sure to thank the secretary for her time in a nice tone.

For the most part, if you cannot reach someone, do not try more than five times or you are wasting time. If the Rich prospect does not call back after five messages, mark that person off your list.

But if it is vital that you contact this particular prospect, you can show up at his or her office once and be very nice to the secretary. Tell the secretary you do not have an appointment, but that you happened to be nearby and decided to drop in. Would she see if Mr. X will see you? If he won't, then give her your card, smile, and ask her to have him call you.

Never underestimate the power of the secretary! Secretaries practically run some companies. They are trusted employees and the boss values this person's judgment (or, believe me, the secretary would be out of a job).

Trust the secretary to get you in. If the secretary likes you, he or she will put in a good word for you. If you are rude to the secretary he or she can probably keep you out. I love secretaries. They have gotten things done for me when the Rich prospect or client was foot-dragging or preoccupied.

If you can't get in, and only if it is imperative that you see this particular Rich prospect, you should do this: Find out what time the person arrives for work or leaves the office; wait outside, look sharp, have all materials with you, and nab the person: "Excuse me, Mr. X, but I really need to talk to you for just a minute."

Your Spiel. One and half minutes is all you have to hook your Rich prospect, whether by telephone or in person. Write and rewrite your spiel on a sheet of paper. Memorize it, but always have it on hand, in case you forget.

Practice reading your spiel into a tape recorder, over and

over, until you can read it without sounding as if you are reading it. You want to say it with life in your voice, too.

- Introduce yourself

- Give your company name

- Get right to the point

- Have a Fact Sheet of important information with you

- Ask specifically if the prospect wants your product or service

Tickler Files. A tickler file card system is very important for setting future appointments with a Rich business prospect.

If a Rich prospect says, "Not now," then ask when you might call back. When you get off the telephone, type the date into the business organizer in your computer. If you do everything by hand, just write on your tickler card the date you intend to call back and key things said by the Rich prospect. Then, place the card in a small file box under the future date slot for your follow-up call.

Handling Rejection. Time really is money. When you cold call, every wasted minute costs you. If people turn you down, you have not wasted your time by calling, because they might have said yes. It is only a waste of time if a person says no and you try to change his or her mind. If you have this trait, eliminate it, because it is a no-win method. You can be more productive using that same time period to politely get off the line with that person and to telephone someone else.

Most Rich prospects will say no nicely, but there are some who are rude to everybody and it has nothing to do with you. I do not care how much money they have, they do not deserve you.

It is okay to feel dejected, as long as you don't give them the power to stop you from dialing the next telephone number and forcing an upbeat tone into your voice with the next Rich prospect.

8. PROFESSIONAL LITERATURE

Professional magazines and newsletters within the industry that interests you will keep you abreast of who the movers and shakers are in the industry.

You can also read the business classified ads in the professional or industry magazines to see if there is someone who might use your business. And you can place business ads in the magazines yourself.

9. BUSINESS CLASSIFIEDS

Follow guidelines for advertising. Usually, newspapers require your business be listed with the Better Business Bureau before they will let you advertise. Also study several ads that grab your attention and seem credible. Then ask yourself what is the most important benefit a Rich client would get from your products or services. Make that your bold headline.

10. PROFESSIONAL, SPECIAL INTEREST, OR INDUSTRY ORGANIZATIONS

If you qualify for full membership in an industry organization, work to become an officer, so that you can become involved with the major players, who are typically Rich leaders within the industry.

11. COMMON CAUSE

Closely related to special interest organizations is politics. I can think of no easier, more direct way to meet the people you want to meet than to get involved—actively involved—in your political party.

An election year will be sizzling hot with energy and the Rich who want to back a candidate will surface more at that time. The key to meeting them is to get active on committees. Also, attend every group function where a candidate (local, state, or national) will make an appearance.

Everyone attending is open for mixing and mingling, so you can introduce yourself to anyone there and chat about the candidate. It is okay to give your business card to people you meet on those occasions. However, give your cards only if there has been a nice measure of rapport, so it will seem as if you give the card for identification reasons and not just to push for clients.

12. TRADE SHOWS

Through associations, you learn when trade shows are being held. Top executives and business owners attend major trade shows. Be sure you have an itinerary of events and calculate which days and events are most likely to attract the Rich you want to meet.

13. SPECIAL INTEREST SEMINARS

Do the Rich attend seminars? Yes, they do. Most of my Rich clients are people who attended my seminars. There is an attorney who gives legal opinions on national television who attended my seminar and then took a consultation. There are two Grammy award winners who did the same thing. Millionaires, heiresses and heirs, psychiatrists and psychologists, brain surgeons and CPAs have attended my seminars.

Yes, the Rich attend seminars. Seminars can be an effective method of showing how your business benefits the Rich. There is nothing wrong with selling your products or services at a seminar, as long as you give full information to your audience, whether or not they buy anything! True, you are targeting the Rich as your primary client base, but not all people who attend your seminars will be Rich . . . yet. You must never underestimate the ultimate potential of anyone.

There are many seminar circuits. One of the biggest and most lucrative is the corporate circuit. Businesses want seminars that can make better, happier workers of their staff. If you are good at it, you can command sizable speaker's fees from the businesses, as well as sell your services or products. And as your fame grows through your success, your speaker's fees grow in digits.

There are also college circuits, spa circuits, executive retreat circuits, cruise-ship circuits, travel destination circuits and learning center circuits. You can do your own footwork of mailing to businesses, telephoning their program coordinators, or showing up in person to talk to them. Or you can find a speakers bureau who can get you into these upscale circuits.

14. ALUMNI GATHERINGS

Some graduates who become Rich never look back at the sacred halls of college once they are gone, but many do. If you were well liked by your peers in college, alumni gatherings can help widen your Rich contacts. Even those who are not Rich will know old college friends who have become Rich (or always were). Once they know what your business provides and that it will help those they know, they will recommend you.

15. ANNUAL STOCKHOLDERS MEETINGS

One of my New York clients told me he went to an annual stockholders meeting and discovered he was sitting next to a wealthy stockholder. He said the man eventually became a business client of his.

16. CHURCH, TEMPLE, MOSQUE

Whatever your spiritual affiliation, you can often find members who would rather do business with someone of their own faith, if they have a choice.

17. FUND-RAISING COMMITTEES

By calling on the Rich to donate money to a popular cause, you are making an acquaintance on a neutral ground. If this is an organization the person considers important, you will have that charitable interest in common. Then, the contact you make has the potential of being translated into a business prospect.

18. HELP THEM REACH THEIR GOALS

My favorite success story is about my brother, Lefty Morris, when he was a young law student at the University of Texas, as told by former state attorney General Crawford Martin.

When he was running for attorney general, Crawford was deluged by young law students wanting to work on his campaign. One by one, he interviewed them and they all gave the same answer—working for him would help their careers. That didn't mean anything to Crawford.

But he was impressed when my brother walked into his office, extended his hand, and said, "I'm Lefty Morris, and I can organize the young people of Texas for you." (Lefty had been president of the Young Democrats for the State of Texas and knew he could keep his word).

Crawford said, "Now that meant something to me!"

The key is this: Lefty said how he could help Crawford Martin attain his goal of becoming State Attorney General. And Crawford won. Lefty became Assistant State Attorney General under him.

If you can help a Rich client reach his or her own goals, you may get their help achieving yours, too.

19. THINK BACKWARD

When horizontal drilling was a new technology, a creative oil man found that most Rich oil and gas buyers were skeptical of the technique and were not interested in buying properties that would not produce well without the new method.

Mulling over his dilemma, he had an idea. He looked through want ads in the newspapers to see who was hiring stock-brokers to sell horizontal drilling investments. He knew those companies would desperately need an ongoing stream of properties ripe for horizontal drilling. He called them up and instantly sold a large property and made a lot of money.

If you cannot penetrate your market through the usual

means, try "thinking backward." Instead of starting at the beginning and working toward the end result, start at the end result and work backward to find your Rich clients.

Anytime the usual way is not working for you, throw it out and try unorthodox methods for finding your Rich clients.

20. BECOME "LIKE-MINDED"

The wonderful message of Napoleon Hill's masterpiece *Think and Grow Rich* is that all the wealth in the world began as a mere idea in the mind of a person.

I want to take that a step further to say that your mind can be connected to the minds of Rich achievers through books about their lives. Choose to associate mentally with the Rich. Do your homework by keeping a biography or autobiography of a Rich person with you at all times. Read one after the other.

You learn a lot about the Rich by reading about them. You learn how they think and what appeals to them. You absorb the common denominators of those of self-made greatness.

Just as important as absorbing their successful qualities is seeing how very human they are. Many times they have endured hardships you never knew they had. Reading about the twists and turns in their lives and how they worked through them gives you the encouragement to persist in the face of self-doubt. It can also give you ideas of how to solve similar problems—or even trigger a link to how to solve an unrelated problem.

Study of the Rich leads you directly to the Rich—through an understanding of motives, mind, and pursuit of wealth.

$\mathcal{B}$eing Comfortable with the Rich

"You only rise as high in life, as your comfort level. And you can increase your comfort level."

—*Ginie Sayles*

You will be comfortable with the Rich when you learn how to be comfortable with yourself—and you can learn how to be comfortable with yourself more easily than you think.

You feel comfortable with yourself when you feel equal to the situation and to the people around you. At those times, you project confidence. Luckily, if you do not feel confident, there are specific body language techniques that project confidence for you so that you will at least look comfortable.

Posture of a Winner. Posture tells the world how to treat you. Posture tells others what to think of you. Even if your posture conflicts with your clothing status, people will subconsciously believe your posture and wonder about the difference.

Posture tells the real story of the real you. Posture tells others if you are tired or energetic or sad or happy; it can convey exuberance, fear, and confidence.

Confident posture is something you learn to maintain, automatically, if you practice it.

What is confident posture? Stand next to a wall and flatten your body against it. Your head, shoulders, elbows, hips, calves, and heels should touch the wall. *Keep your chin level,* not up. And push your shoulders back and down—not up.

Every time you go the restroom, stand next to the wall and do a posture check. When you are not able to utilize a wall, just pull your entire rib cage up as high as you can while standing or walking. When you are sitting, you can get comfortable, but just do not let your shoulders sag forward.

Hands. When a man is standing or walking, his arms and hands should be out from his body, just a bit, with elbows slightly bent. His fingertips should be about an inch and half from his thighs when he stands or walks. This is confident male alignment.

A woman's hands should lightly touch her thighs when standing straight or walking. This is confident female alignment.

Both men and women look more confident if they do not swing their arms much. In fact, swing only from your elbow down, not from your shoulder.

Standing. Face the Rich with the full front of your body while talking to them. Do not turn sideways and talk over your shoulder. This is a projection of fear.

The best business distance to stand is nineteen inches from someone who is about your height. If the person is much taller than you or much shorter than you, stand farther back so that your eye contact seems fairly level with theirs, without your having to bend your head to look down or to stretch your neck to look up.

Walk with Purpose. Do not amble, but avoid rushing, which looks as if you cannot keep up with everything.

Keep Your Conversation Optimistic. Complaining sounds as if life is too big for you. Optimism is faith—and confidence.

Handshake. Shake hands with yourself, right now. How did it feel? It should not be a hard, painful clamp, nor should it be limp. Just solid.

Eye Contact. You may be as honest as the day is long, but if you glance around the room a lot while you talk, people will say you have shifty eyes. Without knowing why, people will be slightly less trustful of you. The same is true if you avoid eye contact or have short eye contact in a one-on-one conversation.

If eye contact is difficult for you, tear out a full-page picture of the face of a man or woman who seems to be looking directly at you. Tape it up on a wall and stand directly in front of it. Time yourself as you maintain eye contact while introducing yourself (pretend to shake hands), while pretending to listen, and while talking to the picture. Or if you have a video camera, set it up, turn it on, and talk while looking directly into the camera as if into a person's eyes.

Voice. Speech trainers recommend a moderate pitch of voice. I have a degree in speech, too, and I disagree with my colleagues in that field. I think a more impressive business tone is just one notch below moderate. It sounds cultured, self-assured, and serious. Just one notch, though.

Right now—in a moderate pitch—say out loud, "This is the best product on the market," as if you are talking to a CEO. Emphasize the words "this" and "best."

Say the sentence again, just one notch below your normal tone, still emphasizing "this" and "best."

If you are naturally soft-spoken, don't change it. Just be sure to emphasize key words in your sentences—and be sure you pronouncing each word distinctly.

If you are loud and cannot seem to do anything about it, you operate at a handicap. The only way to counter loudness is to keep your tone friendly and to be exceptional at what you do. Otherwise, you will find yourself left out, a lot.

Practice talking into a tape recorder and work on the sound of your voice until it is exactly the way you want it.

Moments of Self-Consciousness. We all have those moments, when we feel self-conscious, which projects as inferior or inadequate. Self-consciousness kills the power of your personality.

When you feel self-conscious, you must deliberately fight it by forcing your mind off yourself and onto something else. Ask someone a question and it will draw your attention—and their attention—away from your self-consciousness. And concentrate on every word the person says for a few minutes. Gradually, you will relax and not feel self-conscious.

If you cannot ask someone a question that will command your attention away from yourself, then instantly start asking yourself mental questions about the surroundings. They can be a bit of nonsense, even "I wonder if that lamp is solid brass . . . and the plants look well tended . . . I don't think it is going to rain . . ." This keeps your mind occupied and off yourself.

Being Yourself

Probably the best way to really feel confident is to be yourself. Nice advice, but what does it really mean? I believe that being yourself requires three things:

1. Expressing yourself through your natural energies

2. Being true to your beliefs

3. Having one genuine manner

Express Your Natural Energies

If your natural energies are lively, talkative, and witty, don't attempt to be subdued and shy. You'll only come off disinterested, bored or boring, or worse, snobbish.

If you are naturally Goal-Intense, direct, and positive, why pretend to be otherwise? And if you are naturally reserved, observant, and contemplative, let yourself be that way. Forced patterns will not only make you feel uncomfortable, but may make you look inane.

In other words, don't try to be anything. Just be.

It is your personality that takes the phoniness out of the rules of behavior that we all must follow. It is your personality that kicks the fakeness out of your smile. Your personality puts life and conviction into any statement you make.

Ultimately, flowing with your natural energies helps you feel at ease with yourself, and when you are comfortable with yourself, you are comfortable with anyone, including the Rich.

Whatever your natural energies are for expressing yourself, do concentrate on the word "happy," because happiness magnifies the best in any natural energy. When your smile is genuine, you're not only you, you're the best "you" you can be.

Stay True to Your Beliefs

You were born with one primary job in this life: to take care of yourself.

Being true to yourself means that you do not abdicate that responsibility just to please someone else. It means that before you commit to something, you must look into your own heart and measure it by your values.

Your values may not be popular, but they protect you—and that is your primary job, remember? The nature of business is compromise, but not if it sells out your values.

A client of mine said he lost eleven years of his life recovering from cocaine, and all because he did not have the courage to live by his own values in the face of social acceptance.

If social acceptance means you have to sacrifice your values, you are looking to the wrong people for acceptance.

At a business-social occasion, you never have to do anything you don't want to do, if what you have to offer in the business is worthwhile.

So if you are in a situation you don't like, just check your watch and say you have to be somewhere and that you will get back later to those attending. Or if something is suggested that you do not value, you can simply say, "No thanks" or "Sorry, fellas (or ladies)."

Don't act offended or give lectures. Don't make a big deal about your values. Just live them.

If anyone scoffs (true Pedigrees will not), just smile and hold your ground. I assure you, the Rich will secretly respect your loyalty to yourself. And they will trust you.

You are the values you live. Stay true. That is being yourself.

Have One Genuine Manner

To be yourself at all times means that you have one genuine manner that is the same with all people, of any socioeconomic class. Your one genuine manner can pay off in business.

One of my celebrity clients told me of a situation that happened to her:

A woman journalist was waiting in a hotel lobby to interview my client, when a woman entered the hotel, smiled, and greeted the waiting journalist as she passed. But the journalist did not smile or speak. She only glared at her, then with a lift of her chin, averted her eyes. Most journalists are nice to people, but, according my client, this particular journalist was not.

A few minutes later, the journalist learned that the woman she had just snubbed was the celebrity she was supposed to interview. She had not recognized her in casual dress and a new hairstyle.

When the journalist realized her mistake, she rushed to the celebrity, smiling and gushing her hellos. The celebrity made a polite excuse to cancel the interview.

To save your best manners for people you think are Rich or "somebody" reflects negatively on you. No one is going to respect your self-importance. They'll just think you're a snob.

Have one genuine manner that is the same at all times with all people. It frees you from phoniness and allows you to be yourself at all times. And as I've said, being yourself is the key to true confidence, enabling you to comfortably associate with anyone—including the Rich.

$\mathcal{D}$ress for Success—For Him

> *"I . . . recently saw a sequin-trimmed jacket and mistook its wearer for a member of the band, not a guest."*
>
> —*Letitia Baldridge,*
> The New Manners

Twenty-eight seconds is all you have to sell yourself. That is as long as it takes for the Rich to categorize you as someone they would like to know or to do business with.

Clothing is a language. You can identify a priest by his clothing, or a policeman by his clothing. The way you dress communicates who you are in your world.

$\mathcal{D}$RESS THE PART

When dressing for business success with the Rich, you are better off targeting a look that appeals to Rich Pedigrees, even if clients are Flamboyants or Status Rich. The Pedigree look is classic and always in good taste.

Shirts

Dress Shirts. The ideal business shirt is a white, long-sleeved, plain-point-collar or round-collar dress shirt. (Never wear a short-sleeved dress shirt—especially without a jacket.) Your ideal shirt has no taper, a button cuff, one pocket, and long tails. The preferred fabric is a pure, fine pima cotton.

You should have as many white dress shirts as you can, but no less than five. Try to accumulate eight white dress shirts over a period of time. It is also okay to have a few colored dress shirts that you can wear with your business suits.

Casual Oxford Shirts. Especially for young men casual business dress can include button-down oxford shirts with slacks, chinos, even denims occasionally. You want a smooth roll on the collar. Warm weather oxfords look good in stripes or solid colors with white collars.

Sweaters

Cashmere V-necked sweaters or sweater vests over your shirt and tie, worn with flannel pants and a jacket, look handsome and elegant in cold weather.

Pants

Classic pant styles have no pleats. They are straight leg, and have 1¼-inch cuffs that break on top of your foot and are barely above your heel in your bare feet. You want narrow waistbands and narrow belt loops, with pockets exactly on the seams, and back pockets with flaps. Your basic wardrobe should include one pair of black wool slacks, one navy pair and one pair of gray flannel pants, as well as three pairs of Chinos for a casual look.

Sport Coats and Blazers

Jackets dress you up, even in jeans. Be sure your jackets are two-buttoned, single-breasted jackets, with natural shoulders and classic lapels. They should have no taper and pockets with flaps.

The length of your jacket should be to the middle of your hand when your arm is relaxed at your side. Your shirt collar should show a half inch above your jacket collar. Your shirt cuff should show a half inch below your jacket cuff. Your jacket should button exactly in the middle of your belt. A good jacket will be lined and have smooth button-holes and good-looking buttons.

Sometimes a less expensive jacket can look expensive if you just have the buttons changed. For example, leather buttons can make a tweed jacket snap with class.

Be sure leather buttons pick up the natural color of the tweed. If you have a black houndstooth jacket, have black leather buttons and black leather belt, shoes, and watch strap. If you are wearing a brown tweed jacket, make sure the buttons, belt, shoes, and watch strap are brown.

Other touches for tweed can include a thin leather trim on pockets, on the elbows, or on the underside of a collar. And you do want real leather, not fake leather.

You need different jackets for different times of the year. A lightweight navy blazer, a white jacket, and a cream-colored one are staples for the spring and summer. Your white jacket will look good with light blue or navy pants; your cream-colored jacket works with brown or tan pants. The fall and winter call for a navy flannel blazer, a houndstooth or herringbone jacket, and a black or brown wool jacket. Your wool navy blazer looks best with gray pants, and all navy blazers look great with brass buttons that have an insignia, or even better with your initials monogrammed on them.

Alternate your blazers and pants with suits, and you won't have a locked-in look or as high a cost in clothing as if you try to have a whole wardrobe of business suits.

Business Suits

Business suit jackets follow the same guidelines as blazers: two-buttoned, single-breasted, no taper. Invest in good quality. Well-made suits may be expensive, but they can last a lifetime. You should own a gray pinstripe wool-worsted suit, a dark blue silk suit, and a dark blue wool-worsted suit. For spring and summer you may want to add a lightweight blue suit and a pale gray suit.

Long Coats

If you live in or travel to a place that has temperatures below forty degrees you're going to need a coat. A long black overcoat or a gray herringbone wool coat that is well below your knees is best. Everyone should own a long trench coat in navy, black, gray, or tan.

Classic Color Combinations

You will see color combination trends come and go in fashion magazines. And, in your private life, you can follow them to your heart's content. But when dressing for business, stay away from fashion trends and stick with serious-looking clothes. Wear brown leather accessories with gray, brown, tan and sometimes blue; wear black leather accessories with blue, black, and gray.

Underwear

You may be invited to the gym with your Rich client. If, for some reason, you will be seen half-dressed, be sure you won't be embarrassed by holey-moley underwear or a lower-class style.

Long boxer shorts in plain white cotton are classiest. Naturally, your comfort is more important, so plain white cotton briefs are an alternative—but stay away from bikini or thong styles. Although a few patterns or pastels are okay; white is your best bet because it can be kept spotless by adding bleach to your wash load of whites. Colored or patterned underwear can fade.

Some might think indulging in silk underwear is the way to go, but silk is pricey and can be hot. Cotton breathes and absorbs moisture, keeping you more comfortable. If you want to, you can buy your underwear from Wal-Mart, K-Mart, or Target. Remove the labels, which is classy anyway. Be sure you have at least ten shorts that have no holes, stains, or frayed edges. A man can never have too many pairs of underwear.

If you wear an undershirt, make it a T-shirt style, rather than the muscle shirt style. Plain white is standard.

Socks

Silk socks look nicest with business suits and formal wear; cotton socks are okay for casual business wear. No argyle socks for business.

Your basic collection of silk socks should include two pairs of black, two pairs of dark gray, two pairs of dark brown, and two pairs of navy socks.

The skin of your leg should never show, even when you cross your legs in any manner; therefore, socks need to be high on your calf and to stay up. If washing causes loss of elasticity, invest in a pair of black garters to hold up your socks.

Shoes

Black wing-tip shoes and brown lace-up shoes are basics. If you can afford English handmade, lined, and well-finished wing-tips, get them. If not, get a close approximation. Be sure they do not have wide soles that extend much beyond the shoe. This is your best all-around business shoe that can also take you to many formal occasions. You may also want a pair of black or brown loafers as an alternate business shoe and to wear with your Chinos.

Be sure you keep the soles and heels of your shoes in good shape. It does not cost much and it adds life (and comfort from shoes that are well broken in) to your shoe wardrobe. Shoes should be repaired at least every three months and polished before each wear. Do it yourself the night before or splurge and get them shined. Use a wax polish instead of liquid, because liquid can cake on your shoes, and over time, the buildup of liquid polish damages the leather. If you have buckskin shoes (white bucks in the South), buy the recommended cleaner and shoe brush from the shoe store or a shoe repair shop.

Be sure to have a pair of black rubber rain shoes to pack into your briefcase, to easily slip over your shoes. Put a shoe cloth in your briefcase, as well, and touch up your shoes just before a meeting. Details like this contribute more on your projection of self-confidence than you can imagine.

Accessories

Never wear diamond-studded anything during business. It diminishes your credibility.

Watch. If you cannot afford an expensive 18-carat gold watch, buy the face of an antique watch in 18-carat gold or one that is gold-plated and add a really good leather-strap watchband.

For dressy occasions, leave the leather-strapped watch at home. On these occasions an entire 14-carat (or better) gold watch is appropriate. A gold-plated watch is okay, except that it wears away over time and you will have to have it replated.

Silver-toned or steel jewelry does not look as expensive as gold. Some people combine steel with 18-carat gold and that is fine, but it is still not as dressy as all-gold.

Rings. If you are married, a plain gold wedding band without diamonds looks best. Some men wear college rings, but they can look a bit pedantic.

Cuff Links. These should be small, flat, plain or monogrammed (preferred) cuff links in gold or silver. Wear only the two-button types that snap together, giving you a button on each side of your cuff.

Ties. According to my contact at Hermés, the standard tie width is three and a half inches. Tie lengths vary according to the height of a man, but nothing looks worse than a short tie or one that is too long. You will be correct if the point of your tie rests at the bottom of your belt buckle. And do not wear tie tacks or tie clips. However, a tie pin is elegant.

The four-in-hand is the tie knot of choice. Windsor knots are only to give bulk to the knot in weaker tie fabrics.

Belts and Suspenders. Black leather belts from Coach are reasonably priced, have good workmanship, and are enduring. Thin gold or silver tone belt buckles that come with the belt are fine; or you can have small monogrammed gold or silver belt buckles bought separately. When you can afford it, a 14-carat-gold belt buckle or sterling silver belt buckle—or a combination sterling silver with 14-carat gold inlay—is a nice Rich look.

Leather-tabbed suspenders (no clips) can be worn instead of belts to add "character." There is something distinctive, traditional, and endearing about suspenders. Can you imagine Larry King without them?

Key Ring. You want a monogrammed gold or a silver key ring that disengages the car key so you can give valet parking attendants only the key to your car and not the rest of your keys.

Wallet. Get a smooth black or brown leather wallet with your initials monogrammed in the center in block letters.

Hats. The guideline with hats is that you must really feel so comfortable in them that you forget you are wearing them. If so, you will look good in hats and wear them well. If you have an iota of self-consciousness in a hat, don't wear it. And men's hats are never worn indoors. The instant you enter a building or house, remove your hat.

Eye Wear. For business, be sure your eyeglasses are round or slightly oval (according to your face shape), in either wire or tortoiseshell frames. This look in eyeglasses can enhance your image of competence and intelligence in the minds of the Rich.

Sunglasses can be the kind that change from clear to dark automatically if you are in the sun. Or you can opt for all-black frame and lenses in classic Ray Ban sunglasses and be in good form.

Briefcase. A simple, plain black leather briefcase that is sufficient to hold whatever you need to carry is all you need to look smart and successful. You do not need the $2,850 ostrich leather burgundy attaché.

Like your wallet, you can monogram your briefcase for a nice touch. Monogram directly onto the leather on the upper broadside, beneath the handle, or on a gold, brass, or silver medallion.

Miscellaneous. Cell phones in the new models are smaller and look better than the bigger, bulkier models of a few years ago. Pocket electronic organizers are not necessary, but they are nice and time-saving.

Everyone needs an umbrella. A large, black umbrella with a carved wooden handle is classic. You can also have a silver or brass handle, which you can have monogrammed.

Note on Monograms: Standardize your monogram. Don't have one style of monogram on your shirts and another on your wallet and another on your jacket buttons or buckle. Choose one style and use it for everything.

Read Chapter 21 for detailed instructions on how to shop for your wardrobe so that you look sharp and save money.

Business Wardrobe Considerations

There are three other considerations you want to be aware of in business dress:

1. The part of the country you are in
2. The nature of your business
3. The business occasion

Many Rich businessmen in the Southwest wear pressed dark blue jeans, a white dress shirt, reptile cowboy boots, and a hand-tooled leather belt with a handsome silver-and-turquoise—or just plain silver—belt buckle. For a business lunch, they add a tie (possibly a string tie) and a sport coat. This is a trustworthy, genuine, good-old-boy look, valued for its humility, although business suits are sometimes worn as well.

On the West Coast, businessmen may wear T-shirts with jeans and a blazer, long-sleeved knit shirts (buttoned up, all the way) with trousers and sport coat, or open-necked shirts and khakis and no socks. And yes, some wear a business suit.

In the far North, business suits are always correct, but casual business wear can be outdoor gear, such as a corduroy shirt, pants, and a jacket, or a turtleneck sweater, pants, and a jacket.

Dress shirt, tie, and khakis are as casual as you should get in business with the Southern Rich. Add a jacket if going out of the office. Otherwise, wear a suit.

On the East Coast, the rule is simple: a business suit, period.

Naturally, the nature of your business can dictate your attire. If you are selling sailboats or ski equipment, you can dress accordingly, but you score points for always looking clean and neat.

Above all, appropriate dress for the occasion is expected. Apart from unusual regional styles, the following dress guidelines will keep you appropriate in your business meetings with the Rich:

Job Interview. Definitely a suit. White dress shirt with plain point collar and button cuffs, lightly starched, and ironed, with a silk tie. Shoes must shine.

Business Lunch. Lunch with a Rich client or Rich business associates will typically be in a better restaurant, a corporate dining room, or a private club, so wear a suit. If lunch is low-key at a local sandwich shop, it still won't hurt to wear a coat and tie.

Office Setting. If you are visiting a Rich client in his or her office, wear a suit.

Dinner. Avoid wearing brown suits in the evening.

PERSONAL GROOMING

You can put on the most expensive clothes and still not look the part if you have poor grooming habits.

The Richest act you can perform on your own body is to give it

1. A daily shower with shampoo
2. Antiperspirant
3. Brushed teeth
4. Fresh underwear
5. Fresh socks
6. Clean, trimmed nails.

Create an easy ten-minute regimen for grooming that you look forward to—and soon your body won't be able to tolerate anything less.

Never try to save money or time by re-wearing yesterday's underwear or socks because they don't look dirty. Yesterday's clothes are not fresh and that is enough. This simple choice can make a world of difference in your self-esteem and projection of personal pride.

Smoothly Shaved. A classic look sells you best to the broadest number of Rich clients. Your classic look includes no sideburns, no whiskers, and no "shadow" during business hours—even if it looks sexy in men's magazines.

A mustache must be neat and clean-looking and can make a very young man or a baby-faced man look more mature. A goatee is not preferred, but if worn, keep it neatly trimmed.

Hair. A short, side-parted haircut without sideburns is a classic business look. If you must wear your hair long, have your sideburns short and pull your hair back into a neat ponytail. Military hairstyles look authoritative, but they can also project an unyielding nature. A dated haircut—such as a California surfer of the sixties or a seventies antiwar revolutionary or an eighties new wave look—projects that you may also be outdated in your thinking.

Fad hairstyles project an unstable personality and a weak sense of self. Severely short or severely long hair, uneven lengths, or wild colors make you look immature and as if you are trying too hard to get attention.

Above all, do not try to hide balding areas by combing your hair forward. It draws attention to the baldness and fools no one. If thinning hair disturbs you, look into hair replacement techniques that you can shampoo, style, and play sports in. Too often a hairpiece looks like a hairpiece to other people. A full head of hair does look virile, so consider the permanent methods of hair replacement.

On the other hand, complete baldness—meaning the head is shaved, leaving no hair whatsoever—has been tested and proven to be considered just as virile as a full head of hair. Italian dictator Mussolini and the late Broadway actor and movie star Yul Brynner were both advised to shave their heads completely to add to their virility and it worked!

Gray hair has been tested for public perception. It was found that people with gray hair were considered less energetic and their ideas viewed as "probably outdated." When the hair was colored, the same people were viewed as more vigorous and their same views were better received. This is why many of our former presidents who were past their prime opted for coloring their hair. And coloring your hair can make your own skin tone look better. If you wear a neat mustache or goatee, keep it colored as well.

Silver temples on a man in his late thirties or early forties looks distinguished and it projects experience and credibility. Silver hair can also look elegant if you are in your forties or fifties and if your clothes are an extremely fine quality, your posture is perfect and your manners are flawless. Past the age of sixty-two, however, most silver hair begins to have the same effect as gray hair.

Hands. One of my successful clients said, "Rich men always have white knuckles and nails. A man can wear expensive suits and shoes and drive a good-looking car; but I always look at a man's knuckles and nails."

Any man can upgrade his looks by keeping a natural bristle wooden nail brush at his sink (purchase one at a drugstore). Use it *every time* you wash your hands at home.

It only takes a couple of seconds. Rub the brush over your soap and quickly scrub nails and knuckles of both hands. Rinse the brush and replace it. Rinse your hands and dry them. Another plus of this habit is good health. Disease is spread more by unwashed hands than by anything else.

Fragrance. This is strictly optional. A clean shower scent is fine, but if it makes you feel great to wear a men's cologne, do it. Fragrance is one area where you cannot stint on price. Only the more expensive men's fragrances will do. Cheap men's colognes smell cheap.

*   *   *

The saying is that the clothes make the man, so dress the part and project the right image. I'm not advising you to break the bank to put together a designer wardrobe, but a neat look with a few key pieces is an investment that can have huge dividends.

$\mathcal{D}$ress for Success—For Her

> *"When I look my personal best, I am powerful."*
>
> —Georgette Mosbacher

A sophisticated business look will be more successful with the Rich than any other style of women's business dress. A sophisticated business style is a combination of classic modesty with a touch of glamour. It looks serious but feminine, respectable and authoritative. It is not a seductive look, and it is not a neutered or emasculated look.

$\mathcal{D}$RESS THE PART

Shirts

Dress Blouses. Blouses should always be tucked in, and slightly bloused at the waistline. Collars can be pointed, round, or scalloped. You should leave the top button open or wear a full, soft scarf tie at the neck. Blouses should be silk or 100 percent cotton. You can wear a variety of colors, but make sure you have a classic white cotton blouse and a white or pink shirt with a large black, navy, or red foulard bow.

Oxford Button-Down Shirt. For more casual days, you might want to wear an oxford shirt—bright white, light blue, or pale yellow.

Sweaters

Turtlenecks in cotton, cashmere, or a silk blend look sharp under a blazer. A classic navy or bright white turtleneck is a smart addition to your wardrobe. It is correct *not* to fold the collar down.

Dresses

A Black Dress. A solid black dress is too severe and dressy for daytime unless you add a clip-on white collar and white cuffs or a short, striking, neatly tied scarf (not the flowing kind because it looks too dramatic and evening-y for business). You can also wear your black dress with a short red blazer and red accessories or with a tapered white blazer and black and white accessories.

For formal or evening business events, wear your little black dress with pearl earrings and a pearl necklace.

You do not want to bury yourself in black, so wear it sparingly. Most women who wear black do so to feel safe or to hide figure flaws. Black is aging and looks best on women in their twenties and early thirties.

Cotton Dress. This dress wears nicely above the knee, but is okay below the knee, too. A fitted skirt is fine for the office if it is not tight.

Pink, rose, solid red, turquoise, or blue are good colors for this dress. Add matching accessories in pink, rose, red, etcetera. If the dress has a rounded collar, add a large navy foulard bow and you will have a crisp business look. If this dress has sleeves above the elbow, add a white cotton blazer.

Circle-Skirt Dress. A dress with a circle skirt looks best when the top of the dress is fitted, with long sleeves, and the skirt swirls low, around the calf or exactly mid-knee. In wool or a good knit, this style is flattering to the figure in navy, along with lightweight navy stockings and navy flats or low heels. Wear with a colorful, patterned scarf for business.

Silk Wrap-Dress. You need a good figure to wear this style. The ideal dress is knee-length or above, long-sleeved, in solid cocoa brown. Wear it with only a thin gold watch and round gold earrings. If the V-neck made by the wrap-dress reveals cleavage, wear a pink scarf (so good with brown) long enough to wrap around your neck and criss-cross into the V made by the dress.

For evening, turn the look sexy by removing the scarf, and add a thin gold chain that disappears into the V.

Skirts

Hem lengths for women's skirts in the business world have probably wrought more controversy during the twentieth century than any other aspect of women's clothing. The best rule of thumb for the conservative business world is to be fashionable, but avoid extremes.

When skirts are very short, be sure yours are not shorter than three inches above the knee. Mid-knee length is ultra-conservative but it is always acceptable for business. Avoid extremes with longer skirts, too, which can look very elegant with the hem between your calf and ankle.

The cut of your skirt is a matter of both fashion and body frame. Circle skirts are flattering to any body style, emphasizing a slim figure and making a fuller one look trimmer. A-line skirts are either in or out of fashion, and you will look dated if you wear them when they are out. When they are in, they are excellent for a tailored, slender look on women with fuller hips. Likewise, straight skirts are either in or out. When they are in, be sure yours are not too tight for business. A straight skirt in a half-size larger can make a woman with weight problems look slimmer.

Pleated skirts are designed for two figure types. Women with thin legs look best with pleats from the waist; but women with fuller legs look better if the skirt is fitted three inches below the waist, with pleats beginning just above the thigh.

Whatever the hem or cut, look for the following fabrics, colors, and combinations for your clothing.

Flannel Skirts. Stick to solid colors—gray, brown, and black. This skirt is simple enough to wear with a blazer and tailored blouse to create a business look, or to wear with a silk blouse and pearls for cocktails at someone's house.

Cotton Skirts. Great for spring and summer, cotton skirts in solid navy, white, and classic red are indispensable. Plaid or discreetly patterned lightweight blazers and plain blouses in white or pastels give these a nice look for business.

Full Or Swing Skirt. A solid-color swing skirt can be fine for business if you wear a short, military-style jacket and turtleneck with it. And wear flats; leave the pumps and boots at home.

Pleated Skirts. A pleated skirt in blue-and-green plaid looks good with a blazer in one of the colors from the plaid. Your shirt can pick up the other color.

A black pleated skirt can be worn with a black blazer, white shirt, and bright red vest.

Pants

Flannel Pants. Black or navy and gray are your staples. For business, wear a tailored shirt, with or without a ribbon or scarf bow tie, and a dark or red jacket. A solid turtleneck with flannel pants is dressy casual. Always wear leather flats with your slacks.

Chinos. If you need a casual look, Chinos are an option. Keep to straight-legs and without a cuff. A tucked cotton blouse counters the outdoor look of khaki. Add a navy blazer and you have a casual business look that is crisp but comfortable. Low or flat heels are the only shoe option.

Corduroy Pants. A rich-looking chocolate brown pair can be worn with a sweater-vest over a long-sleeved cotton shirt and a wool jacket or a corduroy jacket that exactly matches your pants. Woven-leather belt and loafers are the accessories of choice.

Blazers

A blazer in classic red will likely be the star of your wardrobe. Have one in a lightweight summer fabric (cotton, linen, linen-blend) and one in wool. Classic red adds a splash of instant confidence and class when worn over a simple dress, with a skirt and sweater, pants and a blouse, or jeans and T-shirt. It is also terrific when teamed with gray flannel.

Have a lightweight navy blazer for warm weather, and one in wool for when the weather turns cool. Navy is always pretty with a white dress or white trousers and red shirt, and is a classic with Chinos or a Khaki skirt.

Wear a black blazer as an accent piece to tie together black pumps or flats, belt, and briefcase. A black blazer with a hound-stooth dress, jumper, or pants looks especially neat.

For summertime, a white blazer is essential. You'll achieve a striking monochromatic look when you wear it with a white shirt and pants. It is also very nice over powder blue and other pastels.

A Scottish tartan plaid blazer in wool is beautiful for business with a solid color skirt that picks up one of the colors in the plaid and a turtleneck that picks up a second color in the plaid. In the summer or fall, a madras plaid jacket over a yellow shirt with chinos or a khaki skirt is nice.

Suits

For business, women can alternate sophisticated business suits with streamlined dresses and skirts, worn with blazers.

A gray flannel suit worn with a tailored-style pink silk shirt, ribbon tie, and small silver earrings is a winner for business.

Year-round silks or silk-blend suits are also good investments. Classic red, with covered buttons and worn entirely with red, and a classic black worn with black and white accents—or for a real power play worn with red accents—are winners.

For summer, a white linen suit with all-white accessories looks very sharp. A blue striped seersucker suit with white accessories is a good second choice. Be careful with seersucker; sometimes, it does not work well for business.

Long Coats

A loose-fitting, ankle-length winter coat in black, red, or camel with a full, rounded collar and lapel is timeless. Add a cashmere or wool tartan scarf. You will also want a year-round trench coat, preferably in classic red, but acceptable in navy, black, or tan.

Underwear

For a smooth look in straight skirts or business slacks, use adhesive pantyliners in pantyhose and do not wear panties. Bras must be comfortable, so be sure you are properly fitted and that the cups are smooth for sweaters or T-shirts. If your clothes are heavy enough, you can wear any color and style you like; otherwise, dark clothes should have dark underwear, light clothes should have light underwear, with champagne colors preferred over white. And be sure bra straps will stay securely in place. You don't want to be distracted by worrisome bra straps while you are in a business meeting.

Socks and Stockings

Sheer skin-toned stockings or very sheer navy or black hose are standard. In the summer you may want to add ivory-colored stockings; stay away from white. In colder weather you can get away with black opaque tights.

When you wear pants, you can wear trouser socks in black, navy, or ivory. Make sure they fit properly; socks sagging around your ankles look very sloppy.

Shoes

Every woman I know loves shoes and probably owns more shoes than she really needs. That's okay, we all have our indulgences. What you must have in your closet is a basic pair of pumps and flats in both classic red and black. Feel free to buy shoes in all other colors, as well. If good-quality and worn with the appropriate clothes, they can pull an outfit together and look dynamite.

Keep in mind that strappy sandals and stiletto heels are never appropriate in a business setting. Also, many women have taken to wearing running shoes with their business suits to commute to and from work. I don't think this ever looks good and all your shoes should be comfortable enough to walk in.

Accessories

Accessories do add your individual personality to your look, but the key is to keep them simple, classic, and elegant.

Pins. An antique pin in real gold, worn with everything, can be your trademark. Or you can have a small gold pin monogrammed with your initials. Wear pins on the lapel of your blazer or to attach a scarf on your dress. You can also pin them to a cloth or scarf belt.

Rings. Upper-class hands are adorned by meticulous care and little else. A single gold wedding band or diamond wedding set is all you wear if you are married.

Rings for every finger and between every knuckle is for teenagers in an identity crisis or for women who don't know any better. You don't want your hands to look like the artificial ones used at a retail display counter. An array of rings is out of place in business.

Bracelets. If you wear bracelets for business, be sure they do not clink noisily or jingle and that they are not a distracting style or size for business.

Earrings. Earrings in yellow gold or white gold and flat or round balls or knots are best for business.

Watches. Add a lizard watchband to an antique watch with a classic-style face and you have a good-looking watch for business or casual wear. A ribbon or cloth watchband is also acceptable. For dressy business occasions, a thin, gold-banded watch is lovely.

Wallet. A small, trim leather wallet that fits in your jeans pocket as well as in your compact handbags is preferred. You can have it monogrammed.

Belts. Woven and smooth leather in classic bright colors, as well as black, are good year-round. Brown is optional. Orvis offers leather belts with a zipper lining you can tuck money into. This can be an alternate to carrying a purse—and offers back-up security funds.

Briefcase. The more slender the briefcase, the more elegant it looks. You do not look dragged down, or as if you are lugging a weighty case. Be sure your briefcase has a shoulder strap you can add for times you are really loaded down.

If you carry a laptop computer, use only a traditional black leather briefcase, not a computer case, for security. A thief recognizes a computer case in an instant and may think you are an easy target as a woman. If you carry your laptop in a traditional briefcase, thieves will think you only have papers inside.

Handbags. For business, you are better off not carrying a purse. Just tuck a slim powder-base compact, lip pencil, mascara, and other essentials into a flat zip case and tuck it inside your briefcase, along with your wallet and a few neatly folded tissues.

If you want to carry a handbag, make it as small, trim, and flat as you can for business. Shoulder-strap options help when you maneuver both purse and briefcase to meetings.

If you intend to carry the same purse every day, have it match the color and leather of your briefcase. Otherwise, your purse should match your shoes and belt exactly.

Accessory Colors

Red—or any other color—can be a neutral as much as black or tan when it comes to accessories. And red goes beautifully with everything. For example, red accessories look outstanding with a yellow outfit, with a white outfit, with a black outfit, with a blue outfit, with green, with pink, with purple. Likewise, green accessories are fabulous with a blue, red, yellow, or white outfit.

Try to have at least three colors for your accessories. Either navy or black, classic red, and possibly green.

Don't play it safe and only go with black and brown. It's boring, unimaginative, and definitely not Rich.

Eye Wear. Eyeglasses that are round or slightly oval (according to your face shape) in either wire or tortoiseshell frames can enhance your image of competence and intelligence in the minds of the Rich. Plus, they add refinement.

Sunglasses can be the kind that change from clear to dark automatically if you are in the sun. All-black frames and lenses by Ray Ban are classic.

Have a monogrammed fabric, needlepoint, or leather case for your glasses.

Note On Monograms: Standardize your monogram. Don't have one style of monogram on your shirts and another on your wallet and another on your jacket buttons or buckle. Choose one style and use it for everything.

If you monogram your briefcase, have it put directly onto the leather on the upper broadside, beneath the handle—or on a gold, brass, or silver medallion.

To look great and save money, read Chapter 21 for detailed instructions on how to shop.

Miscellaneous. A small, digital-analog cell phone adds business efficiency and personal safety when you are not in your office. Pocket electronic organizers are easier to manage than notebooks. A fold-down umbrella that tucks into your briefcase, along with rubber or plastic overshoes keep you dry when rushing through the rain to a business meeting.

Business Wardrobe Considerations

Business styles in this section of the book are appropriate for women in any part of the country and are more homogenous than men, who vary in business dress according to region.

Above all else, dress appropriately for the occasion in your business meetings with the Rich:

Job Interview. Always wear a serious gray or navy suit; but a white lace collar and lace handkerchief peeking from your jacket pocket keep you from looking too severe.

Business Lunch. A dress with a jacket is fine, as is a suit.

Office Setting. If you are visiting a Rich client in his or her office, wear a suit.

Dinner. A solid color knit or silk dress with pearls. No cottons. A jacket is unnecessary.

Personal Grooming

It is imperative that that you have impeccable grooming habits. If you don't, all the designer clothes in the world won't help you look Rich.

Begin every day with

1. A shower and shampoo

2. Antiperspirant

3. Brushing your teeth

4. Fresh underwear

5. Fresh stockings

6. Nail care

Never try to save money by re-wearing yesterday's panties or bra because they don't look dirty. Yesterday's clothes are not fresh.

Taking proper care of your clothes will help them last longer and keep them looking better. When you get home at the end of a busy workday, remove your stockings and drop them into your bathroom sink. Draw up cold water with a touch of bubble bath. Leave it to soak.

Hang up your suit, even though it will be going to the cleaners with your other suits at the end of this week.

Later, when you are in the bathroom again, drain the water, rinse your stockings and fold them into a towel. Hang them up to fully dry.

Hair Removal. Always keep your legs and underarms smoothly shaved. Stubble looks awful showing through sheer stockings or shirts. Unsightly facial hair should be plucked, bleached, waxed, or removed with electrolysis. New methods of laser hair removal are becoming popular and may be a good investment.

Hair. An all-one-length or softly layered or tapered haircut that is no shorter than your chin and no longer than your collar, is a classic look that takes you from business to the opera in perfect style. Learn three ways to wear your simple wash-and-go haircut. Have a style for business, a style for fun, and a way to dress it up.

Simple, well-cut styles take you from business meetings to cocktail parties with just a change of hair ornaments, if you like. Thin tortoise headbands keep hair out of your eyes while you are working, as do neat bows or tortoise clasps that hold your mid-length hair at the nape of your neck. For evening events you may want to wear rhinestone barrettes or combs.

You can also wear your hair swept back and up, as long as you don't wear it in the mussy, sexy up styles that are not meant for the office.

The Rich are not as likely to trust you with their business if you have a strange haircut, because you do not seem to trust yourself enough to be yourself in a simple way. You seem too insecure. A dated haircut projects that you may also be outdated in your thinking.

Gray hair does not look distinguished on women. It tends to make them look tired and washed out. The only exception is silver gray/pure white hair (think of the model Carmen or Barbara Bush). But even these looks are maintained with treatment from a professional colorist. I highly recommend going to the salon to get a consultation and to color your hair. The color will look natural and will compliment your skin tone. Be sure to go for touch-ups regularly; nothing looks worse than your roots showing.

I don't advise you to over bleach your hair, go for harsh black, or try an unusual color (eggplant, purple, maroon etc). And definitely don't get thick frosted streaks in your dark hair. These looks can appear cheap, or are just too trendy for business.

Hands. Hands should be well cared for. Apply hand cream daily to avoid dry, chapped skin. Nails should be short, manicured, and natural or painted a classic red. Make sure your cuticles are clean and not ragged, and chipped nailpolish is a definite no-no.

Fragrance. Clean, subtle, spicy scents are best for business.

Cosmetics. Makeup is a must, but should be understated. That fresh-scrubbed face might look healthy, but it doesn't look professional. A light layer of natural-looking makeup, a neutral blush, brown and beige eyeshadow used sparingly, mascara, and classic red lipstick are all you need. Stay away from frosted makeup—it's definitely not right for daytime—and make sure your lipliner, if you use it, is the same color as your lipstick.

Permanent Cosmetics. Natural-looking permanent cosmetics for your eyebrows if they are weak or for your lips can save time and keep you looking good. Do not get glamorous permanent cosmetics. Avoid permanent eyeliner; but if you do have permanent eyeliner, have it only as a very thin line close to your lashes.

Be very careful if you elect to have permanent cosmetics. Let only a board certified cosmetic surgeon refer you to a practitioner. Even then, get references, and be sure the person has been in business for *years*. Meet the person's clients. Get references. Find out where the person was trained and if he or she has certification.

The idea of a business style is to look serious, trustworthy, and competent. To accomplish this, be clean and very neat in your grooming. De-emphasize sex in your business looks, but do not try to look masculine. The ideal is to be classy and professional.

$\mathscr{R}$ich Business Practices

" 'Richness' is at least as much a matter of character, of philosophy, outlook and attitude, as it is of money."

—J. Paul Getty

Long before this book was even thought of, I used to ask Rich clients and Rich friends what the one most significant trait was in a person they did business with. I soon learned that no one could limit the choice to just one trait. Rich clients look for a package of qualities in a businessperson. Over time, however, I kept hearing certain traits crop up again and again.

I compiled them into a list of the twelve most important traits the Rich seek in a business associate. Once they were compiled, I asked my clients and friends to put the traits in order of importance to them. The order below was the result of combining their choices. The number one trait may surprise you. It surprised me.

1. *Love your work*. It seems that most of the Rich want to work with people who love what they do. Passion for your work virtually guarantees superior quality.

2. *No ambivalence*. Many of the Rich said they want to work with a person who has no ambivalence about success— they want to work with someone who passionately wants to succeed. This is especially important if someone approaches them for a partnership or an investment.

3. *Honesty*. This is the one I expected to be first, and clearly, it is important. No one wants to work with someone who is dishonest. If you find a wallet, you return it. When you pay for an item and the cashier gives you more change than you are supposed to receive, give him or her back the excess. The Rich said it is the little things like this that impress them.

4. *Independent thinker*. You do not have to butt heads with the Rich who can make or break you, but you will be better off in the long run if you express your true belief in a matter, if asked. You are not a disagreeable troublemaker, but you are not a yes person.

5. *Not petty*. This was another trait the Rich mentioned that I had not expected. Keep business records, they said, but not personal score. Score-keeping of who did what to whom and when drains the sap out of rapport.

The Rich will not respect you if you are a pushover or a patsy, so you should, of course, stick up for yourself when needed. But people who do not burden themselves and others with petty complaints usually have a benevolent spirit and a generous heart, both of which command client loyalty.

6. *Consistent action*. Anyone can hop eagerly into a new project when the excitement is high, but it is the individual who continues to maintain a high productive profile when the newness has worn off who keeps the respect of a Rich client.

7. *Accept responsibility*. Be careful with this one. You must be willing to accept responsibility for your actions. But if there is possible liability, do not jump in and volunteer that you are responsible or offer to pay anything, thinking you are being noble. You might end up eating those words in a lawsuit! Instead, if your Rich client confronts you about something that might have legal implications, tell the client you will look into the matter. Then, contact your attorney and work out a solution to the problem.

8. *Originality*. You must bring something new to the table or there is no reason for your Rich client to be interested. If all you have to tell the person is what everyone else is saying, you

are probably too late. If you can point out unique views or so-lutions, you will show yourself as valuable.

9. *Client-oriented*. The Rich do not want you to kowtow to them, but they want to know that you have their best interests at heart when you do business together.

10. *Keep your word*. If you say you will be somewhere at a certain time, *be there*, on time. If you commit to something, do it. Of course you want to use written contracts in business, be-cause it is a good business practice, but your word should also be your contract.

11. *"Has more money coming in than going out."* That's how one of my Rich clients described the type of person he wants to do business with. If your Rich clients sense you can't take care of your own money, they won't want you to touch theirs.

12. *Professionalism*. The Rich I talked to emphasized that your level of professionalism is important. They defined it as

- Promptness
- Appropriate dress
- Respect of their time with succinct presentations
- Providing neat, easy-to-follow charts or support mate-rials
- No undue bravado, but matter-of-fact pointing up of skills or talents that separate you or your company from the run-of-the-mill in accomplishing common goals
- Thoroughness, and pausing to answer questions
- Leaving on time; if you said it would take you only fifteen minutes, don't stay forty-five—P.S. *top salespeople are the ones who end the meeting*

BUSINESS MEETINGS WITH THE RICH

You've finally gotten an appointment with that Rich business prospect. You've impressed the client with your initial pitch and your character. Your suit's pressed and you're excited about the big day. But are you really ready? Can you handle yourself in a business meeting—from the lowliest hello (actually, nothing is lowly) to the reading between the lines of ambitious players? You must be prepared, and to be prepared you need to practice. Even if you only take ten minutes and walk through your presentation, you will be far better off than if you don't. Try these time-tested tips:

• *Simulate the scene of the meeting.* To internalize information, you should act out scenes in your mind or in front of your mirror or video camera.

• *Shake imaginary hands and speak.* Literally get up off your sofa and walk about in your living room, speaking your part in a pretended situation. It only takes a minute or so and yet it can mean the difference between being in command of an actual situation or feeling ill-at-ease.

• *Anticipate questions.* Write down anything someone might ask you in a meeting. Tape record yourself making the presentation and listen to it. If you saw someone else make this presentation, what else would you want to know?

• *Practice your eye contact.* Set objects (pillows, vase, plant, cat or dog) in a semicircle around your living room with a mirror in the center. While you practice your presentation, let your eyes move from left to right to left again, pausing only half a second on each object, while you speak.

Business meetings work better when you rehearse your understanding of information, work out the bugs, and add your own personal touch. You can also benefit from role playing with a spouse or friend who can think of real questions you may be asked.

The Purpose of the Meeting

Purpose: the key is to know that the stated purpose of a meeting may not be the real purpose. Likewise, what one person says he or she wants in the meeting may not be what that person *really* wants.

Everybody has a purpose in the meeting, including you. Determine the primary purpose of everyone who will attend the meeting. Let that purpose be a filter in your mind for whatever each person says, or however he or she reacts to what you or others suggest.

Then, determine *your* primary purpose. Let your body language and territorial positioning follow suit according to your purpose. Are you there to gather information? Or are you there to lead the meeting? Are you there to persuade or to influence the outcome of the meeting?

If Your Purpose Is: To Gather Information

If your primary purpose is to gather information, follow these guidelines.

• *Position yourself nonthreateningly.* In every meeting, there will be dominant territories, which are usually the front, center of a room, or the executive desk in the office where the meeting is being held, or the head of a conference table. If you stand or sit in dominant territories at the meeting, you may intimidate or cause skepticism and therefore not learn everything you need to learn. Sit to the side, along the front of the meeting area, but not in the back, if you can help it.

• *Dress very conservatively* in grays. Men should wear a solid gray or gray striped tie.

• *Have a low-key friendliness before the meeting.* It is important that you talk to people so that you do not appear fearful or mysterious, as if you have a hidden agenda.

• *Pay attention.* While you gather technical information, analyze the underlying psychology of those present. Determine four key things:

1. Who is really in charge of this meeting? It may not be the person hosting it. It will be the person who seems to innately lead the meeting in the direction it takes.
2. Who is the ultimate decision-maker about the issues being discussed at this meeting?
3. Look behind what people are saying. What could be hidden agendas or personal ambitions not spoken? How could

each person benefit from the position he or she is promoting, minimizing, or criticizing?

4. When the person who is hosting the meeting is not around, what does everyone say about the issues under discussion? You don't care, really, what is being said about the person, per se; you care what is being said about the issues when that person is not around.

• *Talk to learn, not to express yourself.* Talk should not consist of your opinions, or you may never find out what you came for. When the meeting is under way, listen. Ask questions to clarify your understanding.

• *Be passive but fully present.* Have a "wheels-turning" thinking manner. Don't bury your head to take notes. Create your own style of shorthand so that you can make quick notes without breaking your attention from the speaker very long.

• *Don't take a position yet.* Do not nod approval or frown about anything being discussed, and be one of the last to laugh at a joke. If you indicate your position, you may not learn other information.

If Your Purpose Is: To Control a Meeting
If your purpose is to control the outcome of a meeting, let your body language and territorial dominance set the pace.

• *Establish appropriate authority.* Control the meeting, first, by scheduling it in your domain—at your office or conference room.

• *Control the environment.* If you must present the meeting in someone else's office, establish your authority by changing the furniture, even slightly. You can do something as simple as to move your chair, or to ask those present to change theirs. Changing the environment in some way demonstrates you feel the authority to take charge of the setting.

• *Dress authoritatively.* Men should dress in a black suit with a solid red tie or red-striped tie. Women in a solid red suit, red shoes and belt, or a black suit with bright red buttons, matching red silk scarf in the breast pocket, red shoes and nails.

- *Use authoritative body language*. The most important part of your body language is to keep an upright posture throughout your presentation. Don't slump or lean on anything.

- *Never come across as pompous*. Appropriate authority is not heavy-handed or imperious. Have a light friendliness.

- *Begin on time*. I have always liked the view that if you wait for latecomers, you punish those who thought enough of you to be on time.

- *Impress by being prepared*. Have everything with you. Make a checklist of every chart, every handout, every news clipping, and every report that supports your information. Have all the simplest supplies at hand: pencils, pens, erasers, paper. Don't impose on others at the meeting.

- *Include everyone in your eye contact*. Have traveling eye contact, from left to center to right to center to left, if it is a large group. If it is a small group, be sure to look at everyone there. Your eyes should not linger more than half a second on each person as you talk. Move your eyes smoothly. Jerking your eyes from person to person looks fearful.

- *Exclude disapproving people from your eye contact*. Do not let anyone throw you by a glare or a frown, or that person will be controlling you. Many speakers will keep courting the approval of that one individual, by continually looking at him or her more than at anyone else. Instead, refuse to be controlled by removing your eye contact from that person. When your eyes go that way, either look at the middle of the person's forehead instead of into his or her eyes, or completely skip the person as if he or she does not exist. You will reclaim your authority.

If Your Purpose Is: To Persuade
You can accomplish your purpose of persuading people to your views, if you effectively accomplish all six of the following:

- *Know your target*. A few days before a highly important meeting, find out the views of each individual involved. Do this by having separate talks with each individual, privately, perhaps over cocktails, lunch, or tea. That way, when the important meeting comes around, you already know who you will have to win over.

• *Don't intimidate*. If a man wishes to persuade, he should wear a blue suit, blue shirt and rose-and-blue striped tie to the important meeting. For a woman, a rose-colored suit with blue accessories will be fine.

• *Soften the environment*. Establish authority in a less formal sitting area in your office, preferably with a sofa and a couple of chairs around a coffee table.

• *Charm and stay in control*. Smile as you greet and welcome everyone and indicate where each person should sit. After people have sat down, pull up a larger chair, facing them. Their eye contact is automatically on you.

• *Make it win-win for as many people as possible*. Begin the meeting within a few minutes of everyone's arrival. State the purpose of the meeting, define the issue to be discussed in terms of those present, and how everyone present can benefit from your proposal. A touch (but only a touch) of flattery as to the contribution each person has made to this effort is fine.

Where to Hold Business Meetings

Ideally, you would want the meeting in your office, but most business meetings with your Rich client will be held in the Rich client's office. However, if your client expresses a preference for going to you and you don't have an office or you are from out of town, set the meeting in a respected restaurant. A brief meeting in the lobby seating area of a nice, centrally located hotel is fine, too. You can make it slightly more formal by meeting for dinner or afternoon tea, whereas lunch or cocktails make for a less formal meeting.

Choose an elegant, well-known restaurant or hotel. If you are known by the personnel, they will be more attentive to advance requests you make. Make advance arrangements for seating, and for settling the bill and tip ahead of time so that no one else can insist on paying. This also prevents the interruption of the bill's arrival.

Restaurant tips are twenty percent of the bill, without taxes and wine, unless there is a wine steward. If there is a wine steward, tip eight percent of the price of the wine to the steward. These other standards should apply:

• Tip the headwaiter ten dollars for setting up the special advance arrangements with you.

• Tip the coat-check clerk a dollar.

• Tip the doorman a dollar for getting you a taxi or calling for your car.

• Tip a valet two dollars for bringing your car around.

Be sure your lunch, tea, or dinner meetings do not run too long. Typically an hour should cover most meetings. Occasionally, a lunch meeting may run an hour and a half. More formal afternoon tea and dinner meetings can last up to two hours.

To succeed in business with the Rich, you need to look and act the part. However, the most important things you can do are be honest, be yourself, and be confident. The Rich can go a long way in helping you meet your business goals and becoming Rich yourself.

Part 3

Socializing with the Rich

$\mathcal{T}$hree Stages of Society Life

> *"Each friend represents a world in us, a world possibly not born until they arrive, and it is only by this meeting that a new world is born."*
>
> —Anais Nin

Many people who have the talent to rise socially never try to enter society because they are intimidated by the very word "society." And it is only because they think of society as an untouchable elite.

Society is much simpler than that. First of all, society is just a group of people who become friends as they do things together.

True, so-called "high society" is a group of Rich people who may know one another only superficially as they gather to support nonprofit causes with lavish parties. But within the superficial glitter, there are pockets of true friendships that formed over time.

And society cannot exist without a steady trickle of newcomers to keep it alive—which is where *you* come in.

So, first and foremost, do not be intimidated by the word "society." It is a place where you find friends.

While many people are intimidated by society, there are those who want to enter and who try to enter, but lose heart and drop out because, after a few months or a year, they have not yet "arrived."

What these individuals do not realize is that society is much like a corporation: you rise through the ranks and evolve into a respected and influential social standing. And all that takes time.

How much time? Well, it takes a few years for you to prove yourself "worthy," and you become worthy as you evolve through three social stages. These three social stages are:

Stage I—Entering Society. You choose a prestigious nonprofit organization as your point of entry. There, you learn the all-important social strata of the organization's leadership. You also work your buns off as a volunteer, doing all the dirty work no one else wants to do, so the Social Rich get used to you and learn you are sincere.

Because some prestigious social organizations are inundated with volunteers, you may be put on a waiting list that could take many years to produce an opening. Don't put your own life on hold for anybody. A very effective shortcut is to find smaller nonprofit organizations that are offshoots of the larger one. For example, a Grand Opera had a subsidiary Opera Theater, which was an opera education tool that took opera to schools and churches and cabarets.

Often, you get into an offshoot quickly, and still make a reputation for yourself among the old guard who run the parent organization, by getting to know them during shared events.

Another way around the long waiting period is to find out the names of the Rich who are involved in the large organization and identify their separate "pet projects."

For example, a Rich woman who was influential in the opera company of a major city also loved modern dance. So she set up a small nonprofit modern dance company. One of my clients who wanted to meet her bypassed the long waiting list of the opera company and volunteered for this woman's small nonprofit dance company. There was no waiting list for this smaller but nonetheless prestigious nonprofit company. My client did excellent volunteer work and not only met the Rich woman, but came to know her through the company's small social galas. This busy socialite became so endeared to my client, she eventually scheduled tea together with her, twice a month.

Stage I lasts an average of one to three years (up to five years in New York City).

Stage II—Social Acceptance. You will know you have entered this stage because you will be invited to some or all of the eight primary social functions listed in Chapter 23. You will become enough at ease with your Rich friends that you will reciprocate by hosting some of the eight primary social functions, too.

Stage II is an exciting period in your life. Most people are happy to stay in this stage, indefinitely. You really don't need to go higher. But if you want greater social responsibilities, you may be in Stage II an average of five to eight years, before you move on to Stage III.

Stage III—Social Leadership. You have arrived! Your social evolution is complete as you accept very responsible leadership positions that are high-profile in the community. You may or may not find yourself accepted in close friendship with the Rich, but they recognize your value—and you can socialize with them on some level. This, in itself, provides you ample opportunity to reach your ultimate social goals.

Stage III lasts for the rest of your life, if you handle your first leadership role successfully. As you age, you will step aside, but you will always be influential.

This part of the book—"Socializing with the Rich"—is designed to help you through the three stages of society, pointing out major signposts along the way to keep you on course.

Three Obstacles to Rising in Society

When people seem unable to evolve through the three stages of society, I have found it is usually due to one of three serious obstacles.

1. Unwillingness to add missing layers Of Class

2. The tendency to only rise as high as one's "comfort level"

3. The hindrance of old "friends"

1. Missing Layers Of Class

No one has all the layers of Class (see Chapter 2). Every Rich person you meet will have some of them missing, whether or not you know it. But try to have at least ten of them—for the quality of your own life—and to propel you more successfully through the three stages of society.

2. You Only Rise as High as Your Comfort Level

Because you will only rise as high as your comfort level in society, the trick is to become increasingly comfortable with the trappings of wealth. You do this by consciously exposing yourself to as much of a Rich lifestyle as you can afford, without over-spending.

You accustom yourself to fine art through museums, through attending auctions (whether or not you buy), through volunteer efforts and social events. Increase your comfort level to Richness by owning "pieces of wealth." You may not be able to afford a house full of fine antiques, but you can probably afford to buy one fine antique or one really good work of art. Pieces of wealth keep your desire alive and your progress on mark.

And if you cultivate as many of the fourteen layers of Class as you possibly can, you will find your comfort level automatically rising, so that you mix well with any category of Rich, from Pedigrees to Celebrities.

3. The Hindrance of Old "Friends"

If your old friends are true friends, they will be happy for you as you work your way up the social ladder. They will never talk about embarrassing past moments or how you looked before you had your teeth capped. Good friends do not criticize your goals or try to limit your achievements. *Those are the true friends—and the friends you should keep for life.*

But not everyone you grew up with and called your friend deserves you. Some people who have known you all your life may not let you improve, especially if you began in circumstances lower than theirs and now you have far exceeded them.

Unfortunately, their negative side comes out and they remind you of an embarrassing gaffe you made years ago. They take opportunities to tell people they "knew you when" and then relate a tale that presents you in the limited way they knew you. When they do this, they are trying to strip you of your power—letting you know that you aren't "really" the wonderful high achiever that you think you are, that you are still the lowly, inferior little being they took pity on.

If you stay involved with them, thinking that you love them and they love you, you are actually just trying to earn their approval—which you will never get. And you are allowing them to have petty victories over you with cheap potshots that chip away your hard-earned self-esteem. These people do not deserve your friendship.

The easiest way to move into new and higher social circles is to move to another city, region, or state, or move to a new country altogether. People accept newcomers better than people they have known all their lives. In a new location, no one has a preconceived idea of you that limits their opinion of how high to let you rise.

Where should you go?

You can't have what you want in life if you don't go where it is. To quote a Rich sportsman, "If you're fishing for marlin, you have to go to the ocean. Not a mountain stream."

Find a "progressive" city that has not yet reached its prime or peaked out. It will be a city of energy whose electricity you can feel—in fact, it throbs through your soul with excitement.

For me, it was Dallas. I had lived in many major cities, but when I moved to Dallas, I knew, instantly, I belonged there. The air felt perfect on my skin in every season. The slant of the sun put a perfect cast on every building and tree.

When you are in the right place for you, you'll know it. And everything will fall into place—the right opportunities, the right job, the right place to live, the right friends. This doesn't mean you won't have to work at it or that you won't have problems. Of course you will, but underneath it all, you *know* you are exactly where you are supposed to be.

My husband Reed and I met and married in Dallas, and though we have not lived there for years, Big D was the right city at the right time for my career, my love life, and my friendships.

Is there a city beckoning you? Visit first, to see how it feels. It won't take long for you to know if it's where you belong.

$\int$tage 1—Entering Society

"The human heart yearns for the beautiful in all ranks of life."

—Harriet Beecher Stowe

As you enter society, you will find five social strata of the Rich. Whereas only two or three of the five may show up in exclusive, private clubs, all five strata will be evident in art or charitable societies.

1. RICH SOCIAL FOUNDERS

Pedigrees and Flamboyants fill this stratum for the most part. These are the Rich who believe their city should have a ballet company, or a yacht club, or a historical society, or an art museum, and have considerable influence to bring it about.

Pedigrees and Flamboyants have the clout to persuade corporations and friends to contribute and to join the new organization. They, themselves, give handsomely of their own money and time.

Because of the prestige of the Founders, the organization has prestige. Annual fund-raising is turned into lavish social events. Photographs of those attending a fund-raiser splash across the society pages and it becomes the event of the year.

If the organization is over twenty years old, most of its Founders will be over the age of fifty-five. As the Founders grow older and newcomers learn the social ropes, the torch passes from the Founders to a slightly younger generation of emerging leaders. But even as new people fill the positions on the board, the Founders retain a quiet power in the background.

Personalities of Rich Social Founders

The social personalities of Old Money Founders are easily identifiable when you have been around them awhile. Whether Pedigree or Flamboyant, the two social personalities of Founders are:

Authoritative. You will know them by their forthright manner. Usually they talk a little on the loud side, but not in the shrill pitch associated with lower classes. They have an open friendliness with a no-nonsense cast to it.

Polite Reserve. This will be a man or woman who speaks so softly, he or she requires you to focus your full attention on the person's face in order to understand what is being said. The softness of speech is refinement, not shyness, and clear, open-faced eye contact underscores that fact. These people have a distant friendliness.

Body Language of Rich Social Founders

Old Money whether Pedigree or Flamboyant shows up in a body language that is contained. Founders are still, but not stiff. Arm movements are usually close to their bodies. Gestures are typically from the elbow, rather than from the shoulder.

Pedigree Founders' facial expressions are also more contained. They smile, but not broadly. They may lift an eyebrow and nod. There are few exaggerated facial expressions. Flamboyant Founders are more animated and outgoing.

Socially, both the Pedigree and Flamboyant Founder wears formal clothes as comfortably as sportswear. Whether their personalities are authoritative or reserved, the Pedigree Founder has has a manner of casual elegance.

2. RICH SOCIAL CLIMBERS

Do not underrate this stratum, for Rich Social Climbers are the financial life's blood—and social life's blood—of the performing arts, the historical society, or an art museum.

Mostly made up of new money—especially the Status Rich who are between the ages of thirty-five and fifty—Social Climbers donate their way into an organization and into society.

Rich Social Climbers enjoy the new prestige they paid for with hefty donations or exorbitant membership fees. It is not that they care about the organization or the art or sport all that much, but they love the limelight of being photographed at opening night galas or tournaments. They compete with one another in lavish designer clothes, impressive jewelry, showy cars, and one-ups-manship in their private parties. All of this makes them the darlings of the media.

Most of all, Rich Social Climbers love mixing with the city's power brokers and old money. It means they have arrived.

Personalities of Rich Social Climbers

Rich Social Climbers express their personalities in one of two ways:

Sparkly. Like the expensive jewels they wear, Rich Social Climbers titter with excitement on opening night of any social gathering. They ooh and aah over one another and are truly caught up in the thrill of their new social world.

Observant. Thoughtful of others, this Rich Social Climber observes others and carefully takes in the full scene before responding. Sincerely friendly, these Rich Social Climbers are well liked by most people in the organization.

Body Language of Rich Social Climbers

Status New Rich Social Climbers can be identified by their natural body language or else by their studied body language. One of the two following body language styles is typical of Rich Social Climbers:

Dynamic. By and large, most of the body language of the Rich Social Climber will be larger, less contained. They gesture in large circles, away from the body. They may even gesture from the shoulder. Their faces are very expressive. They smile broadly and laugh heartily.

This Status New Rich Social Climber is quite charismatic, with an unself-conscious animation that sparks interest from others.

Old Money Imitation. A new money Social Climber who has studied the Rich and been around them a great deal may adopt some of the mannerisms of Old Money, as movie actor Cary Grant did, rather remarkably.

3. SNOB APPEAL SET

Most of the Snob Appeal Set have marginal wealth, but even Status New Rich go through this phase of social development. These are valuable people in their own right. They are motivated toward self-improvement and will, in time, grow into a meaningful relationship with society.

During their development, they may not really understand cultural arts or upper-class sports—they participate solely because the Rich do. Throughout this period of their development, designer labels are an important crutch to overcome their feelings of insecurity.

Personalities of the Snob Appeal Set

The Snob Appeal set have one of three personality styles:

Eager. Hungry to be counted among the social elite, this Snob Appeal personality openly courts conversations with the social who's-who in attendance. They may make the mistake of fawning over them, but, at least they have the courage to try.

Intimidated. Watching social leaders mix and mingle easily with each other, this Snob-Appeal person feels safer on the sidelines, and feels important just attending the same event.

Belligerent. This behavior is especially evidenced by the

Status Seeking Rich as they pass through the Snob Appeal phase of their social development.

Body Language of the Snob Appeal Set

Body language of the Snob Appeal set is often touching. It is either shy and awkward with poor posture and self-consciousness gestures or totally affected as they try to do what they hope is right. Both behaviors are a natural part of learning and will fade as the Snob Appeal Set acquires understanding, skills and confidence.

Unfortunately, when they first become genuine appreciators, they become snobs of the worst sort—and look down on (or ridicule) anyone who does not have their new level of understanding.

There was a young physician who arrived late with his wife and another couple to an opera performance. Once the curtain has been raised, no one is allowed to enter the performance hall until intermission because light pouring into the darkened seating area from an open door is distracting to the performers and to the audience.

When ushers would not allow the physician's group into the performance, he became bellicose.

"Do you know who I am?" he shouted, "I am *Dr.* John Doe! Who are you? You are a nobody who seats people, that's all! I'll bet you don't even understand opera. I paid a fortune for each seat for the four of us—and you can't keep *me* out!"

Likely as not, the doctor had only a smattering of knowledge about opera himself, or he would have known enough not to be late. Clearly, this Snob Appeal man was not a season ticket holder. He had bought expensive seats to one performance of the opera for his wife and the other couple just to impress them.

4. PASSIONATE SUPPORTERS

Passionate Supporters are involved in an organization because they truly love the art or sport, or believe in the cause. They may or may not have wealth, but because their adoration is sincere, they are embraced by the Founders—and, therefore, by everybody else.

There was a woman whose father was a music professor and her mother a voice teacher. They made a modest but decent living, and their daughter grew up listening to operas. She did not have large sums of money to donate, but she gave volumes of time as a volunteer to a local opera company. It was easy to see that she was neither a Rich Social Climber nor of the Snob Appeal Set.

She happily took on any volunteer task, and spoke glowingly and intelligently about various composers, performers, conductors, and the history of it all. Opera was a genuine part of her, and she was a passionate supporter of it.

The Founders felt she embodied the type of person they had founded the company for, and they adored her. Because the Founders adored her, the Social Climbers included her. Because the Social Climbers included her, the Snob Appeal members cozied up to her. She was in society, and she was not Rich.

Personalities of Passionate Supporters

Unlike the Rich Founders who are evaluating the organization's progress during the evening, unlike the New Rich Social Climbers who are there to preen in their glitterati before flashing cameras, unlike the Snob Appeal Set who are trying to learn about the art, and unlike Celebrities who have been fund-raising trophies for the event—the Passionate Supporter is there for the pure enjoyment of the art and wants only to share that enjoyment.

Passionate Supporters care more that you love Verdi than whether or not you have money and talk eagerly to you, if you do, hence their personalities vary with naturalness from a wellspring of sincerity.

Body Language of the Passionate Supporter

Passionate Supporters have a zestful body language that leans intimately close to share their enjoyment of the performance with you. Their faces shine with intensity and their gestures court your reaction to the artists or performers.

5. CELEBRITIES

Celebrities are the trophies of fund-raising for organizations. Celebrities are also the trophies for the Status Rich and the Flamboyants to pose with in the newspapers. And frequently, the Celebrity Rich become friends of Flamboyants and the Status Rich.

Historically, however, Pedigrees have not become personal friends with the Celebrity Rich, because gentle people should only have their names in the news three times in their lives—to announce their birth, their marriage, and their death. Traditionally, they consider publicity-seeking vulgar. However, Pedigrees appreciate the contributions of Celebrity Rich, and they will graciously host or attend a party in their honor to show their appreciation.

One final factor: most Celebrity Rich are entertainers, and Pedigrees hire entertainers, but don't socialize with them. Pedigrees often consider the Celebrity lifestyle unsavory. Fortunately, such stuffy thinking is fading and stiff rules are bending, but you will find some Pedigree stalwarts who believe the lifestyles of Celebrity Rich erode good values.

Personalities of Celebrities

The personality of a Celebrity is usually a public personae, but not always. Most Celebrities are genuinely gracious. They freely give smiles, sign a few autographs, pose for the press, and shake hands with Founders, while they keep moving, slowly, through the crowds that typically gather around them. Still, their public personae is part of their income, so if they are known for being outrageous or surly, they will display a bit of that personae, even for a social event.

Body Language of the Celebrity

The body language of a Celebrity is meticulously planned to project a desired image for that Celebrity from attention-getting dress and hairstyles to whether or not they hold hands with their escort. Their facial expressions are animated, their body language relaxed and confident.

Social Strata and Friendships

The Rich may socialize with each other for a "cause"; but friendships are another matter. Pedigrees consider the Flamboyants an amusing oddity in the old money and tolerate them; but are more likely to have limited friendships with Practicals and Rollers, whom they consider authentic, than they are with Status New Money or Celebrity Rich.

Status New Money, Flamboyants, and Celebrities have more in common for friendships with each other; and though they are awed by Pedigrees, who shun them, they themselves shun Practicals and Rollers.

Study Your Social Stratum

You want socially prominent friends, and there is nothing wrong with that. When you join organizations, you expect your social life to be fuller. And you want the most influential people there to recognize your value, and to include you. Certainly, that is an honorable goal.

Operate with pride from whatever your position is in life. If you have new money, don't be embarrassed to be a Rich Social Climber. Go ahead and donate your way into society and enjoy it to the fullest. Social Climbing is a time-honored tradition that society cannot exist without. Besides, you will have great fun and make a lot of wonderful friends.

If you are a Pedigree or Flamboyant who is new to a community, you will find a natural affinity with the Rich Founders. Follow the methods of the Social Climbers at first, and make donations that get you noticed and approved.

If you do not have money, then I urge you to bypass the Snob Appeal set and mimic the behavior of a Passionate Supporter. The key is to study an art or sport or cause thoroughly and to learn it better than most people. Be devoted to it, for its own sake. Then, throw yourself into volunteer work, spouting devotion along with real knowledge. Since you cannot donate money, donate time. Be willing to do things no one else is willing to do. Make your volunteer work so good, so reliable, that you become indispensable.

Take your mind off the goal of being liked, off of making an impression, and focus on the goals of the organization. What are the goals of the organization? How can you help? And do you really want to? Learn as much as you possibly can about the organizations you choose to support. When you focus on a non-personal goal and work on it as a happy team player, the by-product is good friendships, even with the Rich. If you are able to make the organization better through your efforts, and if you are not an objectionable personality, you, my friend, can penetrate the elite society in that group.

eighteen

26 Ways to Meet the Rich Socially

> *"If you want to be Rich, you must do what the Rich do."*
>
> —Aristotle Onassis

Give yourself a full two and a half to three years to succeed in any of the methods given below that you choose as your entrée into society. People need time to get to know you, to trust your commitment, to warm to you. Sometimes it happens sooner, but be willing to give it that much time at least. And choose only those activities that pique your interest or curiosity. Telephone organizations and get on their mailing lists. Familiarize yourself with their literature. Get involved.

Socializing with the Rich does not have to cost an inordinate amount of money. In fact, there are some activities that do not cost much at all.

But some activities are expensive. I have included both, because some people have the money to do both.

Straining to keep up is impossible in some categories. But do not let marginal income stop you from acquiring friendships and familiarity with the Rich. Richness is something you can grow into.

To help you determine which activities you can afford, I have put dollar signs—just as restaurant and hotel guides do—next to a social activity to indicate how expensive it is.

$—inexpensive
$$—moderately expensive

$$$—expensive
$$$$—very expensive

1. Go to Auctions—$

Whether or not you buy anything, go to a few auctions.

An auction is only as good as the auction house or the estate being auctioned (i.e., the level of wealth). Fine antique furniture auctions are the best. Some estate auctions can also be good. Art auctions are iffy, but you will want to attend a few. If it is a rather nondescript collection, you will find mostly nondescript people. Even then, there will usually be one or two Rich bidders with eclectic taste wandering through to see if they "discover" new talent.

With a silent auction, there will typically be a cocktail party first, where you write your bid on a sheet of paper beneath the art. If you are going to participate in the open auction, you will then be issued a numbered paddle that you lift up when you bid.

You can meet: Pedigrees, Flamboyants, Celebrities, Status Rich, and even Roller-Coaster Rich, when their finances are on the upswing.

2. Take Prestigious Art Classes—$$

Ask several art supply stores for the names of the most prestigious artists in your area who give lessons. Ask the same question at some of the better art galleries. You can even telephone regional art magazines and inquire about top artists who give lessons.

Then, telephone the artists, visit them, and take lessons. I've found that the classes of the best artists who give lessons are filled largely with Rich widows. Most of them take art as a form of therapy. Typically, these are lovely, fine women who make very good friends. And they become connections for you, as well as friends.

You can meet: Pedigrees and Status Rich.

3. Volunteer for the Arts—$

For a membership fee in the women's guild or the men's association for the opera/ballet/symphony, etc., you receive newsletters and invitations to coffees, which are often in the homes of Rich guild officers. Men's groups tend to meet for lunch or breakfast in a restaurant to discuss goals for the art group.

Volunteer Rule 1: Learn to say no. Never agree to do anything that you might not be able to fulfill. This rule is very important.

Volunteer Rule 2: Learn to say yes. Be willing to take tasks you are not particularly fond of.

Volunteer Rule 3: Work your buns off! Whatever you do—do it the very best it can be done (as if you are being paid for it, but, of course, you are not, which is a "class act" for you).

Volunteer Rule 4: Do your paperwork. Documentation of your duties is important.

Volunteer Rule 5: Choose an art form that truly appeals to you, so you will find your involvement interesting.

You never know where your volunteer activities can lead. One of my married clients began making more money and wanted to upgrade his social life. He volunteered for a major theater in his city, thinking he would just hand out programs or such. And for a while, he did. But when he was needed to help with sets, he began working backstage. Eventually, he was prompting lines on the sides to anyone who needed it.

And then, a year and half into his volunteer duties, one of the directors asked him to audition for a lead role in an upcoming play. Astonished, he nevertheless gave it a shot and landed the part.

His reviews were wonderful, and he was approached by an agent who wanted to get him parts in other major cities. He declined, but his subsequent acting for "benefits" (all the money raised from ticket buyers goes to charity) bought favor with patrons. Soon he and his wife became friends with social leaders.

You can meet: Celebrities, Pedigrees, Status, and Flamboyants.

4. VOLUNTEER FOR A MEDICAL CHARITY—$

If you cannot afford to be a patron to a medical charity, then consider being a volunteer for a medical cause you believe in with all your heart.

All of the volunteer rules in number three, above, apply to in this case, too.

You can meet: Practicals, Pedigrees, Celebrities, and Status Rich.

5. VOLUNTEER FOR A POLITICAL PARTY—$

Nowhere can you meet more of the very people you want to meet than by getting very, very active in your political party. Work on committees as much as possible; you can develop friendship and connections that can be invaluable.

During elections, your committee will be invited to "watch parties" that are usually held in the homes of influential leaders in the party.

And, yes, the same volunteer rules apply here, too. You want people to think of you when they think of forming an important committee. You gain stature that way.

Find out if new, special events are coming up, then go to the organizational meeting. Volunteer to be on the steering committee.

And, by the way, being a delegate at a convention is unbeatable fun and work. Keep asking how you can become one. Keep saying that you want to be a delegate, and you stand a good chance of becoming one. Be willing to be an alternate, so that if someone cannot go at the last minute, then you can.

Socializing is the heart and soul of politics.

You can meet: All Rich profiles—Pedigrees, Flamboyants, Celebrities, Status Rich, Practicals, and Roller-Coasters. They all have political interests to protect.

6. CULTIVATE A HOBBY—$$

What do you love to do, apart from your career? When you have free time, what do you like to piddle around doing?

Whatever it is has the makings of a hobby. And a developed hobby has the makings of social friends if you get involved in groups from Rich neighborhoods.

You will need a basic level of competence in a skill before you jump into a well-established group of hobbyists. If you have not developed your hobby interest to that degree, take lessons. Classes usually cost a modest amount, and there are supplies to be bought. Also, subscribe to magazines and other publications on the subject of your new interest.

Nurture your curiosity. Nurture your skill. Have patience. Be consistent—which is easy when you choose something you love or find fascinating. Attend lectures on the subject. Join national and regional associations. Look them up in your Yellow Pages, the *Encyclopedia of Associations* at your public library, and ask your class instructor.

Locate those associations in the Rich neighborhoods and get involved with your new hobby.

You can meet: Pedigrees, Status Rich, and a few Practicals.

7. BE A COLLECTOR—$$$

To become a collector you need a basic level of knowledge about collectibles in your area of interest, and you need money to build your collection. Not all collectibles are expensive, but a bona fide collector does not buy anything unless it meets the standards the collector has set for his or her collection. The Rich usually try to build a collection that has investment value. So value is one of the standards typically set by the Rich for their collectibles.

Choose a collection that appeals to you. Research it in the library. Subscribe to publications for collectors.

You can meet: Pedigrees, Flamboyants, Status Rich, and Celebrity Rich. The Rich may be secretive about their interest in an item and may conceal their identities or their wealth in order to buy at lower prices.

8.   LEARN AN UPPER-CLASS SPORT—$$$

Practically any sport that costs money will have its fair share of Rich enthusiasts—from flying souped-up balloons around the world to skydiving or gliding.

But the five common "social sports"—sailing, horseback riding, snow-skiing, tennis, and golf—are more practical for developing Rich friends.

Learning the sport should be only moderately expensive. Participating with the Rich can run into a bit more money. If done frequently, it can be expensive—but worth it!

You can meet: Serious Pedigrees, snow-bunny Flamboyants, driven Status Rich, and "where-the-action-is" Celebrities.

9.   TAKE IN UPPER-CLASS SPECTATOR SPORTS—$$

Polo and other equestrian competitions are upper-class sports you can enjoy from the grandstand. And whether or not you play tennis or golf, you can learn enough about it to become an appreciator at country club tournaments.

Not all upper-class spectator sports are stuffy, either. It is fine to root for football teams or to enjoy a thoroughbred horse race.

You can meet: Team- or horse-owning Flamboyants and Status Rich. At thoroughbred racetracks, they will be in the clubhouse area.

10.   GET RELIGION—$

Whatever your faith, if you want to make friends as a couple or as a family, or even as a single adult, find worship services where the Rich go and join. You'll meet people, and maybe enrich your spiritual life, as well.

In America, the greatest number of Rich worship in the Episcopal denomination of Christianity and the Jewish religion. But not just any Episcopal church and not just any synagogue. The ones with the most prestige are likely to be the oldest Episcopal church in town or a newer one in the Richest neighborhood.

This is true for Jewish worship, too. However, all denominations and all faiths have houses of worship with affluent members.

There are some faiths that do require a paid-up membership in order to attend. If you belong to such a faith, find out if there are reciprocal visits when in other cities. Then choose the Richer houses of worship for your faith in that city.

You can meet: Pedigrees and Practicals—and a few repentant Roller-Coasters who take an active part in religious events.

11. TAKE A CRUISE—$$$$

Of course, some of the Rich own yachts, but the upkeep of ownership is expensive for something they may not use as often as they would like.

Instead, many of the Rich are sharing the expense and adding a brand-new concept to Rich cruises. For one and a quarter million dollars or so, you can buy a permanent floating residence (or vacation house) aboard *The World* of ResidenSea from *Christie's* Real Estate division in New York City (505-983-8733). It is "a new concept that combines the ease and convenience of a private home with the mobility, services, and facilities of a luxury cruise ship."

The ship has two hundred fifty completely furnished permanent residences and—here's the good part for some of you—one hundred eighty-three smaller guest suites. Complete with a helicopter landing pad, casino, live entertainment, cocktail lounges, game room, and library for books and music, the ship caters to the Rich. You have several restaurants, fully equipped exercise facilities with instructors, jogging track, tennis courts, salon, and spa. A golf professional is available to advise you on the driving ranges, putting course, and computerized golf simulators. To top it off, there is an international house of worship, state-of-the art business center, and complete medical facilities available around the clock.

For the Rich who do not opt either to own a yacht or a residence on the beautiful *World* of ResidenSea, there are traditional cruises. But the Rich are very selective in their cruise lines. *Sea Goddess I and II*, as well as Seabourn Cruise Lines, offer luxurious, intimate, small ship cruising for a hundred to two hundred fifty passengers. The *Royal Viking Sun* and the *Vistafjord* can offer a slightly larger cruising experience for seven hundred fifty passengers.

The *Crystal Harmony* and the *Crystal Symphony*, with passenger capacities of nine hundred sixty each, provide a very grand scale of cruising—and the *Symphony* is very, very popular with the Rich.

And the fifteen-hundred-passenger *Queen Elizabeth II* (known affectionately as the *QE2*) still stands for luxury cruising on the grandest scale. There are Rich passengers who virtually do not leave.

If you want to socialize with the Rich on a cruise, you must have first-class passage that seats you at one of the high-ranking tables or the Captain's table if that is the Ship's protocol. You should also change clothes two or three times a day—and never be seen in the same outfit more than once.

Favorite cruise seasons for the Rich vary. November through March are popular times, and some of the Rich spend every Christmas and New Year's on a cruise. Warm weather cruise wear comes on the market soon after Christmas for January through March cruises, which are good months for the Rich.

You can meet: Pedigrees sailing to London, Flamboyants sailing to Monte Carlo or to the Orient, Status Rich on a round-the-world cruise, Celebrities sailing the Mediterranean with a return on the Concorde, and Roller-Coasters sailing the Caribbean to celebrate a success.

12. PLAY GAMES—$$

Classic games such as contract bridge or chess are not the mainstay of society they once were, but there are still Rich aficionados of both games.

Learning the games may not cost much, however, memberships in the Rich circle of game players may entail a little expense. Still, it should be affordable.

Many expensive hotels have Rich residents, and you often find weekly card games going on. For years, when my husband and I were in the Century City Hotel Towers in Los Angeles, we ventured into an area known as the Living Room and encountered a group of Rich ladies playing bridge with a movie star who lived there.

I encountered one of the women in the ladies' room. While we both touched up our lipsticks, we chatted amiably. By the time I left the ladies' room, she had praised her cosmetic surgeon so much, she even gave me his name and telephone number, along with her name and telephone number. She had asked if I played bridge, but I answered that I don't. If I had been a bridge player, our rapport was such that an invitation to play would have been imminent.

This meeting could have been as available to you as to me.

You can meet: Older Pedigrees and older Celebrities who love the classic games.

13. ATTEND BREAKFAST, LUNCH, AND TEAS—$$

If you go to breakfast, lunch, or tea only once or twice, you might strike up a conversation or friendship with someone, but it is not likely. However, if you go to the same place on a frequent basis, over a period of time, you may see many of the same people again and again, until a nodding acquaintance becomes a greeting and then a casual conversation and possibly friendship.

I have a friend who developed a society friendship while having lunch at the Palm in Dallas. She struck up a conversation with a woman at the table next to her, who was alone and waiting for someone. By the time the woman's late guest arrived, my girlfriend had a new friendship with a multimillion-dollar socialite. And they have stayed good personal friends.

14. ATTEND INVESTMENT SEMINARS—$

Most investment seminars are free. Telephone stockbrokerage firms and ask if they hold seminars. Seminars specializing in tax shelters for people in high tax brackets are the ticket.

You can meet: Practicals, Status Rich, and Roller-Coaster Rich, usually. Pedigrees and Flamboyants are a possibility, but they often have a team of money managers, lawyers, and accountants who triple-check one another's financial moves—and whose firms have been with the family for a long time.

15. BE INTRODUCED—$

Before you move to a new community, take inventory of the Rich people you know in the town where you now live. Do you have friends who are Rich? Relatives who are Rich? Are there Rich parishioners you know through your religion?

The next time you see them, casually mention the city where you will be moving, then ask if they know anything about the location. They may say, "I know some people there."

If they don't say it, ask them if they know anyone in the city where you will be moving. If they do, stay casual as you ask questions about their friend. "Does she enjoy the symphony as much as you?"

At that point, they will probably volunteer information. "Not really. Beth prefers the ballet."

Later, before your move to the new city, telephone your Rich contacts and ask if they would mind if you contact their friends, since you will be new in town. Get the names and telephone numbers. (This takes a little moxie—but those with moxie usually get what they want.)

When you arrive in your new city, telephone your Rich contacts' friends and say, "Hello, Beth Smith. This is Jane Doe. I have recently moved here from Cityville and your good friend Julie Jones asked me to call you. Julie and I belong to the same church. Julie knows I have been involved with the Cityville Ballet for a number of years and said you are just the person to direct me to similar activities here."

Be sure to mention something the two of you have in common. Eight times out of ten, Beth Smith will feel obligated to her friend to give you an opportunity to prove yourself of social merit. She will probably invite you to dinner or for drinks at her club.

This tactic is especially effective with golfers. All you have to say is, "Bob Jones said you and I might enjoy playing golf together because we have a similar handicap." No golfer will pass up that opening.

You can meet: Contemporaries of the Rich who gave you the friend's name, who may turn out to be a good contact for you in your new city.

16. MEET THE RICH THROUGH YOUR CHILDREN—$$

Enroll your children in schools where children of the Rich are enrolled. As they make friends, you will get to know the parents. Rich schools often have parent volunteer programs. Join and meet other parents. This social activity can lead to friendships and to a wider, more influential social life.

You can meet: Pedigrees, Flamboyants, and Status Rich parents.

17. GO TO PET SHOWS—$$$

Exotic cats and rare-breed dogs are expensive pets. Some of the Rich buy them as show pets. Training for show costs money as does traveling to the shows themselves. Many Pedigree and Flamboyant owners have someone else to train and show their dogs, but they are often present for the show. Keep your eyes open for owners.

You can meet: Pedigrees, Flamboyants, a few Status Rich, and an occasional Practical who loves purebred dogs.

18. TAKE CLASSES—$

Postgraduate classes in expensive, private colleges sometimes have Rich adult students. I became close friends with a Rich divorcée when I took a master's-level psychology course at Trinity University, and our friendship has outlasted the six-week course.

Continuing education classes for adults are another surprising resource for Rich friendships. For one thing, the fun or unusual topics are often those that colleges and universities don't teach. Famous speakers and authors sometimes circulate for seminars of these schools. Seminar classes by book authors who have received a lot of publicity will usually have several Rich people in the audience.

You can meet: A cross-section of society, including a few Pedigrees, Status Rich, Practicals, and Roller-Coasters.

19. KEEP FIT—$

This can be as simple as a daily walk or jog in Rich neighborhoods. If you do it day after day, you will see certain people repeatedly. After a while, you can break the ice during warm-up stretches and initiate polite conversation. In time, mutual curiosity and trust can allow expanded conversation, possibly friendship. One of my clients followed this advice and during her daily walks in a Rich neighborhood in Los Angeles, she became friendly with a woman who is the wife of a very famous movie producer.

Wear a variety of outfits so you are always fresh-looking. Clean white shorts and shirt with sneakers is an attractive look.

You can meet: the Rich who live in that particular neighborhood if you go on a regular basis. However, check out who walks or jogs at different times of the day—early morning, noon, and an hour or so before sunset.

20. VISIT SPAS—$$$$

One of the best ways to rank a spa is by its chef. The food must not only be outstanding, but it must also fit the health purposes of the Rich who go there. The quality of the treatments of the spa—such as specialty massages, wraps, and other exotic restorative treatments—are a close second to the chef. Third is the overall ambiance of the spa and other activities that are offered. And, of course, high price ensures exclusivity.

Most of the Rich escape to spas for psychic renewal through physical pampering or toning. The spa is a retreat, and they are there to relax and to regain control of their well-being. If you do not detract from the sanctuary that is being sought there, a spa can give rise to new friendships.

Many spas are designed around group activities. Other spas

are built into resorts with the idea of socializing as a part of psychic renewal. You have ample time to meet other guests by participating in scheduled activities or sports.

The *Zagat Survey of Hotels, Resorts, and Spas* ranks spas according to quality and top amenities. They even include the "power scenes." I also like *Spa Finder* magazine for lush photographs of places and individual stories of activities.

You can meet: Flamboyants, Status Rich, Roller-Coasters, and Celebrities at the best spas.

21. TRAVEL TO RESORTS—$$$$

To socialize with the Rich, go to a resort when it is "in season." Peak season prices are very expensive, but if you only spend a few days there, and if you have money enough to spend on the activities for which the resort is known (golf, say, or tennis), you may be able to cultivate a few Rich friendships that extend beyond the season.

How will you know when a resort is in season? By the prices.

Bargain prices are off-season because they're for times the Rich are not usually there. However, you can go during off-season to familiarize yourself with the resort, if you like. Sometimes, there will be a few Rich who love the place and go there whatever the season.

Some resorts still have a dress code, eliminating jeans or T-shirts. It will be listed in the resort literature, or you can telephone before you go and ask if there is a dress code.

Andrew Harper's Hideaway Report is another of my favorite "inside" sources of quality resorts where the Rich can be found.

You can meet: Pedigrees at less-known resorts; Flamboyants, Status Rich, and Roller-Coasters at well-known resorts. Other Flamboyants and Celebrities will be at private membership resorts.

22. BUY SEASON TICKETS—$$$

Season ticket holders commit their money to reserve seats for every performance of the theater, ballet, symphony, or opera for that season.

The best tickets are usually boxes, center orchestra, and grand tier—and for *opening nights only*. In some cities, the social demand for opening night tickets is so great that you must be a season ticket holder to attend.

Why is opening night special to the Rich? Because they want to see the first performance. Typically, the first performance has a new and fresh energy from the performers. In some cities critics attend preview performances; but in other cities the critics are at opening night and this first performance can make or break the show. In those cases, the Rich like to compare their view of the performance with the next-day newspaper review. And there is one more perk for the Rich on opening night: social photographers for the newspaper society page will be snapping shots.

Long gowns, jewels, and small, unpretentious opera glasses (avoid lorgnette style) are ideal for women on opening night. Men wear tuxedos. True, you will find an assortment of people in a wide range of dress, but formal attire is appropriate. Although if you are in a community that dresses casually for the performing arts, you do not want to be an eyesore in formal dress. Ask what to wear when you buy your tickets.

Sunday matinees will have a few Rich season ticket holders, usually much older and too reserved for glamorous opening nights. Less formal dress is best for these afternoon performances. A dressy suit with pearl buttons for women, and a dress suit for men will suffice.

If you buy good season tickets, you will often sit next to the same people, performance after performance. It is perfectly all right to speak and, over time, to make occasional comments to your neighbor.

You can meet: In the better seats, Pedigree and Flamboyant Founders, and Status Social Climbers.

23. BE A PATRON—$$$

If you have attained a level of affluence that provides a large amount of "disposable income," you can enhance your social standing and benefit from a tax write-off at the same time by donating sizable sums of money to a charity or art.

Be sure the charity you give to has an active social life connected to it. The ballet, symphony, opera, and major theaters are flooded with galas and balls you will be invited to if you are a patron or sizable donor.

Medical charities for children, such as the Make a Wish Foundation that helps make wishes come true for terminally ill children, are thick with social benefits, often including celebrities, and it is a wonderful cause.

You can meet: Pedigrees, Flamboyants, Status Rich, and Celebrities.

24. DO SOME FUND-RAISING—$

If you have a talent for raising a lot of money, quickly and easily, you will be cherished by any major nonprofit organization. If you do not have Rich contacts to ask for money, or if you are too uncomfortable asking anyone for anything, do *not* get on the fund-raising committee. You will embarrass yourself by not being able to bring in very large donations.

Most of the time, the Rich have friends they have done social favors for and can call those people and raise thousands of dollars in just an hour. However, if you are successful in a career, such as the stock market or commodities, you can sometimes call on some of your Rich clients for charitable donations. Bringing in large sums of money impresses everyone on the fund-raising committee—and raises your "Social Quotient."

25. ASK FOR TRAVEL REFERENCES—$

If you are planning a trip and you know someone Rich who has frequented your destination, ask if they can refer you to places and people there.

Often the Rich who frequent an area will either stay with friends or lease a villa because they expect to entertain while they are there.

The well-traveled Rich can save your trip by referring you to the best restaurants, clubs, theaters, and hotels. They can also refer you to leasing agents for good rental property. And best of all, they can refer you to people who will make your stay memorable.

You can meet: All of the Rich profiles in fascinating cultures.

26. PARTICIPATE IN EQUESTRIAN EVENTS—$$$

Equestrian competitions are taken seriously by the Rich. The relationship between the rider and the horse is most important in their evaluations.

It costs, but if you are now earning a lot of money, this can be your ticket. If your involvement is serious and your skills excellent, you will be respected. Respect is the basis for solid friendships and you can move into social circles you could not have entered before.

The Rich are always involved in horse-related events—everything from polo; Arabian or Appaloosa show horses; English sidesaddle competitions; horse breeding; horse training; and horse investments; to harness, quarter, and thoroughbred racing. And of course, they will attend major racing events, such as the Kentucky Derby.

You can meet: Pedigrees, Flamboyants, and Roller-Coaster Rich.

$\mathscr{L}$iving Rich

*"If you want to be Rich, you must . . .
live where the Rich live, even if it is in
an attic."*

—*Aristotle Onassis*

Think of your mind as being a cup of hot water. And think of
Rich neighborhoods as a rare, exotic tea filled with all the flavors
of the Rich lifestyle—the traditions, the value systems, and the
mannerisms. This is a very important mental picture because
when you get an address in a Rich neighborhood, you will find
that you have not moved into a Rich neighborhood at all. *You
have moved the Rich neighborhood into you.* And like the tea
steeping in hot water, all the qualities of the Rich lifestyle steep
into you. If you later move away, then just as when you remove
tea leaves from hot water, you will see that the water is not water
anymore. Now *the water contains all the same properties as the
tea!*

If you met me, you could tell that I am from Texas because
I have the regional speech of a Texan. Why do I speak this way?
Because *Texas is in me.* And even if I am not in Texas, it does
not matter—Texas is still in me. If I moved to another part of
the country and lived there a number of years, my Texas drawl
would be modified by absorbing the speech patterns of the new
area, because I would absorb a new flavor of environmental tea.

When you were a child, you had no choice over the flavor
of tea that was being steeped into you—and many people spend

years of their adult lives, and a lot of money with psychologists, trying to change the flavor of the tea that was steeped into them.

But you are an adult now, and you do have control over the tea that you allow to steep into you.

So if you wish to change your life in a deep, lasting, and significant way, change your environment.

A very interesting client of mine came to America from a depressed country in Europe because she had a dream of going into business for herself.

When she arrived, she had a total of four hundred dollars, a small child, and no relatives or friends here. When she saw the prices of apartments, she panicked. Scouring rental classifieds, she finally found a room to rent in a house that she could afford and still have some money left over. That, in itself, tells you what kind of place it was.

"Ginie," she said, "It was in a slum part of town. And the house was so filthy that I had to sanitize it to make it habitable. But I could keep a roof over our heads until I found a job."

She found a job within a few days, but still she did not move to a better part of town. After all, she would have to save money to finance her dream.

By the time she came to me, she had fulfilled her dream of owning her own business, which was doing quite well. Her child was now seven years old. I pointed out to her that fear was holding her back, and for her child's sake, as well as her own, she had to change the "tea" that was steeping into the child's mind, as well as into hers, by moving into a Rich neighborhood in her city.

A few months later, she arrived for another consultation filled with excitement about the changes in her life. She had leased a guest house on an estate. Instantly, that qualified her child for the best school district. Her child made friends with wealthy children at school and, of course, the mothers met her, liked her, and admired her move to America. In fact, they took her under their wing socially, included her in many events, and invited her to dinner when they had an extra man.

Her entire life changed (and so did her child's) because she changed her neighborhood.

Living in a Rich neighborhood is not at all prohibitive, if you scour the area for good deals. Look for older houses, or smaller houses, if you are married and have children. If you are single, you can rent guest houses on estates or an apartment in an older building, or you can look for older houses or condominiums in areas bordering the neighborhood. This can be one of your smartest moves, even if you end up in a garage apartment with only a few amenities. You see, what you are really paying for is your neighbors. The Rich do this themselves. They could build mansions in cheaper parts of town and have lower property taxes. But they gladly pay higher property taxes in order to "buy" the neighbors that cost the most to have.

DECORATING YOUR HUMBLE ABODE "RICHLY"

As friendships develop with the Rich in your neighborhood, or the Rich you meet or work with as a volunteer, you will naturally visit one another. That means you must make your apartment or home available to visits.

Your home can be a beautiful masterpiece if you have money and can have decorators help you out. But if you can only afford a one-bedroom apartment, do not let this frighten or deter you. Keep in mind that when people respect your work and the values you exhibit in day-to-day living, they love *you*.

But even if your place is small—and your funds limited— you can still turn your home into a welcoming sight for your new Rich friends.

Don't even try to compete with the quality of decor a Pedigree, Flamboyant, Status Rich, or Celebrity can afford. But you can emulate style, color, and taste very effectively. And you will be even more effective if you concentrate on making your place comfortable, inviting, warm—and clean.

Choose a Theme

Sportsman Theme. Many of the Rich (especially Pedigrees) have a hunting theme of ducks or a fishing theme or a nautical theme or a horse theme in their dens, studies, libraries, offices—and sometimes throughout the house and even on their clothing. There will be framed prints, monograms, decorative pillows, needlepoint chairs—all sporting the duck or the fish or a horse or an anchor. They may even have horse prints or collectible antique duck decoys or fishing hooks or nautical paraphernalia handsomely and prominently displayed on shelves, on walls, and in glass display cases.

Furniture can be large, comfortable pieces, in a composite of styles, as long as they blend together well.

Southwestern Theme. A Southwestern theme is easy and inexpensive enough to develop. It does not require a lot of furniture because rooms can have an airy, spare look, as long as it does not seem cold.

A solid-color sofa can be done Southwestern style by draping a large native American rug or blanket sideways across one end of it and piling native print pillows in several sizes at the other end of the sofa.

Giant clay pots can serve as end tables if covered with glass, tiles, or rustic wood. Top them with black wrought-iron lamps. Hang native prints in rustic, wooden frames on the walls and furnish your apartment with oak or pine furniture. A tile or wooden floor is best, but if you have carpet, scatter three native area rugs throughout. Complete your Southwestern theme with giant and smaller cactus plants.

Scottish Theme. Combinations of plaids (not more than three types with complimentary colors) in decorative pillows and throws can give your solid-colored sofa a Highland theme.

An old bagpipe can be a decorative item. Pictures of kilted marchers playing bagpipes can be framed in brass and matted with plaid fabric. Navy, red, yellow, and white are your colors, with brass accents in lamps. Mahogany furniture reproductions work well with a Scottish theme. This can be a classy look.

African Theme. Black, red, white, and copper are colors that work well with this theme, along with large, leafy jungle plants. Panga-panga furniture on grass-mat area rugs with well-made tribal masks, Congo drums, voodoo dolls, ropes of stone necklaces and chunky wooden and copper bracelets displayed next to pots painted with African designs create a dramatic style. Be careful this does not have a cheap import-bargain-store look to it. If you do it carefully, it can be beautiful. Elegant and fine furniture from Africa is available nationwide in African Odyssey Stores. Ask for the Railwoods Collection—or call 505-448-1902 to order a catalog.

Oriental Theme. Spare, low, oriental furniture in black against a gray wall with small pieces in red as relief can build an oriental theme. Oriental art in thin black frames can complete this simple style. You do not need much, but whatever you have should look expensive. Ornamental bonsai trees add a nice touch.

Intellectual Elegance. Mahogany-finished bookcase walls, filled with old and new hardback books, a set of encyclopedias and a large dictionary, are the prominent feature of this style. A globe on a Mahogany-finished stand, an old leather chair and ottoman, a corduroy upholstered sofa and wingback chair with needle-point pellows, big blue-and-white porcelain lamps on old end tables, an old coffee table, ivy plants, and Turkish rugs set a theme of intellectual elegance.

Create a Focal Point

When people walk into your place, what do you want them to notice first? If the focal point of your room is spectacular, you do not have to put as much money into the rest of the room, although it should harmonize well enough not to distract from the focal point. Consider the following as potential focal points to your room:

A Fireplace. A fireplace can be made a focal point if you buy an especially beautiful mantel for it. Or you can have a dramatic work of art that is not terribly expensive over it.

A Piece of Furniture. One giant chair that has an unusual design or color or upholstery can be a focal point. A large, beautiful credenza can bring instant and repeated compliments from visitors.

Natural Assets. A view of the ocean, the mountains, or lush, swaying treetops if you are on the second floor of an apartment building, can be the focal point of your room. No curtains lets the view stand alone. Molding can frame the view.

Art. A beautiful painting or sculpture that you have created, or that was created by a member of your family or by a friend, will have meaning to you, as well as be eye-catching. Be sure it is good, though. Otherwise, you may want to buy a beautiful print or save up for a work of art that really thrills you.

A very nice touch of art is from the heart—framing a niece or nephew's kindergarten art in beautiful frames and hanging it all together. A Rich woman did this with the art of all her grandchildren.

Today, you can have a print of a masterpiece that looks as if it is the original that hangs in the Louvre or the Smithsonian. But if you opt for this, have only one.

Cluster of Objects. If you have a collection of unusual items—whether or not they are expensive—cluster them in a large enough display that they instantly catch attention. They can be beautiful, unusual shells, family photographs, china, or crystal figurines.

Be willing to experiment. I once bought an enormous, framed print of a pelican painted in pastels, and hung it low, next to a chair. It occupied the space an end table would have normally taken.

It was an inexpensive picture and I really don't know why I hung it in such an offbeat way, but every time we had visitors, they instantly commented on how much they liked it. Be willing to follow an unusual instinct.

Add Pieces Regularly

You don't have to buy everything for your place at once. But do make a plan and set a budget.

Start simply with one good basic sofa. Sleeper sofas are sensible if your place is small.

Staying within your budget, go to sales, shop consignment stores, classified ads, and garage sales in good parts of town. Try to add an important piece of furniture two or three times a year.

$\mathcal{T}$HREE COLORS IN A 70–25–5 PERCENT RATIO

The key to coordinating a small house is to have three colors and to combine them in a 70–25–5 percent ratio. For example, if you choose pink, pale yellow, and blue in your living room, you might use 70 percent pink, relieved by 25 percent pale yellow, and 5 percent blue accent pieces. Your kitchen might be 70 percent yellow, 25 percent blue, and 5 percent pink. Your bedroom could be 70 percent blue, 25 percent pink, and 5 percent yellow. Your bathroom might be 70 percent pink, 25 percent blue, and 5 percent yellow.

You can combine these colors in plaids, stripes, polka dots, florals, and solids in various rooms. This creates stimulating variety, yet keeps a serene coordination to your apartment or house.

This is a winning ratio for decorating easily, beautifully, and confidently with color.

Accessorize Simply

The fewer doo-dads and whatknots you have, the better, especially if you do not have someone to keep everything dusted for you. They may look great the first day you set them out, but if you get busy, you may not notice dust gathering on them, but your friends will.

Try to have real plants—gigantic and lush with large, shiny leaves. Remember, these are living things, so take good care of them. If you cannot take care of plants and yet your room begs for them, buy very real-looking artificial plants.

A combination of old and new hardback books can make colorful additions to bookcases and tabletops.

Pets

Animals require a lot of care. If you want a pet and can care for it well, consider getting one from the Society for the Prevention of the Cruelty to Animals (SPCA) or another good animal shelter.

But if you are single and want to go to happy hour with your friends after work instead of home to walk your dog, don't get one. It will end up being an unhappy experience.

Besides, animals can make your place smell like a zoo to others, even if you do not smell a thing. It takes daily, consistent grooming and frequent washings of your pet to keep your apartment sanitary.

Aquariums are probably the most attractive and trouble-free, but keep the little fish fed and the tank cleaned, regularly.

China, Crystal, and Silver Service

You do not have to have matching sets, although a good line, such as Wedgewood China, can usually be bought reasonably priced at large department store sales. Otherwise, create an eclectic set of beautiful dinner pieces from various antique stores.

Cleanliness Is Next to Richness

The old saying that "cleanliness is next to godliness" may be clichéd', but the wisdom of the words applies to your apartment. Take it to heart, because cleanliness is certainly next to Richness according to the people you want as friends. Sure, there are a few Rich eccentrics who live in filth, but they are not the friends you want.

One of the characteristics of successful people is that they are meticulous. That, my friend, is merely a habit—and habits are formed by creating a routine of behavior until you do it automatically without thinking about it anymore.

Create a simple routine for keeping your apartment clean at all times. An hour once a week won't do. You need a regimen that you incorporate into your natural activities, every single day. As soon as you wake up, make up your bed (you can get it down to two minutes). When you get out of the shower, sprinkle cleanser into the tub, toilet, and sink and using two long brushes to scrub briefly, then rinse. When you use something from the kitchen, immediately wash it and put it away. Take two minutes to whisk a magnetic duster, over everything before you leave each morning. Toss yesterday's newspapers in the trash, stack mail and magazines neatly, straighten cushions on furniture before you walk out the door. Vacuum and do laundry on weekends.

If you have trouble throwing things away and are overwhelmed by the clutter, especially papers you may want to save, then stuff it all into plastic bags and put them out of sight. If you have too many of them, rent a storage space and you can go visit your clutter anytime you want to.

Neat, clean—that is your pattern.

Set the Tone of Personal Pride in What You Have

When you open your door and invite your friends inside, do you apologize for anything? Do you feel conscious of how little you have or how it reflects on you?

Your attitude sets the tone for your home. Apologize for nothing. And do not behave as if you are ill-at-ease. Even if someone drops by without telephoning first (which *you* will never do to anyone), you must not apologize for how your house looks, even if it happens to be messy (which is rare, these days, right?).

Your attitude should instantly be bright, friendly, and hospitable. That is the graciousness a home either has or lacks, regardless of the furnishings. And you are the one who creates it with your welcoming glow.

At least keep decaf and regular coffee beans, a herbal and a regular tea, milk, sugar and plain shortbread cookies on hand to offer anyone who visits. Set a simple, welcoming tone.

For more elaborate visits, have available an electric teakettle, whole leaf tea in tins instead of tea bags, a porcelain teapot, a silver or silver-plated tea strainer and a tray to carry it all from kitchen to coffee table, or a tea cart to roll it.

You can offer espresso or cappuccino if you have an espresso maker. But do not offer instant cappuccino. Breadmakers are popular and easy, so you can make delicious sweet breads in no time.

If the weather warrants it and if you have a fireplace, a low flame in the hearth is a welcoming touch of hospitality.

Your home is your castle, and though you are the king or

the queen, when the Rich come to visit, treat them like royalty. And they *will* come to visit if you're in the right neighborhood, part of the right organizations, and forming the right kinds of friendships.

$\mathcal{Y}$our Social Wardrobe

*"Birds of a feather flock together. And
one of the ways they identify each other
is by their feather."*

—Ginie Sayles,
How to Marry the Rich

A social wardrobe must be either dressier or more casual
than your business wardrobe. The main thing to strive for is a
"social look" in your clothes, just as you have a business look
in your career.

One of the biggest differences between the upper class and
other classes when it comes to social wear is that upper classes
are comfortable in dressier clothes and do not rely on denim,
which is a staple of the lower classes.

In the last quarter of the twentieth century, however, the
street fashion of jeans entered the realm of the upper classes;
but the trend seems to be reversing again leaving denim to drift
back into the lower classes.

Even so, there are parts of the country where jeans will always be revered, even by the upper classes of that region.

Never wear jeans to a social occasion unless it has been suggested as acceptable. And if you do wear jeans, observe the
guidelines for wearing them that are included throughout the
Men's and Women's Social Dress sections.

Men's Social Dress

Men do not need to add as many new pieces to create a social wardrobe as women, because their business suits can double for many occasions. And a man's alternate business attire of sport coat, slacks, and tie with loafers can take him to a relaxed social event. However, brown suits are traditionally out of place after 5 P.M. Blue or black are best for evening.

Suits

Black Tie. For black tie events, wear only a tuxedo. Today's tux has a black satin shawl collar and satin seam on the pants. Wear it with a white, French-cuffed tux shirt, shirt studs, gold or black onyx cuff links (two-sides, not swivel), black bow-tie, black socks, and black patent shoes. Wear a dressy black vest.

Off-beat touches, such as collarless shirts and plaid vests are best worn among very close friends; but if you are still on-the-rise, socially, stick with today's shawl-collared tux.

A white tux coat is worn between Easter/Passover and Labor Day or on warm-weather cruises.

Dark Blue Suit. A good suit for dressy evening social occasions that are not black tie. A white or light blue shirt, bright blue silk tie or pink-and-silver tie, dark blue or black socks, and black wing-tip shoes pull it all together.

Gray Suit. This suit is good for dressy morning or afternoon social occasions. One of the sharpest looks for a gray suit is to wear it with mahogany brown lace-up shoes and mahogany brown belt. This is now a preferred alternate to the traditional gray with black shoes and belt. White shirt and silver-gray silk tie complete the look.

Jackets

Black wool jacket, navy blazer with monogrammed brass buttons, and a gray or white jacket are all acceptable.

Pants

Gray Slacks. Slate gray pants, worn with brown belt, white shirt, light gray V-necked sweater, and brown loafers, is a Rich casual look.

Moleskin Pants. Wear these with a blue wide-striped shirt, gray socks, brown brogues, and dark jacket.

Black Pants. Black slacks with a blue shirt that has a white collar, blue-and-silver silk tie, sheer black socks, black wing-tip shoes, and gray or black jacket is a dynamite evening look.

Khakis. Team khakis with a cotton shirt of any color, a blazer and tie, and loafers, and they will take you almost anywhere that is semicasual.

Dark Blue Jeans. Always dry clean your jeans. Wear them pressed, with a white shirt, any color blazer, and loafers. Add a tie if you want. This outfit is good for meeting a date at Starbucks.

Light Blue Jeans. This pair can be machine-washed. Wear your light jeans with a tucked-in T-shirt, belt, and sneakers. This is appropriate attire for washing the dog, cleaning the yard, or relaxing around the house.

$\mathcal{W}$OMEN'S SOCIAL DRESS

Women should not wear business-looking suits socially, unless the occasion calls for it. However, sweaters, skirts, and dresses that are worn to the office can double socially, if they are accessorized differently.

Add some of the following to your wardrobe:

Skirts

Turquoise Short Skirt. Worn with a lemon linen shirt, thin, yellow belt, a white jacket with large turquoise native American brooch on lapel, and yellow sandals or white ballerina flats, this creates the type of outfit to wear when you go shopping or get together with a group of women for a casual visit. Add a small white or yellow straw bag to complete the look.

Long Cotton or Silk Wrap Skirt. Wear this with a halter top for very casual cocktail parties, or for pool or beach gatherings at a clubhouse. This skirt can be a solid color or have a bold print or Haitian design. Large hoop earrings and strappy sandals work well with this look.

Straight or Flowing Velvet Skirt. In solid black, wine, dark green, or bright red, this is wonderful for winter holiday dinners and socials. Wear your velvet skirt with a simple satin or silk blouse (of any color) and a striking belt or belt buckle. A matching velvet jacket is very dressy. Add velvet flats or pumps, if possible. A jeweled or lamé blouse turns this from elegant to glamour for a very festive, very dressy occasion—like New Year's Eve.

Full Taffeta Skirt. In solid black, emerald green, or ruby red, the taffeta skirt has ultimate femininity when paired with an ivory satin-and-lace blouse with billowing sleeves and a black velvet cummerbund. The blouse can be an antique, adding all the more elegance to its look. Your only jewelry should be small diamond or pearl stud earrings. Wear flats or pumps, preferably in taffeta or fabric. This is ideal winter holiday wear.

Pants

Dressy Fabric (Velvet, Taffeta, Silk) Pants. These pants can replace its counterpart skirt, so that instead of wearing the velvet skirt, you would wear velvet pants. They look especially nice with a lacy antique blouse and a short velvet jacket. They also look great with a black silk or satin blouse or sweater and a jeweled belt buckle.

Leather Pants. These are acceptable for dressy resort wear and holiday wear. Without pockets, the straight legs are smooth-fitting, but never tight. You don't want to look like a rock star. A tucked-in turtleneck, smooth belt, and two bangle bracelets or a charm bracelet finish the look. Wear dark, ankle-high boots with dark stockings.

Chinos. Always a good choice with a pink shirt, a pale yellow shirt, or crisp white shirt. They wear well with either yellow or red accessories, including flats.

Dark Jeans. Own a dark denim-blue pair that you *never* wash, because they will fade and look like street jeans. Dry clean and have a sharp crease pressed down the center. Wear them with a bright white cotton shirt and needlepoint belt: add a scarf tied like a tie, with a blazer and loafers.

For summer travel and afternoons at an outdoor café, wear your dark denim-blue jeans with a loose red silk shirt tied at the waist, sandals, mesh handbag, and gold hoop earrings. Sleeves can be rolled up.

Light Jeans. A pair of light-blue jeans that you toss into the wash regularly are acceptable. These are worn with T-shirts or polo shirts and tennis shoes. Wear them to Little League games, to a fund-raising car wash, to work in your garden, or just gadding about the neighborhood on Saturday mornings.

Dresses

Plain Dress. Take a solid color dress, and wear a colorful blouse tied at the waist over it. Add at least four bracelets and flats. This look is good for travel and taking tours. Remove the blouse and the plain dress will look different for later in the day.

Silk Dress. Any color silk dress worn with or without a jacket and with matching sling-back heels can go to any cocktail party or dinner.

Coats and Jackets

In addition to your three year-round blazers in red, black and white, you'll want to add a traditional long, camel-haired coat and a shorter, well-insulated zip-up or snap-up coat for outdoor activities. A heavy Satin coat is good for dressy evening wear and a fur coat is dressiest of all in winter.

Accessories

Necklaces. Pearls are basic. A very long double strand of pearls that falls well below your breasts is elegant and dressy. A single strand of pearls just below your collarbone is good for cocktail parties and semiformal occasions. A triple strand of pearls worn as a choker with a diamond clasp is very formal.

A necklace with an unusual gold, silver, brass, pewter, platinum, or copper pendant, worn constantly, can become your trademark necklace, requiring you to wear no other jewelry.

Earrings. Hoops are acceptable for casual wear, and dangle earrings for dressier occasions. Rhinestones or diamonds and other precious stones are formal-event earrings.

Bracelets. Practically all bracelets are appropriate. Gold, silver, precious metals and even enamel and plastic can be worn. Links bangles, cuffs, and mesh styles are fine.

Rings. For society parties, you may bring out a stunning jeweled ring for your right hand.

For occasional casual wear, more than one native American ring with bracelets and necklaces works with native-style clothing. For instance, wearing native turquoise-and-coral silver rings, with a matching slave bracelet and a squash blossom necklace, perhaps moccasins or sandals, and a long, full denim skirt and silk blouse can be stunning and completely appropriate.

Native anything is fine for casual wear as long as it is authentic and coordinated true to native style or native American blend. This is also true for native Hawaiian, Mexican, Haitian, and so on.

Mixing Metals. All gold or all white gold or all pearls can be fine, but some fine jewelry artists today are incorporating combinations of silver with 14-carat gold inlay in bracelets, earrings, and necklaces. It is a way not to limit yourself to one metal. You can combine bracelets of brass, silver, and gold.

Handbags. Socially, you want to have a variety of handbags to match your outfits. But you'll want one main handbag appropriate for the season that you carry almost all the time. Straw bags in every color can match or complement your summer outfits or match your sandals. A small, dressy clutch purse, is the only type of handbag appropriate for evening. Fabric must be dressy enough to match the occasion and your outfit. Beaded bags and small gold or silver-toned metal clutches work for very formal occasions. Evening gowns look better without bags of any sort. Put your lip pencil in your date's tux pocket.

Belts. Woven fabric belts in pastel colors for spring, needlepoint belts, a gold or silver belt, plus several interesting belt buckles, including one monogrammed, will complete your social wardrobe.

Shoes. In addition to the shoes from your business wardrobe, make sure you have black sling-back heels, brown loafers, white sneakers/black sneakers and gold sandals (which will go with anything), suede flats and heels.

Scarves. Tie a short, patterned scarf around your neck and see what it does for a plain blouse and skirt. Wrap a long, thin scarf around your waist and watch a a pair of pants and shirt be transformed. Drape a colorful scarf over your shoulder and belt it to add some pizazz to your suit. Tie back your hair with a scarf for a picnic or barbecue and see how it changes your appearance.

Hair. For dressier occasions, pull one side of your hair slightly back with a tiny-jeweled or solid-gold clasp. A pony-tail is permitted only if you are young and for very casual occasions.

Fragrance. Spicy fragrances are wonderful for outdoor or sports or daytime activities. Florals are nicest for dressier social events and evening.

$\mathscr{H}$ow to Shop

"What are three words that profile the affluent? FRUGAL! FRUGAL! FRUGAL!"

—*The Millionaire Next Door*

Can you afford tailored-to-fit clothes, instead of off-the-rack clothes? You would be surprised at how little the difference is in price and how great the difference is in detail and perfect fit.

Can you afford shoes made specifically for you? What about accessories made to order? Even jewelry. Those may be a little out of reach right now. But keep them in the back of your mind because they are not as prohibitive as you think.

The Rich enjoy this level of clothing, sometimes to the exclusion of any other type of dressing, but mostly as part of a mix. Pedigrees, for instance, have clothes, shoes, and accessories made (sometimes they even commission their own dinner china), but they also shop at L. L. Bean and Talbots. They like quality and classic styles, whether tailored or store-bought.

If you will keep quality and style as your guidelines, you will be surprised at your shopping success on a budget. There are five-thousand-dollar outfits that add no value to your appearance, and there are ninety-dollar sale items that can make you look Rich when accessorized correctly. And whether you are a man or a woman, always, always, always buy good accessories that you can wear for up to two years. They really will make a difference.

$\mathcal{N}$EW CLOTHES

Buy new clothes mostly for your own morale. Resale items are a perfectly viable way to shop, no matter how much money you have, but to make it your only way of dressing yourself can have drawbacks. Apart from feeling that you deserve something new, the clothes in resale shops may be on their way out of style, so you will likely not get as much wear out of them.

To buy new clothes at cheaper prices, look for

- Custom tailoring shops

- Closeout houses

- Outlet malls

- Less expensive retail shops

- Knockoffs

Find a Reasonable Tailor for Custom Clothes

My husband's tailor always came to his office with samples and to check his measurements. This service adds expense to your custom tailoring cost, but if you can go to a custom tailoring shop, your cost is reduced—and you get a great custom look for less money.

The Custom Shop, a national chain headquartered in New York City, makes beautiful shirts, ties, and suits for both men and women at reasonable prices. There is nothing quite as impressive as a custom-made shirt with your initials (not your name) tastefully monogrammed in a diamond shape or in small block letters (the best two styles) on the left side of the shirt. If there is no breast pocket, put the monogram in the center of where a pocket would be. Place it so that the monogram does not show when you wear your jacket. The Custom Shop can also monogram buttons for some of your jackets. If you can't find a Custom Shop in your area, call 212-223-3600 to locate the nearest one.

Closeout Houses

The Neiman-Marcus closeout store is Last Call in Austin, Texas, where they send new merchandise that has not sold, even on sale. You can buy new Armani Suits, new St. John knits, and fine new shoes, handbags, and accessories for incredibly low prices. Saks Fifth Avenue, Nordstrom's, and Filene's have closeout houses, too.

T. J. Maxx is an exceptionally good chain close-out store that offers wonderful buys on brand-new merchandise that big department stores and retail shops did sell. You can buy everything from Ralph Lauren and Kenneth Cole belts at a steal, to fine housewear items, bedding, crystal, fine lingerie, coats, expensive perfumes, gourmet foods, and children's toys.

For gifts as well as your own clothing, close out houses can be a Mecca. Be sure the merchandise you buy is not damaged, because they sometimes have those items, too. You may want to look at them anyway, because there are some good buys in perfectly good clothes with only a minor repair needed.

Outlet Stores

Outlet stores were intended as closeout houses, but they became so popular that, to meet demand, some stores added merchandise just for the outlet store market. There are some designer outlet stores where you think you are getting an expensive item for less, when in fact you are not. According to a *48 Hours* program on outlet stores, some sell clothes that are made with cheaper materials and the designer's label stitched inside. This merchandise is of inferior quality, so just because it has a designer label doesn't mean you're getting a bargain. And some outlet stores knock only five dollars off the price of their merchandise, so no big savings there.

Still and all, I think a lot of outlet stores have good buys, if you shop carefully and look for quality fabrics, not labels.

Less Expensive Retail Shops

Episode, Georgiou's, and Caché are three national chains of reasonably priced, basically good-quality clothes for women. You can buy brand-new in-style outfits for less money. For men, Jos. A. Banks, Bacharach's, and J. Crew are three reasonably priced chains. Macy's and Lord & Taylor have some of the best prices on new merchandise for men and women every time they have a sale.

KNOCKOFFS AND FAMOUS DESIGNERS' SECONDARY LINES

A dead giveaway that you do not have money but that you are trying to look as if you do is to be seen in "affordable designer wear." The masses may not know that it is a secondary line, but the Rich do.

Some designers simply license their names to a cheaper line of clothing. In other words, *they do not design these clothes themselves.* Most of the time, they never even see the secondary line. You will be paying far too high a price for the cheaper line, and you are only paying for the name.

Top-of-the-line knockoff designs can be of far, far better quality than most secondary lines of famous designers.

Knockoff designers (I was told Calvin Klein started as a knockoff designer) study the fashion runways in Europe to see what the upcoming trends are going to be. They make sketches of them, come back to America, and make clothes that look like the ones from Europe—but alter them just slightly. The clothes are known as "knockoffs."

Victor Costa has long been known as one of America's top knockoff designers, whose clothes are beautifully made. Several years ago, I heard him interviewed on a television program in Houston. He was talking about Ivana Trump when she was married to Donald and constantly in the public eye. She had to wear something different and look glamorous every day.

I was surprised to hear that Ivana would buy thirty new outfits from Victor at the beginning of every season, and she paid about five hundred dollars per outfit. A season is ninety days. That means she wore each outfit three times. She needed an extensive wardrobe, but she didn't spend an exorbatent amount of money on it.

If this story is true, she purchased top-quality American

knockoffs, which are just as good as the European designer labels and far less expensive. How smart of her!

Even major department stores such as Neiman-Marcus (their Galleria Label) and Saks Fifth Avenue (Real Clothes label) carry knockoffs that are sold under the store's private clothing label. Do not use the term "knockoff" when you shop there, however, or you may not receive a favorable response. Just ask where the clothes are that are sold under the "store's label."

Many wealthy people include well-made knockoffs in their wardrobe.

Resale Clothes

It is okay to shop resale when your budget just won't allow a new purchase for something you need. Be very, very selective in every purchase, because some resale shops can be grossly overpriced. But if you are careful, there are some great bargains to be had in the following categories:

• Consignment stores

• Thrift shops

• Altering quality seconds into new styles

Consignment Stores

There are excellent consignment and resale shops for both men and women throughout the country—and you would be surprised to know they are used at times by some of the Rich.

Most Rich women never wear the same evening gown more than once, so many of them pick up a beautiful gown on consignment, wear it, and then reconsign it.

Consignment stores that support Episcopal churches or leading charities are usually good. And those in the better parts of town tend to carry very fine items.

There are books on resale shops in some states and regions. Many of these books list the labels the store specializes in and note the condition of most garments and whether or not they are overpriced. If you cannot find a book on resale shops in your area, look up Resale Shops in the Yellow Pages and call before you go there. Ask which labels the shop carries most. If the salesperson is vague, ask if the shop has a particular label you like in stock and how many items they have in your size.

A real plus with consignment and resale shops is accessories. You can stock up on a variety of coats, scarves, great leather belts, handbags, shoes, even briefcases, hats, and costume or real jewelry.

When you find a good consignment store, get to know a salesperson there and give him or her your size, preferred labels or styles, and your telephone number. Ask the salesperson to give you a call each time the store receives a new shipment and to set aside those items that are your size in a preferred label or style.

Thrift Shops

One Rich woman I know who has great taste wears expensive clothes combined with Thrift Shop finds. She told me it satisfies a creative, fun side of her. And she is amused when people rave over an item she bought at a thrift shop.

As with consignment stores, you have to be careful of what you buy, but if you are familiar with quality and price, you can find real treasures in thrift shops. They offer you an opportunity to try new styles and to have some fun with dressing.

Alter Quality Seconds into New Styles

A beautiful actress in New York City lives penuriously while waiting to be discovered, but she looks like an heiress every time I see her. Her secret? She shops Goodwill thrift shops in New York, where she buys a thousand dollars' worth of used Chanel suits and Armani jackets. Then, she takes them to a talented seamstress who alters all her outfits into current looks for a small cost.

DETAILS FOR LOOKING GREAT

Details can make or break your look. I'm sure you have seen a woman all dressed up for dinner at an expensive restaurant, looking beautiful, like a model—until you notice that her hand-bag is a beaten-up brown leather shoulder-strap bag that should only be carried with a pair of jeans.

Details make the difference. Observe the following shopping details:

Buy Only Comfortable Shoes

Even if you wear a five-thousand-dollar outfit, there is no way you can look stylish if you are half-limping. And you cannot look good if your face is scrunched with silent pain.

Cost does not make comfort. A few years ago, I paid over three hundred dollars for a pair of famous designer flats with a bow on the toe. The shoes had been measured to fit, so I kept expecting them to become more comfortable after a few wear-ings, but that never happened.

I travel a lot, so I carry only a few pairs of shoes with me and they have to be comfortable. Just before one of my seminars in San Francisco, I knew I could not wear the shoes that evening. We were staying in a hotel on Union Square, where there are a lot of stores, so I dashed from one to the other, looking for a pair of plain black flats, but did not find any in my size. Then I saw black flats in the window of The Limited.

For twenty-five dollars, I purchased a pair of plain black ballerina-style flats because they felt good. And to this day I wish I had bought a dozen pairs. They were the most comfortable shoes I ever owned. Interestingly, Rich friends and clients often inquired where I bought the shoes.

Be sure inexpensive shoes do not look cheap, though. My ballerina flats from The Limited had a quality, classic look.

Expensive shoes are not necessarily better made, either. I was ready to buy a pair of red suede designer high-heel shoes until my husband noticed the rubber tip on the bottom of the high heel was backward on one shoe. The store offered to pay to have it repaired if I bought the shoes, but I felt that if some-thing so important as that had been shoddily put on the shoe, I did not trust the manufacturer.

Color-Key Your Social Wardrobe

What if you went into a flower garden and all the flowers were brown or gray? You would think the flowers were dead, right? And would you buy a black-and-white television when you get a color TV? Of course not! So why would you dress in drab colors when you can don yourself in all the hues of the rainbow?

Most people have too much black, gray, brown, and beige in their wardrobes, which makes them look boring, poor, and average. Unfortunately, some people think the Rich wear dull neutrals most of the time to be understated.

That is simply not true. The Rich love beautiful colors and wear them more often than the average person. Bright colors make good fabrics look richer. The colors of royalty are brilliant red, gold, bright white, and sometimes royal blue and bright purple (not dark purple).

Choose three colors that look good on you and build your wardrobe around them. That way, you have a variety of clothes and always have colorful accessories to wear with them. Each year, you can choose three new colors—or keep two of them from last year.

Color creates energy. Repaint your life in exciting, living color!

$\mathcal{Y}$our Social Personality

> "When a man is gloomy, everything
> seems to go wrong; when he is cheerful,
> everything seems right!"
>
> —*Proverbs 15:15*

A happy personality, a caring heart, and a sharing manner are the three most important keys to social success. Add a few basic skills, and you will be perfectly at ease socially.

$\mathcal{H}$APPINESS IS THE "CLASSY" PERSONALITY

"I like myself" is an underlying message of happiness. Whatever your complexes, insecurities, or fears, you can outwit them and project confidence if you decide to project happiness.

In the Christmas musical *Scrooge*, the ghost of Christmas Present sings, "I like life. Life likes me." That is the essence of self-esteem—to *choose* the view that you like life and that life likes you. Happiness is the essence of self-esteem.

People are so starved for happiness that if you have it, they just want to be near you. They feel you must be special if you are happy, that you are superior somehow. And they hope that if they can just be close to you, that your happiness might magically rub off on them.

I think of happiness as being like a fire in a fireplace. People are drawn to it like a magnet. They are warmed by it, brightened by its light, and they respond to its energy.

A happy personality does not have to be loud or overdone. It can quietly sparkle in your face, your eyes, your voice. Let people reach out to you, to warm themselves in your happy glow.

Happiness makes you worth knowing.

What If You Are Not Happy?

Psychology tells us that if you do not feel happy, you can choose to smile, and the action of smiling sends a message to your brain that you are happy, which releases endorphins that make you *feel* happier.

Happiness does not mean you have no problems, but it does make them lighter. Minor irritations, habitual criticisms, ongoing dissatisfactions are choices that can be changed with a simple decision to project happiness and let the rest go. Only the deep grief of loss qualifies as a reason to temporarily set aside a happy state. In most other respects, we can make the courageous choice of facing each moment with happy anticipation, which banishes fear.

Socially, happiness works like a magnet that attracts the very people who are most worth having as friends.

For the next three months

• Walk slightly faster.

• Look about you with anticipation.

• Concentrate on expressing joy in the tiniest actions of life— your bath, your meal, your exercise, your daily tasks, your interactions with service people and friends.

• Look upon your own life as if it is full and exciting and you would not change places with anyone else for anything (choose this attitude whether or not you feel it . . . yet).

• Laugh easily. If you spill something, laugh instead of cursing.

• Choose something to enjoy about everything you see. When you think "What an ugly display," or mentally criticize someone's outfit, your face turns sour and your energy slows down. *Choose* instead to replace the thought with something you do like, such as "What a pretty shade of yellow." If you think you cannot do that, then you are choosing not to.

• If something or someone is really offensive, turn away from it and seek something you like and move toward it. Do not give the offensive sight power by acknowledging it.

• If there is a wrong in the world that you feel should be righted, work for it and *speak of the solution* and the happiness it can bring.

• Don't think about the past. Have a forward-moving energy about you. Anticipate life.

One of the best signs of the refined Rich is that they control their happiness by not allowing the petty behavior of others to rob them of their own happy view. True, there are some disgruntled Rich in this world, but they have to pay people to be around them. And they are to be pitied because they suffer more from their own misery.

A Caring Heart

When you care enough about others to inquire about them because they are people and not because of how much money they have, and when you genuinely listen to them and respond, you have a caring heart. And having a caring heart also helps your self-esteem. If all your energy is focused on someone else, you cannot possibly be self-conscious or worry about what others think.

Like happiness, a caring heart can be developed, but make sure it is sincere. If you do not really care about a person, but you are asking questions because this is an important person who can get you into society, you will be only as successful as your ability to *seem* caring. Over a period of time, it can be strenuous to paint on a superficial gloss of caring about people when it is not from your heart. Little by little, manipulative motives become transparent and leave you unfulfilled.

People—Rich or poor—will sometimes disappoint you, yes.

Accept it. Then keep in mind that people are human and make mistakes, but it is this humanness that binds us together and makes people worth caring about.

For the next several weeks, practice caring in the following ways:

• *Look beyond the words someone says.* When someone is talking to you, ask yourself what this person needs from you. Most of the time, it is that you truly care about what they are saying; when you care, it validates them.

• *Be fully present.* Stop whatever you are doing for a moment, and turn an attentive eye fully on the person. If the tale is a lengthy one and you are both busy, after a thoughtful pause, resume your task, but really listen. If you are working on something together, continue to work, but stay mentally focused on the person.

• *Respond throughout.* From time to time, glance up while the person talks, and make eye contact. Make occasional remarks such as "Remarkable" or nod your head to acknowledge you care.

• *Summarize to let the person know you listened.* When the person finishes talking, smile and briefly summarize what he or she has said in one sentence. "Oh, I see. You believe that new playground equipment will be less expensive than building a new playground. I can see you have given this considerable thought."

Even if you are not in favor of this suggestion, you are not immediately dismissing the worth of this person's view. You are caring about this person's need to be valued, to be of service, to have input, to be recognized.

• *Do not offer advice.* Advice undercuts confidence in the other person. Give encouragement. Even if you are asked, say, "I can not possibly advise you, but I have always been impressed with your good judgment."

• *Don't steal the person's thunder.* Do not bring yourself into the other person's story. If the person has just told you about a trip to a place you have visited, it is not necessary to say so at this point. Just say, "Did you like it?" or "Would you go, again?" or "How often do you go there?"

However, it is all right to say, "Yes, I have been to Bali. What did you like best about it?" Keep your questions directed to the other person's excitement about the trip. You can share your story about Bali another time.

• *Care enough to remember the other person's interests.* When you see someone you know ask about his or her children, or parents' health, or some especially good news.

Care Without Being a Doormat

Caring does not mean you erase yourself. Caring does not mean you subjugate yourself to others. That is not healthy.

Caring means that you value other people because you already value yourself.

• *Care but say no.* If people ask you to do something you do not feel good about, say no. If they directly ask if you believe in something that you don't, say no.

• *Don't take sides.* Two people who compete today may be best of friends next month. If the conversation is a complaint about someone, your silence can be interpreted as taking sides with the other person. Instead, interrupt laughingly and say, "Jack, you have had an exasperating experience. Whatever this is about, you'll see it will clear up by itself." Then change the subject in a light, unoffended way. If you refuse to get into social catfights, you will build trust.

• *Notice who the real leader is.* For the first year in a new circle, form friendships slowly. Be equally nice to everybody— always—but don't eagerly jump into the first friendship offered, or you may end up with people who could be damaging to your social goals. Have coffee with anyone, but wait until you have observed the social hierarchy of the organization before you become identified as chummy with anyone.

When you realize who the lead person is, do not gush or pursue him or her openly, but be sure that person is made aware of your accomplishments in the group, without bragging about it. Perhaps during a meeting you can ask a question about a project that leads into a comment about your efforts. Make the lead person like you and everyone will like you.

• *Push a little but don't seem pushy.* Persistently putting yourself around the Rich who may not seem accepting at first, is no different from letting the neighborhood dogs get acquainted with you. At first they may growl or bark, but in time, they accept your presence.

A Sharing Heart

A sharing heart is the basis of entertaining. And don't let the word "entertaining" intimidate you. It is nothing more than enjoying people so much that you simply share whatever level of abundance you have, without shame or pretense. And they will adore you.

Even the Rich? Yes, when you become friends through a common interest.

And, remember, you don't become friends with "the Rich" as a whole entity. You become friends one at a time, with individuals who happen to be Rich.

"But what I have isn't enough!" you cry, "I would die if they saw what little I have. I could never entertain them on the same level they entertain!"

Don't snub yourself with such an attitude. As long as you live in a good part of town, you don't have to live in anything grand. A few easy ground rules can have you enjoying your Rich friends in their social functions and occasionally entertaining them with ease.

Study the next chapters to learn eight basic social functions that you can attend with the Rich and how to host them yourself.

ʃtage 2—Social Acceptance

> *"I always felt that the great high privilege, relief and comfort of friendship was that one had to explain nothing."*
>
> —Katherine Mansfield

You will know you have been accepted into the middle rank and file of society when you begin to be invited to the eight social functions that most govern society life. And as your friendships grow, you will want to host some of these events yourself, even if they are on a modified level.

1. COFFEES AND TEAS

Coffees are small gatherings that are held in the morning, between nine and eleven o'clock.

There is a difference between someone inviting you to "a coffee" and someone inviting you to have coffee. "A coffee" is a small social gathering. Having coffee is a casual chat among friends over a cup of coffee.

Coffees are sometimes referred to as "morning coffee," whereas teas are often referred to as "afternoon teas." Tea traditionally begins at three in the afternoon and lasts until five o'clock. Since the cocktail hour officially begins at six (but often starts sooner), tea can run until five-thirty.

Social coffees and teas are laid out exactly alike:

• A table large enough to hold service for the number of people invited to the social

• A white damask or lace tablecloth

• A centerpiece of fresh flowers

• China teacups in saucers with paper lace doilies to absorb spills, and silver teaspoons on the saucers or next to them

• Strainers for tea

• Lemon slices, skim milk, cream, sugar, sugar substitute, and honey—in silver, china, or crystal containers

• Appropriate serving spoons, forks, or tongs

• Dessert plates with dessert forks

• Small, lace-trimmed cloth napkins

• Service plate of crustless finger sandwiches

• Service plate of berries or fruit salad with serving spoon; separate cup of topping for the fruit or salad, with serving spoon

• Service plate of pastry or scones with serving tongs; separate cups of fruit preserves for scones, with serving spoons

• Service plate of cookies with tongs

• Bowl of mints or chocolates with small serving spoon

• A silver coffee and tea service at one end of the table with decaffeinated coffee, regular coffee, and tea (whether the gathering is a coffee or a tea), and if you like, hot water and a selection of herbal teas

• A cohostess, seated behind the silver service, who pours the coffee or tea for each guest who arrives

• Champagne or sherry at afternoon tea if you wish, but not at a coffee; juices at a coffee

Greet the host, then greet others as you line up for your coffee or tea. Sit on a sofa or chair and exchange light talk with other guests. Be sure you keep a very relaxed manner and talk only about upbeat topics.

Morning coffees and afternoon teas are lovely social occasions, used to

- Introduce a newcomer
- Precede a club meeting
- Host a shower
- Host a debutante event
- Serve as a reception
- Pay minor social debts among a group of people
- Honor a special guest in town
- Host a reunion event

What to Wear

Women. Silk suits or silk dresses are on target, but not pants.

Wear pastel pink, blue, or yellow silk suits in the spring; a white or ivory silk suit is perfect for summer. Fall and winter silks or woolens are good in chocolate brown, yellow, red, or navy. Don't wear black, no matter who else does. It is too formal for daywear, especially morning.

Accessorize with high heels or dressy flats and a small clutch purse, not a shoulder strap (you don't even have to carry a purse, if you don't want to). Pearls are ideal, but gold or silver jewelry will be fine.

Men. Wear a suit and tie appropriate to the season. A pocket handkerchief is a dressy touch, if it picks up one of the colors in your tie. Do not wear a casual coat and tie.

2. WEEKEND BRUNCH

Weekend brunch starts at eleven o'clock in the morning and lasts until two o'clock in the afternoon.

A hybrid between a coffee and a cocktail party, a brunch is a buffet that offers breakfast fare:

- A choice of eggs: scrambled eggs, an exotic omelet

- A choice of breakfast meat: sausages, bacon, ham, salmon, chipped beef

- Fresh fruits: raspberries, sliced mango, pineapple

- A variety of breads: toast, muffins

- Fruit spreads: grape, strawberry, orange marmalade

- Optional foods you may want to include (finger sandwiches, roast beef)

- Condiments: half and half, whole and skim milk for coffee, sugar, sugar substitute, honey, salt, pepper

- Coffee, tea

- Bloody Marys

For busy socialites, whose weekdays are often packed with coffees, teas, and cocktail parties, a weekend brunch can be tucked conveniently in the middle of Saturday or Sunday, creating a casual social occasion with family and friends. However, a brunch can be held for all the same occasions as a coffee, tea, or cocktail party.

What to Wear

Dress according to the purpose. If the brunch is held to honor a visitor, ask how to dress. Otherwise, it can be a very casual gathering of friends dressed in anything from jeans to coat and tie.

Most men will be all right in a pair of slacks and cotton shirt (and pullover sweater if the weather is cold). A blazer and tie can be removed, if it is more casual. Women can dress comfortably in pants or a skirt and blouse, and a jacket if it is casual.

3. COCKTAIL PARTY

Cocktail parties are fun gatherings that last from one and a half to two hours. Typically, a cocktail party begins at six o'clock in the evening to give people time to arrive from their busy day; however, many after-work cocktail parties begin at five-thirty.

Because they are meant for mingling, most people stand up at cocktail parties, holding their drinks while they talk. They may stand near a coffee table while munching from their buffet plates, but moving around is the whole idea of a cocktail party.

If people sit down, it is only for a few minutes. Never isolate yourself or conspicuously sit alone somewhere waiting for people to talk to you. It makes you a poor guest and you are not likely to be invited again.

Have fun at cocktail parties. Make a secret goal of introducing yourself to at least five people you do not know. Just say, "Hi, I'm Jake. What's your name?" with a clear-eyed, open smile. Talk no longer than ten minutes to each person until you have talked to everyone.

At a cocktail party, there will be some or all of:

• A range of liquor and mixers, but also soft drinks, mineral water, club soda, and some nonalcoholic drinks

• Open-faced canapés—usually four, with choices of seafood, fowl, or beef—and chicken livers wrapped in bacon

• Finger sandwiches—particularly salmon and turkey

• Crudités of raw carrots, celery, asparagus, green and black olives, and various dips

• An assortment of crackers

• Boiled shrimp, crab claws, or cooked oysters

• Bowls of nuts, oyster crackers, or party mix scattered around the room

If a cocktail party is going to run more than two hours, there will be a dinner buffet table with two choices of hot meats, usually a seafood and roast beef. Additionally, a pasta salad, a hot vegetable, and dinner rolls will likely be available. Tables with chairs will be set up for dinner.

Cocktail parties are the mainstay of society. They are used to

• Invite new neighbors over to meet the rest of the neighborhood

• Host a group from the office after work

• Repay a lot of social debts at one time

• Have golf or tennis buddies over after a game

• Collect a group of friends together before—or after—going to the theater, opera, ballet, or symphony

• Celebrate anything—a reunion, an engagement, a graduation, or a promotion

• Have a bon voyage party

• Just to get together, drink, and laugh with friends

Cocktail parties can range in size from twenty people to hundreds of people, as long as there is sufficient space to hold the people and you have enough bartenders, drinks, and food.

Even with dancing, most cocktail parties are more fun if the space is not too roomy. If fifty people are invited, but the room was built for a hundred people, the party will appear less successful, even if all fifty show up.

Sometimes small areas are accommodated by "staggered invitations." That means some people are invited from five-thirty to seven; another group from six-thirty to eight; and if there is a third group, they would come from seven-thirty until nine.

If you host a cocktail party for anything other than a few close friends, hire a bartending service and have the food and service dishes catered to your house. If your place is too small, rent a nice hotel meeting room and hire their catering service.

What to Wear

Women. If it is a pretheater cocktail party, wear theater clothes, of course. This can range from a long evening dress to a glittery street-length or short dress.

Men. For a pretheater event, the dressiness of your clothes should match the dressiness of clothes worn by your date or spouse.

Both Men And Women. For all cocktail parties, dress according to the occasion. If it is immediately after a vigorous sport, you should quickly shower and change into casual clothes. If it is after work, you can remove your jacket before or after you get there. If it is impromptu meeting among close friends, anything will be forgiven.

4. WEEKEND GUEST IN THE COUNTRY

The country, the seaside, the mountains: if you are invited to be a weekend guest of the Rich, you are doing well, indeed. And if you are not a financial equal, then you have a special charm that endears you to them. Simply put, they like you.

About a week beforehand, you may receive an itinerary of activities planned for houseguests. Typically, it includes the following:

• The time you are expected to arrive and the time you are expected to leave

• What you are to bring to participate in sports

• Schedule of activities (you do not have to go to all of them), free time for houseguests, meal schedules, any social events

• Clothes to bring

• Names of other guests

• A map and directions to the country house

If you do not receive a weekend agenda, double-check with your host to get a general idea of what clothes to pack. Be sure to take any prescription medication, extra eyeglasses or contact lenses, and packets of Alka-Seltzer. Also pack a good book for free time, and a gift for your host or hostess.

Gifts for Your Host or Hostess. A basket of fruit; a bottle of exceptional wine or brandy—or a good brand of nonalcoholic wine if they do not drink alcohol; a bouquet of flowers; a new hardback best-seller are traditional gifts of graciousness. If you want to give a more creative gift, fine, but do not overdo it or you can look too eager to please. And if you overspend, it will embarrass your host or hostess. The gift should be a simple, warm, and thoughtful gesture.

5. BLACK-TIE EVENTS

Formal dinners, opening night performances, dinner at the captain's table on a cruise, and an assortment of holiday and other social events will require black-tie dress. There will be assigned seating in most cases. Take your invitation with you in case you are asked for it at the door.

What to Wear

Men. Black tie is always a dinner jacket or a tuxedo worn with a black bow tie and black patent leather shoes. Warm-weather cruises and resorts will allow a white dinner jacket for black-tie events. You may see men with a variety of dinner jackets for black-tie occasions, but you will look more respectable in a black tuxedo. If the invitation says "Black Tie," wear only black-tie clothing

"Optional Black Tie" on an invitation means you can wear a blue business suit, but in that case, check with your date or spouse to be sure what she is going to wear. If she will be wearing a long satin gown, put on your tuxedo and smile. Nothing looks worse than a mismatched couple at a formal event.

Women. Short or long, dressy satin, chiffon, or velvet, depending on the season, will be appropriate.

6. WHITE-TIE EVENTS

Elaborate balls—such as White House balls and high-ticket arts and charity balls, relic debutante balls and some weddings will state "White Tie" on the invitation. You will present your invitation at the door, proceed through a receiving line, have assigned tables, dance, and mingle.

What to Wear

Men. There is no getting around it, you must wear a white piqué tie and a black tailcoat, plus a white waistcoat, black trousers, and black patent leather pumps.

Women: Pile on your glitteriest jewelry, buy a pair of long white gloves, and wear a lavish ball gown that Cinderella would envy.

7. FORMAL DINNER IN A MANSION

The trend in America is toward informality, but in the event you are invited to the mansion of your new Rich friends for a very formal dinner, I don't want you to feel ill-at-ease.

Not everything below may occur, but *your* behavior from the time you arrive at the mansion door until you leave will still be the same.

You will receive an invitation in the mail and probably an enclosed, self-addressed RSVP card. Send it back promptly with your yes or no.

If there is no enclosed card, write out a brief note of acceptance: *Mr. and Ms. John Doe accept, with pleasure, your invitation to dinner on Saturday, October 22, at 7:30 p.m.*

If you must decline, write: *Mr. and Ms. John Doe regret they are unable to accept your gracious invitation to dinner on Saturday, October 22 at 7:30 p.m.*

If you cannot go, I suggest you send your RSVP card and also telephone to express your sincere regrets and desire to attend.

If you attend, observe the following:

Arriving at the Mansion

Do not be the first to arrive, but do not be late. Arrive within five minutes after the time stated on the invitation.

If the door is answered by anyone other than the host or

hostess, have your invitation with you if it is required, as you give your name. The host and hostess will be near the door, if they do not answer it. Otherwise, there will be someone to take you to them.

Speak first to your hosts, before you speak to anyone else. Greet them with a happy smile and a light, breezy bit of small talk for only a few seconds: "Hello, John. Hi, Mary. I've been looking forward to this all day. Mary, you look beautiful."

If they have not met your companion or spouse, quickly introduce them, addressing the hosts first: "Mary and John (or Mr. and Mrs. Smith), this is my wife, Julie. She is an attorney for Briggs and Briggs. Julie, this is Mary and John Smith."

Never bring someone with you unless you have cleared it first with the host or hostess.

Do not linger or open a full-fledged conversation, because they have other guests arriving.

After your greeting, move into the area where other guests are mingling. In some cases, if you are a newcomer, your hostess may lead you to a group of people and introduce you.

Glance at each person in the group, smile, and nod, then say to all, "I am glad to meet you."

Show yourself capable of interacting with the group, so the hostess can leave you there without concern and return to welcome other guests who are arriving.

Procedure of the Evening

Formal dinners are typically later than other dinners. A very formal dinner is comprised of the following:

• Cocktails and hors d'oeuvres for forty-five minutes to an hour at the most, and served by uniformed waiters with silver trays

• Formal entertainment, such as chamber opera or chamber music or a pianist or violinist or a famous poet, for no longer than an hour

• Dinner, seven to nine courses, which will last about two hours and in the most formal situations will begin at ten o'clock in the evening, although nine is more usual

• After-dinner drinks and coffee, for about thirty minutes and not longer than forty minutes

The above procedure of events is designed so that everything leads up to the dinner, which is the pièce de résistance and the climax of the evening, with the after-dinner drinks and coffee as a time for savoring the satisfaction of your dinner before going. And do expect the dinner to be grand.

Each event is held in a different room, showcasing beautiful art and collections in the background as well as the architectural beauty of the mansion itself. Each beautiful room is part of the enjoyment of the evening.

The order of events can vary, though. For example, some Rich hosts will have

• Cocktails

• Dinner at eight o'clock

• Entertainment

Some formal dinners will have no live entertainment and a five-course meal, yet still be formal.

Ending the Evening

At the end of the evening, do not leave without seeking out both your host and your hostess, who may or may not be standing together (but probably will be).

Compliment the evening—and make your compliment very specific, about something you particularly enjoyed: "The chamber music spotlighted my favorite composer."

Be sure to praise the dinner: "An unforgettable dinner."

Do not engage them in a conversation at this point. You should already have talked to them several times during the evening.

Once you have said your good-byes, thank them and *leave.* Do not be distracted by some other guest that you decide to say something to. Your last good-bye should be to your host and hostess.

What to Wear

Men and women. Your invitation will specify whether or not this is a black-tie or white-tie event. Usually, it is black-tie.

8. AFTER-THEATER OR LATE NIGHT MEAL

An after-theater meal can begin at early as eleven, but typically starts at midnight and lasts until two o'clock the next morning. It may be formal, but it is more typically laid out like a cocktail party buffet.

However, a late night meal that begins after a night on the town with friends can start when the bars close at two o'clock in the morning and last until three-thirty, or until dawn in younger groups. And, of course, you wear whatever you have on.

As you can see, there are social events for literally every hour of the day. From a morning coffee to a midday lunch, to an afternoon tea, to cocktails, then to a formal dinner, a ball, to a midnight-till-dawn meal—and off to a weekend in the country and Sunday brunch.

That is not likely to happen continually, but there are the Social Rich who enjoy a daily life that includes one or more of these eight basic social functions.

BE AN EFFORTLESS HOST

When it is your turn to host one of the eight basic functions, you can impress your Rich friends most by behaving in an "effortless" manner. Follow these tips and watch everything work smoothly for you:

• *Have your place professionally cleaned.* Don't try to do it yourself. There are too many details you can overlook. You can hire a cleaning service quite inexpensively. Check their work thoroughly, including baseboards.

• *Put away all breakables.* Anything that could upset you if broken should not be at a large party.

• *Your bathroom:* If you do not have a guest bathroom, then spruce your bathroom up to look like one. It must be spotless, of course, in every detail. Close the shower curtain across your bathtub. Have no seat covers on the toilet, no bath rugs on the floor, or bathrobes hanging on the back of the door. No toothpaste, toothbrushes, or mouthwash out.

The lavatory countertop should be clear of everything but the following:

—An attractive container of facial tissue.

—A scented candle burning at all times (even if you have potpourri) during your social event. Bayberry is classic. No fruit scents.

—Tiny individual hand soaps in a dish—or a liquid hand soap in a pretty pump container. Thin "soap papers" are nice.

—Finger towels. These can be small cotton towels, terry-cloth finger towels, or simply washcloths. Roll them and stuff them into a pretty ceramic or glass bowl next to the lavatory.

—Beside the counter, have a tall ceramic container—or straw basket—for disposing of a hand towel after each use (put one in the container, so new guests will know its purpose).

—A small wastebasket.

Memorize these Procedures

• *Welcoming guests.* When people arrive, be friendly, easy-going, and try to put them at ease.

• *Be gracious to nondrinkers.* Lower-class people act insulted, even aggressive, if they find out a person does not drink. Have good nonalcoholic wines and beers on hand for nondrinkers.

• *Show no favorites.* All guests are equal while under your roof. You do not give one iota more talk, time, interest, smile, or eye contact to your best friend or to the person you want as a friend than you do to the boring spouse of one of your guests.

On average, talk to each person about three to five minutes with your full attention, then move on, glancing about you to be sure everyone has someone to talk to and a drink, before you focus your attention on the next person. Move around from one part of the room to the next to talk to people.

If these are all old friends, you need not be so specific and can be very offhand; but when you host a party with a purpose (to impress your boss, to get to know your new upscale neighbors, to repay social debts), it will only be as good as your ability to make sure everyone has a good time.

• *Defer to your guests.* If you are the host, you always defer to your guests when they voice an opinion you may not agree with. The job description of a host is that you keep the event pleasant for everyone, whatever the cost to your personal opinions. You can merely say, "What an interesting idea" or "I have never thought of it that way."

$\mathscr{B}$eing Socially at Ease

*"Remember, no one can make you feel
inferior without your consent."*

—Eleanor Roosevelt

The more casual your manner, the more relaxed you will be.
And nowhere is it more important than when you are dressed
for a formal occasion.

If your personality changes into a stuffy air when you are
dressed up, you need to dress up more often and learn to be
comfortable that way.

Being dressed up requires certain behavior, of course, such
as not walking with big steps and arms swinging wildly, not
sprawling in your chair or exhibiting behavior that looks coarse.
But apart from that, do have a down-to-earth manner. In fact,
the more dressed up you are, the more down-to-earth and relaxed you will want your manner to be. That way you will seem
to own your finery and not as if your finery owns you. This is
the secret of feeling at ease.

$\mathscr{S}$OCIAL SUBTLETIES

It is often the subtleties that make or break you socially. The
way you behave at a business social is not exactly the same way
you behave at a society social. There are behaviors that are acceptable in a business club or at a business dinner in a restaurant

that are not acceptable in a privately hosted social function. For instance:

• *No business cards*. Business cards are out of place at social events. To offer yours to another guest is the height of rudeness, because it looks as if you are using the hospitality of your host to further your own business goals. Social cards can be the same size as business cards, but they are white and have only your name and a telephone number in black letters.

• *Avoid business talk*. Business is supposed to be separate from social occasions—in theory at least—so honor this. Talk about social interests, sports, topics of relaxation, rather than topics that could bring worries to someone's mind.

Also, it can seem as if you are trying to impress someone if you introduce what you do into the conversation, or it can appear as if you are judging someone by their business rank rather than by their personality.

• *If someone you dislike is present, be nice*. When you accept an invitation, you accept your role as guest to be pleasant to all attending your host's function. Trying to avoid a person you dislike reflects badly on you. Speak and say a few words that are completely impersonal.

• *Be careful with opinions*. To use a host's party as your political platform is beyond rude—and it is a waste of time. You will not convince anyone to change his or her beliefs, only that your behavior is inappropriate. You can find yourself shunned and your cause lost by those who might have been convinced by you in a different situation.

If you express an opinion and someone disagrees, you show class by saying, "Very interesting. Our differing views would make for stimulating conversation over coffee sometime." Then smile and move to another group.

*E*TIQUETTE

You cannot be socially at ease if you are worried about whether or not you are doing the right thing, saying the right thing, wearing the right thing, and making the right impression. It makes you self-conscious, and self-consciousness drains away your personal charisma.

The secret is to take a couple of hours one weekend and memorize etiquette. Sketch rough diagrams on paper. Pretend you are in various situations and act out how you would handle them.

Then, dismiss it all from your mind. When you go to dinners or parties, *concentrate on warmth and happiness.* Don't worry, you will automatically do the right things that you practiced, because you will have internalized them. You will seem smooth, effortless, and unconcerned about it. Such behavior exudes true confidence.

People are uncomfortable in the presence of someone who is self-conscious about doing the right thing. But, you won't be self-conscious and they will respond beautifully to you.

Confidence means feeling comfortable with yourself no matter where you are, and no matter who is around.

EMBARRASSING MOMENTS

We have all had them: embarrassing moments that turn our faces crimson and scorch our thoughts for years.

Making mistakes is the common denominator of being human. If you made no mistakes, you would be either a robot or an angel—and you would be completely out of place with the rest of us!

Since it is inevitable that you will make social mistakes like the rest of us, the real issue is how to handle them when you do make them.

The Right to Be Wrong

• *Give yourself permission.* Say these words out loud, right now: "I am willing to make mistakes if necessary in order to learn how to do something." When you make a mistake, mentally remind yourself of these words.

• *Ignore your mistakes.* Instantly and smoothly draw everyone's attention to something else.

I am reminded of a man who, as a volunteer to teenage boys, had been given the assignment of teaching sex education. On his way there, he stopped by a social tea of prominent men and women. For whatever reason, he carried his briefcase into the room and set it on a side table.

After twenty minutes of socializing, he picked up his briefcase and started across the room to leave. Suddenly, his briefcase popped open and photocopied drawings of the male and female anatomy flew out into the room.

To his credit, he simply bent down and began picking them up, saying, "I'll appreciate your helping me gather these. I don't want to be late to the class I teach on sex education."

Instantly, everyone was able to cover his or her own embarrassment by helping him out. He did not get flustered or stumble over himself with panicky explanations. When he had the copies together, he calmly replaced them in his briefcase, thanked everyone, and left.

He later told me it was his most embarrassing moment; but his aplomb in handling it proved to everyone that he had the right to make a social mistake without shame, fumbling apologies, or a scrambling loss of dignity.

Social Conversations with the Rich

When you talk to someone, do you walk away mentally scolding yourself, thinking, "Why did I say that? God, how stupid I sounded! This person will never want to talk to me again!"

If you do, I am here to remove that burden from your shoulders, forever. You see, nobody remembers much of what you say. The only thing they do remember is *what it felt like to talk to you*.

Were you defensive? Were you pleasant? Were you aggressive? Were you funny? Were you argumentative?

In other words, people remember the "emotional imprint" of you, long after they forget the conversation.

If you say "Mary had a little lamb" in an angry tone, and then say it in a friendly tone, you can see it is not the words that carry your message, it is the emotion.

If you sense you are not getting a good response from people

when you talk to them, you need to listen to your tone of voice—
and try changing the emotion in your tone. Emotion in your
voice is far more powerful, for reaching your goals or defeating
them, than you can imagine. Keep your tone upbeat and people
will enjoy talking with you.

Heed the following conversational rules, as well:

• Do not tell how badly anyone has treated you. I don't care
who does, don't talk about it. You position yourself as a loser.

• Do not let others—no matter who they are—dump their
problems on you. Later, when the situation has cleared up, they
may resent you for knowing about it. Just interrupt, glance at
your watch and gently say, "Oh, I am so sorry, but I must make
an urgent telephone call. Please excuse me . . . and, Joel, I have
the greatest confidence in your ability to handle the situation.
Excuse me." And go!

• Never be ashamed of your background. The Rich will put
exactly the value on your background that you put on it. If you
choose to be proud of your family and your background, they
will admire your decency. Never, ever be ashamed.

• If there is scandal swirling in the newspaper about someone, you never mention it and you behave no differently to the
person than you did before—no matter how others may behave.

• Don't "poor mouth." People who are always worrying
aloud—that they can't pay their rent or their car payment, and
that they cannot afford to do this or that—seem to have no self-
respect. And they show little respect for others by parading a
woebegone life that is always a day late and a dollar short.

• Never try to impress others. It always will have the opposite
effect.

• Work on your conversational skills. Learn to "link ideas."
Linking ideas means that you listen carefully to a conversation
and pick out one word that you can use to take the conversation
in another direction.

For example, a conversation has been exhausted about as-
trology. You link the planets to space exploration and take the
conversation a new direction.

$\int$tage 3—Social Leadership

> "What you get by reaching your destination isn't nearly as important as what you become by reaching that destination."
>
> —*Zig Ziglar*

You will know your hard work is recognized when you are tapped to be an officer on the board of a prestigious charity. And you will know you have made it to the top of society when you chair a major fund-raising event, which is usually a grand ball.

$\int$ERVING ON THE BOARD

Most of the time, people who are asked to be on the board of a major social charity are those individuals who bring an important (and free) solution to the charity. This individual may be a journalist who is able to get free publicity for an organization, or an advertising executive who gives free ad copy and layouts, or a housewife who has worked tirelessly for years. These people are rewarded by being asked to be on the board.

Even if you are young, if you have worked very, very hard as a volunteer doing things the Founders would never do, it is quite likely that you can end up on the board.

Over time, you may even become an officer. When you are one of the officers on the board, you have risen to a nice level of social recognition.

If you become president of the board, you have definitely arrived at the top.

Serving as Fund-Raising Chair

When you were in the entry level of Stage I, leaders in the nonprofit organization noticed that you were a volunteer who got things done. For several years you performed your volunteer tasks more quickly and better than most other people. And you either raised considerable money for or gave considerable money to the organization.

For three years now you have been accepted into society's Stage II through social invitations and reciprocal entertaining. You learned effective social behavior and proved yourself an adept guest and host or hostess.

And now you have been asked to chair the most prestigious charity ball in the city.

You, too, have arrived at the top.

What it Means to Be at the Top

When you arrive at the top of society, it means you have power. You have power to influence people. You have power to make things happen.

Being at the top means you will always be called upon to be photographed for the society page when the organization is being publicized. You will gain recognition among people, which gives you entrée to the best parties, the best invitations, the best accommodations, the best opportunities, the best lifestyle. In short, being at the top means the best is yours for the taking.

Being at the top also means you have attained the recognition of your peers in your lifetime and you are honored by them. People who have the money to buy the best talent will listen to you and will be influenced by you. And if you stay at the top for a reasonable length of time, you will have prestige and influence in the affairs of the community for the rest of your life.

$\mathcal{J}$TAYING AT THE TOP

Arriving at the top and staying at the top are two different things. There are other hardworking volunteers who would do practically anything to be an officer on the board or to chair the most prestigious social event of the year.

You will stay at the top if you pull off your tenure successfully. Then you can pass the torch to someone else and you will still be at the top, too. But if you do not live up to your position you lose ground and topple.

How do you stay on top?

• You learn how to handle difficult people.

• You learn how to handle difficult situations.

And the key for doing both is to learn *how to handle yourself* when you encounter difficult people and difficult situations in your new position chairing the ball or sitting on the board.

• *Know what the job entails*. Before you get carried away with your heady new position in society, know every last detail of what it takes to get it done in a timely manner.

• *Have your team players in place*. You may get the glory for getting the job done, but you cannot do it all by yourself. You must know exactly who the people are that you can count on. And be sure these are people you can work with.

• *Make your goals realistic*. You are better off delivering more than you promise, rather than less; so before you outline your goals, try to anticipate every possible deterrent.

• *Carefully document everything you do*. Have short meetings with a typewritten agenda for every person attending. Start on time and finish on time.

• *Don't be a prima donna.* Give a lot of praise, a lot of thankyous, a lot of credit to others as you call on them and and they do things for you.

• *Don't go to pieces*. Remember you are dealing with volunteers, not paid employees. The quickest way to prove the job is too big for you is to throw a temper tantrum or to belittle people.

• *Disarm antagonistic people.* If someone is bitter about your social rise, he or she may glance "meaningfully" and make sarcastic remarks about your proposed plan. If this person comments that what you have done is flashy, give a bright smile and say, "Oh, thank you. I have been deluged with compliments, but it all works so well because I have such good support from people like you." Don't try to explain yourself or deny anything.

• *Keep problems to yourself.* It is tempting, but it diminishes you to carry on about the problems of the job you have undertaken. And if you complain about the people who bedeviled you throughout the project, you are giving them power. Surely, you do not want to do that, do you?

• *Behave with happy ease at all related social functions.* Fake it, if you have to, but do it for yourself and for the sake of the project. Whatever may be wrong, say nothing, and act as if everything is perfect.

• *Be prepared in your personal life.* Make a checklist to have whatever you need—baby-sitters, prepared meals for your children, a backup hairdresser, two outfits (ball gowns or tuxes) and jewelry to wear with either one, and an extra pair of shoes and stockings in case something goes wrong.

Then, have a wonderful time and enjoy the kudos you will receive from everyone for a job superbly done. You've made it, kid!

FRIENDS FOR LIFE

Remember once more that society is just a group of people wanting friends. Sometimes, while working together with people to promote art or science charities, you will find yourself in an arena of egos, agendas, strong personal drives, and voracious appetites for social recognition.

And sometimes these qualities rub against one another and

create conflict. Some of these people never bother to get to know you, while others drop out of your life. Is it worth it?

Yes, because through it all, as you grow, you also find true, deep, and wonderful friendships—many that will last for a lifetime!

Part 4

Romancing the Rich

twenty-six

*W*ho Wants Romance
with the Rich

"You do not have to be poor to want to marry money. The Rich want to marry the Rich, too."

—Ginie Sayles

What if you fall in love with a Rich woman or man? Do you want to risk losing the person because you feel intimidated or outclassed or through simple naïveté?

No. You want to stand an equal chance of enjoying a fulfilling romance, perhaps even marriage, to this person.

That is where this section comes in. It is designed to help you understand some unique aspects of dating someone who is Rich and to help you through some potential rough spots.

Some of you reading this book are single and not involved with anyone at this time, and through business or social events, you may find yourself attracted to a Rich single man or woman and want to pursue a relationship.

And there is nothing wrong with that. Besides, you are not alone. There are four types of people who seek a Rich mate—and their motives may be very different from yours. But then again, maybe not.

Note: In keeping with my book *How to Marry the Rich,* I will use the abbreviated initials RM throughout this section to mean a Rich Mate of either sex.

So who wants an RM? I list them below in order, from the greatest number of my clients to the least.

1. **The Rich**. More than anyone else in the world, *it is the Rich who want to marry the Rich*—Celebrities, Old Money, and Status New Rich. You would think that because they are wealthy, they would not care if their romantic interests have money, but many of them do. Why?

> • *Fear of marrying down.* Heiresses and heirs especially fear embarrassment with family and friends at the prospect of "marrying down." Peer pressure to marry within their class is very real.
>
> • *Desire to improve their social position.* There are a lot of self-made Rich people who have found that money cannot always buy entry to the level of society they want. So they set their sights on an RM of a higher social level.
>
> • *Paranoia.* This type of Rich is so afraid they will marry a gold digger, that they inadvertently become one themselves, seeking someone Rich to marry

2. **High Achievers**. My second largest client base is filled with well-educated professionals—attorneys, physicians, stockbrokers, certified public accountants, successful authors, motivational speakers, models, actors, and educators (professors from Harvard, Yale, and Stanford). These are high-achieving individuals who can take care of themselves, financially, so why do they seek an RM?

> • *An RM can bankroll their business.* Physicians and attorneys often marry for the "silk stocking trade" that a Rich marriage can provide. Many politicians, artists, writers, musicians, and actors find that a love relationship with the Rich can advance their careers. Why go into debt with a bank loan, when a lover or spouse can bankroll you *without interest*?
>
> • *Achievers are reward-oriented.* All their lives, they work for rewards on every level. They have worked too hard to get where they are and just can't go back to dating the types of people they feel they have outgrown. A Rich marriage is their ultimate reward—and proves they have made it.
>
> • *Achievers are too competitive with other achievers.* Love relationships with other career professionals on their

level, can become competitive. High Achievers either need a noncompetitive support system (wind-beneath-the-wings person) or they need an RM who is noncompetitive because that person already has it made.

3. **A Fortunate Few**. These are men and women whose daily lives do not bring them into social contact with the Rich, but through some quirk of fate, they once stumbled into a relationship with a Rich person. They were truly in love with the RM and were crushed when the love affair ended.

This category is made up of salesclerks, flight attendants, waiters, secretaries, schoolteachers, firemen, policemen, middle management workers, blue-collar workers, nurses, and nannies. Now they deliberately seek an RM because

- *The dream was too Good*. Through an RM who was generous and indulgent, the Fortunate Few experienced a *Cinderella* love story that has ruined them for anyone else.
- *They may have serious hardships*. Many of the Fortunate Few are single parents who simply cannot make ends meet. By the time they pay rent, utilities, car payments, and day care, and budget for gas and groceries, they have nothing leftover. They now believe the old adage that you can make more money through a five-minute wedding ceremony than you can by working hard all your life.

4. **Exotics**. This fourth category includes a few centerfold models, a couple of topless dancers, and professional escorts of both sexes.

These individuals make very good money, often through a Rich clientele, but they want a "real" relationship with the Rich for one or more of the following reasons:

- *Exotics often want out of their careers*. After a few years of living high on the easy money of dancing or escorting well-heeled strangers, they begin to feel trapped because it is a career in which they can go no higher. They feel trapped, too, because they can't make as much money in a new career as they now make—and they are used to their large earnings.

They also have to spend a lot of money to keep looking good: cosmetic surgery, cosmetic dentistry, wardrobe, and hair become necessary expenses. So, even though they make a lot of money, they find it hard to get far enough ahead to stop what they are doing.

• *Exotics get too old for their jobs.* One topless dancer said to me, "I started at twenty. Now I'm forty-one and still popping out of cakes at fraternity parties for boys who are half my age and could be my sons." (This woman does not look a day over thirty-five).

*W*HICH TYPE SUCCEEDS IN MARRYING THE RICH?

True, the Rich tend to marry other Rich because they meet socially or are introduced by friends. They also meet through the force of gravity that is natural to their financial level—same neighborhoods, same schools and alumni associations, same charitable causes, same friends, same sports, same hobbies, same clubs, and so on.

But beyond the social opportunities of the Rich, romance with the Rich is just as much the domain of anyone—including you. It does, however, help to have at least one of the following advantages:

1. Self-Motivating Desire

If you have a self-motivating desire for romance with the Rich, you are willing to do whatever you have to do—and to change whatever you have to change—in order to achieve your goal.

• If it means you must go places where the Rich are every single day—and never miss a day—you will do it.

• If it means learning new social skills—you will do it.

• If it means changing the way you dress—you will do it.

• If it means moving to a new town—you will do it.

• If it means changing your neighborhood—you will do it.

• If it means taking risks to meet the Rich—you will accept responsibility for your decisions and do it.

• If it means going expensive places, alone—you will do it.

• If it means dating Rich people you are not interested in because it will be a learning experience and it will lead you to other Rich people—you will do it.

• If it means touch-up cosmetic dentistry or surgery to give you more confidence—you will find a way to have it done.

• If it means learning about art or sports or charities that have never interested you—you will do it.

• If it means working out daily—you will do it.

You will do whatever it takes to achieve your goal.

2. Good Luck

If your entire psyche is honed and ready for an RM, you will find luck happening in the most unexpected ways.

I have found that good luck tends to follow a heartfelt action to help someone else. My glamorous girlfriend Melissa was notorious for giving great parties, but when she invited me to a Halloween costume party, I declined. I felt I couldn't afford a frivolous costume and baby-sitting expenses when I couldn't afford a wonderful educational opportunity for my four-year-old daughter because of my college loan and my car payments.

I was hard at work Halloween night when another girlfriend called me from the party.

"Ginie," she whispered into the telephone, "please come to Melissa's party. There is almost no one here and she is embarrassed."

Instantly, my heart went out to Melissa, so I called a baby-sitter for my four year old, and without a costume, I set off for Melissa's failed party, not knowing this deed of friendship would drastically change my love life.

It was about ten-thirty at night when I picked my way through a row of buildings, trying to find the party room.

"Excuse me," I said to a man walking toward his car, "can you tell me where the party room is located?"

He was silent a minute, then said, "If you will follow me, I can take you there."

But I was not about to go anywhere with a strange man. I shook my head. "No, thank you. I'll find it myself."

I turned away and resumed my search of the buildings, uncomfortably aware that the man had not gone to his car after all, but was following me.

Thankfully, I soon found the party room, which had only a handful of people and no energy. Melissa's face lit up gratefully when she saw me, and as she hugged me, she said to the man behind me, "We thought you were leaving."

"I changed my mind," he said simply, then quietly introduced himself to me as Mike, letting me know he had been at the party beforehand.

I learned from Melissa that Mike was a member of an exclusive tennis club and that one of the tennis professionals on staff there had asked if Mike would give him a ride to the Halloween party. He did give him a ride and the pro invited him inside for a drink. Mike had just been leaving when I arrived.

The next day, my doorbell rang and a florist literally filled my entire apartment with every kind of plant and flower arrangement imaginable, including flowers I never knew existed. All my tabletops, countertops, and floor spaces were filled with flowers.

Stunned at the endless stream, I watched the florist carry in the last huge bouquet made of pink carnations mixed with giant lollipops and a big, fuzzy teddy bear for my daughter.

It was all from Mike, the man I had met the night before at the Halloween party. And I had not given him my address. He had gotten it from Melissa.

The relationship that followed with this very, very Rich man was intensely romantic and thrilling. Among other things, within three months, he paid off my college loan, my car loan, and paid for my daughter to go to the private school for gifted children that I had been unable to afford.

The night before my birthday, Mike flew my parents to Houston for dinner, where he informed my dad he was going to marry me. And the next day, he gave me a surprise birthday party filled with our friends, and he presented me with a beautiful diamond ring.

My heartfelt action to help my girlfriend resulted in very good luck for me. But luck has happened many times for me. I have found that when I respond from the heart to someone's need, an out-of-the-blue streak of luck arrives on its heels. It won't hurt you to try it—and be sure to look for the luck!

3. Knowing How to "Connect the Dots"

When you meet Rich people in one situation, learn to "connect the dots" and use the relationship for another situation. The Rich do this all the time.

For example, elderly Rich women love platonic attention from young men. So if you meet Mrs. Old Guard through church, spend a small amounts of time in conversation with her each Sunday—and mostly listen. Ask specific questions about her interests—such as her favorite garden plants, or favorite opera singer, or in which country she keeps a second house.

She will be charmed by your thoughtfulness if you send an article about her favorite singer, or tell her about a garden exhibit that focuses on her favorite garden plant.

And then, when you just happen to be visiting the country where she has a second home, you can ask for a letter of introduction, or just a list of places to go, or if she knows families there who might have single adults about your age who could show you around. She may even insist you stay in her second house while you are there.

Whatever you do, if you're looking for romance with the Rich, you have to be genuine. Hidden motives and agendas will show through superficial behavior.

Romance with the Rich is definitely possible—even if you don't have money.

When I was a stockbroker, I learned that there are assets that have the equivalent value of cash to someone and these are called "cash equivalent assets."

Your "cash equivalent assets" will be the qualities you bring to the relationship. Perhaps your assets are humor and warmth, serenity and intelligence, sensuous excitement, complexity and sensitivity, and interesting diversity.

You may not have money, but you are not bereft of assets. If an RM is hanging around, it is because that person considers your assets to be equal in value to his or her financial assets. Your quality as a person is an *equal exchange*—and the RM will gladly finance the time you spend together.

Have no guilt because you do not have money. You have the equivalent of it in personal quality. And you owe the Rich nothing for the money they spend on you in a relationship—because you have paid for it in full with the quality of you and your time.

Many men fall victim to the idea that because a Rich woman treats them to dinner at a five-star restaurant, they owe her some kind of service—like bartending her party or cleaning her pool. This is a false idea. If a Rich woman asks you to dinner and you accept, you are agreeing to what was specified—dinner—and nothing more. She paid for dinner because she likes you and she knows she has the money to pay for an extravagant meal, whereas it might be a hardship on you.

Many women fall victim to the idea that because a Rich man takes them to a five-star restaurant and spends lavishly for dinner and expensive wine, that they owe him sex.

Nothing could be further from the truth. You never owe sex because of dinner. You have fulfilled all dinner obligations by your mere presence and charm.

Relationships are a pay-as-you-go proposition, whether people have money or not. We all pay the cost of our time and our emotions with each other. And once spent, we have only bought the present moment, not future feelings.

Have no guilt for the money RMs spend on you. You are worth it.

Also, you should realize that the money your RM spends on you is a way for him or her to express how he or she feels about you. Think about it. There is no greater emotion than love to inspire money spending. You would spend your last cent on your children, and if you love your pets, you spend money on them.

Therefore, if an RM tells you that he or she loves you, but refuses to spend money on you, it is a lie. Money-spending is one of the greatest indicators of love. If a Rich woman tells a man she loves him, but she buys herself an expensive new car when he is struggling to keep his broken-down clunker working, I think we can tell where her true emotions lie. And "lie" is the operative word. Money doesn't lie.

Money always follows emotion—no exception.

$\mathcal{S}$tart with a Million-Dollar Image

"Change your appearance and what you do with your time and your life will change. You're more in control than you think."

—*Ginie Sayles*

When I became a model, the first thing I learned was the power of color. And my personal life changed when I discovered the power of bright red and hot pink, in solid, head-to-toe outfits. It was as if the lights came on in my life and I found myself center stage, surrounded by new, Richer suitors who had never noticed me before.

The colors of love are both pastel and bright.

Men should have a solid bright red tie, a hot pink striped tie, a solid bright red shirt, a pale pink shirt, a light blue, a bright white, and a soft yellow. A black dress suit and two styles and shades of blue suit complete the wardrobe on a budget.

Women need "the little red suit" (silk with matching shoes, belt, handbag) as much as they do "the little black dress" (which should not be worn as often as color). Add a hot pink cocktail dress with rhinestone earrings, white lace blouse with a baby blue skirt, pale pink suit with pink accessories and white pearls, and you are ready to go. A solid bright white dress with all-white accessories has a similar impact as bright red, so you can wear it as an alternate if white looks good on you.

$\mathscr{L}$EARN THE POWER OF STYLE

Men, you will always be appropriate in preppy styles, because preppy is never out of style among Pedigrees, who are the ultimate Rich. When the rest of the style-conscious world stops wearing preppy and claims it is out of style, the Pedigrees continue wearing it from birth to death—and they look askance at those who aren't.

Even so, it is all right to add a few trendy items to your wardrobe, but rely mostly on good Pedigree preppy styles when you are in doubt about what to wear.

Women, however, should not wear preppy clothes when the goal is to attract men. Rich men are not just Rich, they are also *men*—and men respond to a certain look.

Sophisticated styles that are body-conscious (softly draping the body, not embarrassingly tight) attract Rich men. And if you are in the right color, you are irresistible.

Preppy clothing is appropriate for married Rich women because it does not compete for the attention of men. In essence, preppy clothing says, "I am a woman's woman. Your man is safe with me." But body-conscious clothing says, "I am a man's woman and I am packaged to proudly market myself for relationships."

$\mathscr{F}$ABRICS AND TEXTURES

Touch-me fabrics have sensuous allure for relationships. The best are sumptuous cashmere, chamois shirts, corduroy pants, lush silk, crisp satin, and taffeta, which has the added sensory appeal of a crinkling sound. Nubby burlap-type fabrics, thick cable-knit sweaters, and cozy wool are all fabrics that silently ask for a hug.

Such fabrics feel comforting on your body and they are a pleasure to your RM's touch. Worn in bright or pastel love colors, your tactile fabrics make you irresistibly touchable.

*U*NDERTHINGS

Personally, I like for men to wear sexy underwear. It is a treat when a man steps out of a tailored suit and reveals just a G-string or bikini briefs. Wow!

But the key to carrying it off is to be totally unself-conscious about it. If you can't, then wear your trusty boxers. Some women prefer boxers, anyway—and boxers are Pedigree stuff, so they're always appropriate (but not terribly sexy for seduction).

Wear whatever you feel sexiest and most confident in when you plan a magic night of lovemaking with a woman.

Women, sexy lingerie—or nothing at all—under tailored suits are sexy for you, too. And I guarantee it will make you feel sexy even if no one sees what you are wearing. Feeling sexy is the most powerful aphrodisiac; you'll radiate self-confidence and attract men like bees to honey.

Stay away from trashy or gimmicky lingerie. Opt for a variety of silk teddies, satin garter belts with matching panties and bras, lace-topped thigh-high stockings, a couple of sheer bodysuits, tap pants, lacy-cup bra-and-panty sets, silk boxer shorts, and a leopard-print bra and panty, along with an innocent dotted Swiss panty and bra.

Black is always right for lingerie. Nothing is more seductive and figure-flattering than a very sheer black slip. A sheer black slip with nothing but your bare, scented skin beneath it is extremely erotic.

And speaking of scented, when you take off your undies, drop them in the bathroom sink and add your bubble bath. Swish, drain, and rinse. Hang to dry. Fold the next morning and tuck into a lined drawer with potpourri sachets or cotton balls soaked with your favorite perfume.

As far as lingerie to sleep in—my dear, always, always ask a man to give you his shirt (preferably 100 percent silk) to take home and sleep in. I started doing that when I went steady with a boy in the eighth grade and never stopped. I've found that nothing drives a man more wild than to see you in his shirt.

Wardrobe Pieces

For dating an RM, you need at least four dressy outfits, six semicasual outfits, and four casual outfits; but all you really have to do is just follow the guidelines in Chapter 24, "Your Social Wardrobe," and you will be dressed just fine for romancing the Rich.

Hairstyles

Men, go with your natural hair or have a hair transplant if you wish, but avoid hairpieces. Many women—including me—like balding men—as long as you don't comb it over to cover up the bald spots. And if you shave it completely bald, it can look more virile than balding.

Silver hair is mesmerizingly elegant on men in their late forties and fifties, but gray hair past sixty-five can have an aging look, rather than an elegant look. Think of former U.S. Presidents Ronald Reagan and George Bush—both of whom used hair color to keep looking vital in their late sixties and early seventies.

Women can wear their hair long or short, but whatever the style, it should be touchable, shiny, and sweet-smelling. I've never met a man who didn't love to run his fingers through a woman's hair.

Wash and condition your hair regularly, and try a deep-conditioning treatment at least twice a month—if not once a week—to keep it healthy-looking. You also should avoid overuse of heated styling tools (curling irons, hot rollers, hair dryers) to make sure your hair doesn't get dry and brittle.

If you only take one piece of hair advice, it should be this: don't use too much hairspray. It's a major turnoff when a man goes to touch your hair and it feels like a helmet—or worse, this hand gets stuck in a sticky mess. Don't worry about your hair getting messed up; a tousled, windblown look is incredibly sexy. Oh, and if you must wear your hair up, stay away from a tight bun; it looks too severe. Instead, have some tendrils curl around your face; the look is soft and sexy.

As for color, blonde, brunette, or redhead—they all have fun. Just make sure you cover that gray. A male client from Canada told me he stopped seeing a pretty fifty-five-year-old brunette when she let her gray hair grow out.

"I'm sorry, Ginie," he said and winced, "but I couldn't help it. Her age didn't bother me at all, but with the gray hair she looked so much older, and it was as if she didn't care about how she looked."

ℳAKEUP

Contrary to what you may think, men don't like too much makeup. Ask any of them. But that doesn't mean you should go for that fresh-scrubbed look men don't find that sexy either. The trick is to wear makeup so it doesn't look like you're wearing makeup.

Sound confusing? Well, makeup is really intended to enhance and imitate natural beauty. Blush should give you a soft glow—as if you were blushing. It shouldn't look like streaks of war paint. Eye shadow should complement the color of your eyes—and make them appear wider and brighter; thick black eyeliner that makes you look like a raccoon and frosted blue shadow can be thrown away. And do I really need to say anything about lip gloss? Who would ever want to kiss a mouth covered with goopy, greasy gunk? Classic red lipstick is always a winner.

ℱRAGRANCE

Perhaps the most underestimated seduction technique of all is the use of scent. There are four types of scents that are lush and sensuous and work well for romancing the Rich.

• *Fresh scents of cleanliness.* Bubble bath or just-showered clean skin and shampooed hair are irresistible. So are freshly laundered sheets, towels, and clothes. If you never wear a cologne, be sure your body, hair, clothes, linens, and towels burst with clean, invigorating freshness.

• *Fresh scents of nature.* Take advantage of morning dew or a summer rain. Open the window and let the earthy scents of wet foliage and rich damp cedar or pine bark fill your apartment.

• *Welcoming-home scents.* Comforting fragrances of polished wood; brewing coffee, fresh baked pastries, bread, or cookies; fresh flowers; bayberry candles; or pinecones in a fireplace have a welcoming effect on the senses of RMs who visit your humble abode.

Do not use fruit scents because they smell cheap and will only attract flies. My one exception to this is if you grind orange peels into your garbage disposal, which gives your whole apartment a wonderful, citrusy-crisp smell.

You can buy subtle home fragrances, including carpet powder, scented light-bulb rings, drawer liners, and potpourri that will have your Rich dates asking what smells so good. Avoid those overpowering spray air freshners, especially those that smell like disinfectants; they'll remind your date of a hospital—clean but not inviting.

• *Sensuous perfumes.* Spa scents like *Spring Fever by Origins* are favored by the Rich today over heavier, more cloying perfumes. Second to spa scents are light, spicy fragrances. A third favorite of the Rich is the "historic" perfumes, such as Jickey by Guerlain, which is over a hundred years old, or Imperiale for men and L'Heure Bleu for women. Both are time capsules of history in a spray.

You can have a wardrobe of colognes for specific activities—or you can have fragrances for the seasons. Or you may want two good scents: one for day and one for night.

However, you may prefer a "signature" or "trademark" fragrance that you wear all the time and that makes your Rich woman or Rich man think of you whenever your cologne lingers after you are gone. A true signature fragrance is one that is blended specifically for you and cannot be had by anyone else. Rich women often do this.

My preference was to buy a new perfume when I had a new relationship I sensed would be meaningful—and I wore that perfume only when I was with that man. When the love affair was over, I never wore the perfume again. I have always joked that if I ever wrote an autobiography, I would name it *The Fragrance of My Life* because I can be anywhere and if I smell a certain perfume, I instantly remember the special man assigned to that fragrance and that period of my life.

And do use your fragrances to be memorable. Women, carry your perfume in a small atomizer in your purse. Just before slow dancing, spritz it on and it will cling to the shoulder of his jacket. When he undresses that night, your perfume will carry your presence. A lingering fragrance of you can drive him mad when he rolls onto the pillow where you laid a few hours earlier during lovemaking; the faint smell of your perfume in his car the next morning as he drives to work will remind him to call you.

On the day you shop for a fragrance, go by Starbucks first and pick up a quarter pound of whole, unground espresso coffee beans and take it with you. Sniff the coffee beans to clear your olfactory senses before you begin and after every third fragrance. It really works.

To stay in the "now," tell your perfumer that you want perfumes that are not more than six months old. It keeps you fresh, current, and free from older scents that a lot of other people are wearing.

If you want a fragrance that doesn't evaporate quickly, look for perfumes with a base of oriental florals. My magical Ivoire de Balmain has an oriental floral base.

And, of course, layer your fragrance to help it last. Men, you can layer your fragrance with your favorite cologne-scented soap in the shower, matching antiperspirant, a slap of the same scent in aftershave, and a brisk spritz of cologne. Women, indulge yourself in the sybaritic pleasure of your fragrance with bubble bath, soap, or gel, and bath cream or lotion, fully spraying your naked body with eau de toilette and dabbing perfume on your pulse points: throat, wrists, ankles, and between your breasts.

Legendary author and former *Cosmopolitan* magazine editor Helen Gurley Brown suggests saturating a cotton ball with your perfume and tucking it into your bra so it will waft from your bosom.

Enjoy your fragrance all day. Touch up frequently. And remember—walking in a cloud of fragrance can make you feel sexy, luxurious, even Rich.

Fresh Flowers Can Be a Woman's Accessory Fragrance.

A wealthy Texas oil man took me to a nationally televised tennis tournament at the River Oaks Country Club in Houston, Texas.

I have long carried fresh flowers as an accessory, and on that day, wearing a white halter-top sundress and white sandals, I carried several bright pink freesia flowers with a white ribbon tied around them. My hair was slicked back, and I tucked a few matching pink flowers into the black knot of my hair at the nape of my neck.

My date and I were sitting in front-row box seats at the tennis court when one of the television cameramen said, "Your flowers look great!" and turned the camera directly on me.

My date laughed and said, "Looks like you're going to be on the national news tonight, Ginie."

When I carry flowers as an accessory, men always compliment me. Once a man who was standing nearby reached out and lifted my hand as if to kiss it—but, instead, it was to smell the gardenia I carried!

The following flowers are fragrant and beautiful to carry as an accessory:

- Gardenias

- Freesia

- Roses (but they can seem unimaginative so carry more than one for flair)

- A bunch of honeysuckle

- Magnolia blossoms

Flowers that create a pretty effect without scent are:

- Baby's breath

- Queen Anne's lace

- Lilies

- A single ginger torch flower

- One enormous bright sunflower

- Sweet peas or anything that trails from your hand

If you carry a fragrant flower as an accessory, do not wear perfume. If your flower has no fragrance, it is fine to wear perfume.

You can bind a flower stem with a long ribbon to match your dress, and if you are in your twenties, try attaching the opposite end of the ribbon to your wrist in a loose bracelet.

$\mathcal{T}$ELLTALE DETAILS

You can have perfect clothes, hair, shoes, and fragrance; the details will either tie it all together or unravel your best efforts completely.

Check these details in a full-length, three-way mirror:

• A man's nails must be short and spotless.

• A woman's nails must be even lengths. This means all your nails must be as short as your shortest nail. No chipped nail polish on fingers or toes. No ragged edges.

• The back of your hair should be smooth.

• No lint, loose threads, pet hair, or your hair anywhere on your clothes.

• Even hems for cuffs, pants, skirts, jackets.

• All buttons must be secured.

• No runs in stockings. Make sure you're wearing well-fitting socks that are appropriate in color, texture, and style to your clothing.

• Clothes must be well fitting.

• Shoes need to be polished—with no rundown heels.

• No wrinkles or stains on clothes. Clothes should be well-pressed and clean.

• Makeup, hair, clothes, shoes should look good from every angle.

• Knuckles, knees, and elbows should be pink with cleanliness (people notice).

• Jewelry and accessories should be appropriate for the occasion and the outfit.

• No bunched underwear or panty lines.

$\mathcal{B}$ODY LANGUAGE

You want to be relaxed and natural, of course; and you will be with just minor fine-tuning to give you an air of good breeding in the following:

The Way You "Carry Yourself"

The opposite sex will notice you when you carry yourself proudly. And if you don't feel so proud, find a wall to help you.

Several times during any evening (or day) when you will be standing or walking around, go to the rest room and flatten the back of your head, your shoulders, your rear end, your calves, and your heels against the wall. Your chin must be level—not jutted forward or up.

This perfectly aligned posture gives you "presence." You will be amazed (and will thank me) when you see the impact you have on others when you stand tall and proud.

All my practice of good posture paid off when I was a mystery guest on a celebrity game show and a panelist selected me because of the way I carry myself. I was very excited—so find a wall and practice, practice, practice.

The Way You Enter a Room

When you carry yourself with great posture and pause in the doorway to glance about the room, the doorway frames your body for a moment and allows Rich women and men to notice you. While pausing, take time to locate the people you want to meet, and decide, accordingly, where you want to sit.

Also, "read the room"—notice where the center of action is,

because that is where you want to be. Never sit on the sidelines or in dark areas or away from people.

And try not to bounce when you walk up and down stairs.

The Way You Stand

A man looks more confident and masculine standing with his feet about eight to twelve inches apart—or slightly less than the width of his shoulders.

A woman looks more graceful in a dress or suit when she stands with her feet together, one foot slightly ahead of the other, elbows close to her body, her shoulders back. However, there are times when a woman in pants can look dramatic with a bold stance.

Both men and women will be more effective if the front of their bodies fully face the Rich woman or man they are talking to, while standing about sixteen inches from the person.

The Way You Turn

Pivot on one foot when you turn to leave. You can send a slow look to an RM, just as you turn, and walk away from the RM, without a backward glance. It has almost the same effect as lingering fragrance.

The Way You Sit

Do not bend over and feel for the chair with your rear end. A man should walk alongside a chair, pause closely beside it, and settle down into it. A woman should walk toward a chair, and when she is close to it, turn and step back until she feels the chair with the back of one leg, then lower herself onto the chair seat.

If she is wearing a very short skirt or a formal gown, or if she is a bit heavy, a woman looks better with her knees together and ankles crossed. Otherwise, a woman who welcomes the attentions of a male should cross one leg over the other—and not rest it on her knee, but pull her leg slightly higher onto her thigh. It's a very sexy look.

Sensuous Subliminal Gaze

Whether you are a man or a woman, if you sitting next to an RM you are attracted to, cross your leg toward that person, and angle your upper body toward the RM, fully facing the person.

While the RM is talking to you, listen attentively. But, *once*— and only once—during the conversation, slightly part your lips (yes, men, too), focus on the RM's left eye for two seconds, then shift your focus to the right eye for two seconds, then focus on the RM's lips for two seconds. Then, go back to paying full attention to what the person is saying and don't give the seductive look again. This tactic has a subliminal effect that steeps into their subconscious minds.

The Way You Enter and Leave a Limousine

A man is the last to enter a limousine, in order to put his date in first, and he is the first to leave the limousine, in order to extend his hand and help her out—although this is frequently performed by the driver or doorman.

A woman enters a limousine by letting her date or driver open the door for her. She sits down on the car seat and— keeping her knees together—inconspicuously swings both feet inside. To exit the limousine, she waits for the door to be opened for her, extends her hand to her date (or driver or doorman), swings her legs outside, lifts herself out of the limousine, and takes her date's arm.

Cultivating the right image is crucial if you want to romance the Rich, but the most important quality you can have is happy energy. You don't have to be beautiful or handsome. If you're happy and smiling, people will want to be near you because they'll want to see if the happiness can rub off on them. And when you are interacting happily with people around you, it makes you attractive to everyone, including the Rich.

$\mathcal{D}$ay-by-Day Calendar to Meet Your Millionaire

"Any enterprise is built by wise planning."

Proverbs 24:3

Wouldn't it be great to have a day-by-day, hour-by-hour plan to meet the Rich? Well, here it is: a seven-day sample calendar that you can follow to the letter, week after week for twelve to eighteen months.

It's a pretty full schedule, so if you find it impossible to do it all, choose at least one activity per day. However, the more items you can fit in, the greater your chances of meeting an RM.

When you have finished the week, start again the next week, substituting some items from the list of "30 Quick Ways to Find a Rich Date" which are listed in the next chapter. People can order a twelve-month "Find a Rich Date Calendar" from me at the address at the end of the book. It is fully filled in, day-by-day; but if you just follow this guideline, you can fill in your own calendar.

MONDAY
—HIGH FINANCE DAY—
6:30–8:00 A.M. *Work out in a prestigious gym in the Financial District, where I have a new membership. Occasionally ask upscale members questions about the gym. Shower and dress for work.*
8:15–8:30 A.M. *Pick up a latte at Financial District Starbucks*

*or other esteemed coffee shop. Chat idly with upscale busines-
speople in line.*

8:30–9:00 A.M. *Go to work in a job that positions me to meet
the Rich.*

Sometime during the day. *Casually ask Rich boss the best
restaurants so I can have lunch in one of them.*

11:30–12:30 noon. *Have early lunch in Financial District
restaurant recommended by my boss.*

Sometime during the day. *If my job is flexible, attend a
stockholders meeting (I bought a few shares of stock in a local
company that allows me to do this). Try to meet officers and
opposite sex in attendance.*

5:00–6:30 P.M. *Happy Hour in Financial District pubs—eat
there.*

7:00–8:30 P.M. *Attend a tax shelter seminar for high-tax-
bracket investors (call every stockbrokerage firm and sign up).*

*Or if my classified personal ad reaped a possibly affluent
individual, meet in safe and expensive restaurant for coffee
(stay no longer than thirty minutes, get business info so I can
later call and confirm this person's identity and job status). Or
meet candidate from upscale dating service. Or meet a successful blind date recommended by a trustworthy friend.*

TUESDAY
—ARTS DAY—

7:00–7:30 A.M. *Jog or walk in a Rich neighborhood.*

7:30–7:45 A.M. *Rich neighborhood Starbucks for latte. Chat
with Rich patrons in line. Drop off cleaning at cleaners in Rich
neighborhood.*

8:00–8:30 A.M. *Shower and dress for work.*

8:30–9:00 A.M. *Go to work.*

Sometime during the day: *Charm the socks off Rich clients
of the company.*

11:30–12:30 noon. *Have lunch at the Museum of Art tea
shop or take brown bag to eat after I browse a new collection.
If I don't meet anyone while there, I now have new conversational material for when I do. Sign up for guild or volunteer
group.*

5:00–6:30 P.M. *Happy Hour in Rich neighborhood, or attend
volunteer activities.*

7:00–10:30 P.M. *Attend an art opening or opening night of a performing arts production. If able to get two tickets, can take a friend or ask a Rich date. Have great seats and speak to people on either side of me. Mingle at the champagne concession counter during intermission. Can ask Rich man or woman a question or two about the performance. Consider subscribing to opening night performances.*

11:00–midnight. *After-theater drink in bar of luxury restaurant in Art/Theater District.*

WEDNESDAY
—POLITICAL PARTY DAY—

8:00–8:15 A.M. *Sit down at counter for coffee in popular diner near City Hall or Capitol Building if living in state capital. As usual, make small talk with others, starting with server.*

8:30–9:00 A.M. *Go to work. If my work entails cold calls, make them to Rich customers, especially those involved in politics.*

11:30–12:30 noon. *Munch sandwich while scouring the political section of newspaper and news magazines.*

5:00–6:00 P.M. *Happy Hour in downtown political district.*

6:30–10:30 P.M. *Attend political party meeting. Volunteer to be on a committee. If new committee (steering committee) is being formed for an event, volunteer for it. If no meeting, then do volunteer work for party. Find out when a candidate will be visiting the area and sign up for the planning committee or other activities for candidate.*

THURSDAY
—HOBBY DAY—

7:00–7:30 A.M. *Jog or walk (or walk dog) in a Rich neighborhood. Pick up cleaning at Rich neighborhood cleaners.*

7:30–7:45 A.M. *Rich neighborhood Starbucks for latte-/as always, greet Rich patrons I have spoken to before.*

8:30–9:00 A.M. *Go to work.*

11:30–12:30 noon. *Browse shop that sells supplies for hobby of my choice. Take brown bag lunch.*

5:00–6:30 P.M. *Hobby class/quick dinner.*

7:00–8:30 P.M. *Attend a club meeting about my new hobby.*

8:30–10:30 P.M. *Have a drink with a club member after meeting/make a new friend.*

FRIDAY
—TGIF "ME" DAY—

7:00–7:30 A.M. *Jog or walk where I please.*

7:30–7:45 A.M. *Make coffee at home. Straighten apartment.*

8:00–8:30 A.M. *Shower and dress.*

8:30–9:00 A.M. *Go to work.*

11:30–12:30 noon. *Have haircut, nails done for the weekend. Read an autobiography or biography of a Rich woman or Rich man. Brown bag.*

5:00–6:30 P.M. *Happy Hour in an offbeat place I have been curious about. Realize Rich sometimes do this, too, so keep my eyes open.*

7:00–8:30 P.M. *Have date with anybody—if a nice restaurant, keep my eyes open to see if I want to come back alone, sometime. Take home half of dinner in a doggy bag for weekend snack.*

*R*ICH WEEKEND

On weekends, the Rich tend to leave town. They go to the country, the beach, the mountains, a spa, a retreat, a resort, or a getaway. Their choice is often built around sports. They may be spectators going for an alma mater football, rugby, or hockey game; or maybe they are active participant in sports such as sailing, skiing, golf or tennis.

Consider the season and the sporting events of the season, and plan your weekend accordingly, in neighboring affluent areas.

You can take a friend, or you go alone—but go. And enjoy yourself. Make friends with people, whether they are Rich or not.

SATURDAY
—RESORT SPORTS DAY—

7:00–8:00 A.M. *Drive to nearby resort that is in season.*

8:00–8:30 A.M. *Have breakfast in resort coffee shop.*

8:30–9:00 A.M. *Take group sailing or snow-ski lessons.*

11:30–12:30 noon. *Lunch in resort café with a view—preferably with someone from lessons, but otherwise alone. Chat offhandedly with someone nearby.*

That afternoon. *If the resort is not giving lessons but hosting a tournament, attend the tournament. Otherwise, browse the resort shops or the shops in the resort community. Or treat myself to a massage in the resort hotel spa (I deserve it) or other luxury hotel spa.*

5:00–6:00 P.M. *Happy Hour in sports bar at resort.*

6:30–10:30 P.M. *Attend a different evening sports event (e.g., harness racing), spend night in small, local inn. Or head back home for a date with an RM I met during one of my activities last week.*

SUNDAY
—EXPLORE RICH ACTIVITIES—

7:00–7:30 A.M. *Sleep in.*

7:30–7:45 A.M. *Rich neighborhood diner—or if still in the resort community, locate colorful local coffee shop. Chat casually, asking about "things to do" in the area. People are helpful to tourists or newcomers.*

8:30–9:00 A.M. *Visit a church of my faith in the resort community or in a Rich neighborhood (Saturday may be the day of worship in your faith, if so, attend services on Saturday.)*

11:00–12:30 noon. *Have brunch at resort or, if back home, have brunch with a friend at luxury hotel.*

Sunday afternoon. *Attend an estate auction at a respected auction house (some Rich will send agents, others will be there themselves) or prowl through antiques shops in resort community or neighboring communities of the resort. Chat with antiques shoppers. Have tea and scones in tea shop. Invite a shopper to join me or chat, briefly, with people at a table next to mine.*

5:00–7:30 P.M. *Review last week's activities. Prepare for next week's activities. What clothes will I wear? Check them. Do laundry. Shop for groceries in health food market in or near Rich neighborhood. Ask well-heeled-looking shoppers about produce or other products. Don't linger or be pushy, but interact. Have smoothie at Juice Bar.*

8:00–11:30 P.M. *Have a friend over and relax in front of the TV—or watch* Pretty Woman *or* How to Marry a Millionaire *on video. Read sections of this book or* How to Marry the Rich *and go to bed early.*

$\mathcal{R}$ICH VACATIONS AND HOLIDAYS

Offshore banking is popular with many Rich today. This means the Wealthy keep a lot of their money in countries that cater to secret bank accounts. Most of the Rich report their money legitimately to the Internal Revenue Service, and pay their full taxes, so they are not doing anything they shouldn't do. However, their money is safely out of the clutches of other people, such as private investigators who might try to find out how much they have for unfair lawsuits or punitive ex-spouses. There are many small countries or island countries that cater to the offshore banking desires of the Rich.

There are four major areas for offshore banking, and some of the Rich have money in banking havens of all four areas:

• *Europe,* including Switzerland (less popular with the Rich today, because security is not as tight as it once was), Jersey, the Isle of Man, Austria, and Liechtenstein.

• *The Caribbean*, including the Cayman Islands, Nevis, Belize, Barbados, and Aruba.

• *The Bahamas,* which are not actually in the Caribbean, including Nassau (which is thirty minutes from Miami) and the Turks and Caicos.

• *The Pacific,* including the Cook Island.

The Rich take frequent vacations to visit their money (i.e., meet with their foreign bankers for business updates, etc.) and they write off part, if not all, of the vacation as business expense. Many of the Rich have vacation homes in their banking havens.

Vacations in these areas can be very profitable for you, too. The scenery is usually beautiful, and the towns are small and intimate, which means there are a limited number of restaurants and bars—so you are likely to encounter the Rich in one of them! Locate the poshest hotel in the area and pay for a temporary membership in the private club. It may cost a hundred dollars (possibly two hundred)—but if you want to mix and mingle with the Rich on vacation, this is a *must*.

The Rich will always be where money is—so follow the scent

of money, but with any vacation, make plans to have fun whether or not you meet an RM. Many RMs take their dates with them, so have a backup plan.

Sports Vacations

Locate the best skiing areas and go there. They will be filled with Rich women and Rich men.

Women should also locate the best fishing areas of the world. When Cabo San Lucas was new, a client of mine met a wealthy man fishing there with his buddies, and they continued to see each other for two years.

Horse races and equestrian events are loaded with Rich horse owners or competitors. In *How to Marry the Rich* I tell you specifics about spotting the owners at races. Equestrian events will be an even better resource for you if you get personally involved in riding.

Since shopping is a sport for many women, a Rich woman can be found in the shopping Meccas of Paris, Milan, Hong Kong, and New York, among other places. Most of them do not buy in department stores, but in exclusive boutiques.

A man can often start a conversation with a woman when she is either shopping, stopping for coffee in the boutique-lined boulevard, or having lunch or afternoon tea in the area.

twenty nine

30 Quick Ways to Find a Rich Date

> *"Hope is the thing with feathers that perches in the soul, and sings the tune without the words, and never stops at all."*
>
> —*Emily Dickinson*

Romance lends itself to a little more derring-do and fun methods for finding the Rich. And do have fun. You attract RMs more easily when you are having fun, because you are more relaxed and more open and responsive to the moment, which adds a happy energy to your face and makes you attractive.

Here are the places and schemes to make it happen. Revise your calendar every week to add one of these items.

1. START A DATING SERVICE FOR THE RICH

When I was single, I was asked to write an article on dating services for a singles magazine and I discovered that a lot of dating services were started by singles who wanted to meet a mate for themselves. They were able to scope out the available recruits for themselves under the guise of business—and make money at the same time.

One young woman on the West Coast got the word out that if women would supply her with photographs and résumés, she would approach the Rich men she knew. In reality, she didn't know any Rich men personally. She had her own eye on certain

Rich men she wanted to date, but she needed the legitimacy of running a dating service as entrée to meet them.

When she had collected enough photos and résumés of women, she registered her business name and contacted the Rich men to schedule appointments.

Dressed like a knockout for her appointments, she spent the first ten minutes taking information from each RM and trying to determine if he seemed interested in her. If he did, she showed him photos of less than desirable candidates, often ending the meeting by being asked to dinner by the RM.

If he were polite, but obviously not interested in dating her, she whipped out the photos of her most desirable women and signed him up for her service. Every such interview had the benefit of either producing a Rich husband for her or a Rich customer for her dating service. Neat, huh?

2. JOIN DATING SERVICES

Avoid putting your own money into a dating service that has been in business less than ten years. Always see if a dating service is listed with the Better Business Bureau. Get references and *check the references* of the dating service. See if the dating service has a good refund policy. And be sure they cater to an affluent clientele.

Doing all of the above is the best way to be sure a service is financially sound, well established, and has a verifiable reputation. But there is something else, that women should know: some men who belong to one dating service may belong to several. The men in the dating services often get to know one another and frequently compare notes with one another about the women. For example, they may tell one another who will go to bed and who won't, what she will do in bed, and how they rate her sexually.

Of course, not all men do that, but it does happen, so beware.

Realize that women over forty do not fare as well as younger women in most dating services, so you could end up spending a whole lot of money for nothing. However, if a woman over forty is trim and has taken good care of herself, she might be able to do all right. The best thing to remember is the adage that a dating service might be able to get you a date, but they cannot create chemistry between you and that person.

Still and all, what is wrong with having a date? For all its drawbacks, I still think you should try this and every avenue open for meeting the Rich, including dating services that have a good ten-year track record.

3. TAKE A JOB IN A BUSINESS DISTRICT

Jobs in business districts are great, as long as your company does business with well-heeled clients and you are able to interact with them. I became a stockbroker for this very reason.

I realized that the Rich have to do something with their money, so if I were in a career that helped people "do something" with their money, then I would meet those people who had money to "do something" with—hence, I would meet the Rich. And I did.

4. TAKE ADDITIONAL JOBS TO MEET THE RICH

If you have a job you love, stay just where you are. But if you have not found a career, begin trying on a few that interest you. Here are just a few ordinary jobs where my clients successfully met the Rich:

• Concierge in an exclusive hotel. *Married a Rich businessman.*

• Tennis Pro at a resort. *Married a Rich divorcée.*

• Flight attendant for private jets. *Still dating Rich owner.*

• Working in a fine auction house. *Has dated several Rich investors in antiques.*

• Steward on an expensive cruise line. *He said the cruise line gave the male employees a large box of condoms and told them to be sure the Rich women had a good time. He now lives with one of them.*

• Hostess in a posh restaurant. *Dated several Rich men she met while working there.*

• Attendant at a well-known rehabilitation center. *He became engaged to a Rich woman he met there.*

• Job with major performing arts organization. *Dated celebrity performers and Rich patrons.*

• Secretary for oil company. *Married company president.*

You may want to work part-time for celebrity golf tournaments. The word is that Lee Trevino met and married a woman who was working at a golf tournament. Work weekends or moonlight at jobs where the Rich are. And whatever career you are qualified for, be sure you apply it to Rich areas. For example, if you are a nurse, work at the hospitals that cater to the Rich.

5. FOLLOW YOUR INNER CURIOSITIES

Make a list of five things you have always wanted to learn how to do but never had the time for. A typical list might look like this: 1. skydive 2. painting 3. horses 4. be a tour guide 5. play golf. . . .

Curiosities are your soul talking to you—and if you listen to it, and follow it, you will find your life becoming an adventure. In fact, your curiosities will lead you to the exact people you want to meet—if you will apply all your curiosities to affluent groups of people.

The woman who made the list above had always been attracted to horses but had never been close to a horse, she just thought they were beautiful animals. I told her to pay special attention to her curiosity about horses and to follow her interest in them.

"Visit every club that has anything to do with horses," I urged. "I don't care if it is a Rodeo Fan Club or an English Side-saddle Riding Club or an Arabian Horse-Buying Club—I want you to visit any group that has anything to do with horses. Don't join until you have visited first, to see if these are people you want in your life."

She did this, and at one of the groups she attended she met a wealthy rancher and they instantly clicked.

The nice thing about following your inner curiosities is that when you meet an RM, you already have something in common and something to talk about.

Follow your curiosities. Some of them may seem like dead ends, but keep following curiosities and you will see your life blossom with new friends, new dimensions of your personality, and new people to date, some of whom can be Rich.

6. FAKE A MISTAKE

If there is an RM you would like to meet, find his/her office building and observe what time the RM leaves each day. Then, go to the floor the RM's office is on and stand next to the elevator as if waiting for it to stop. But don't get on until your RM shows up to ride down. Pretend you are looking for another business in the building (pick a name from the building directory in the lobby). Ask questions about it.

If nothing takes on that day, you can try one more time by being in the building to ride up when the RM does, as if you are going to the business you were looking for before.

7. GO TO GAMBLING CASINOS

Find out where the best shows are, because gambling will be going on just outside their doors. The Rich will be going to the best shows and they usually arrive early and gamble before going to see the show. They will often stop to gamble there again when the show is over.

Stand at one of the dice tables nearest the theater door. You do not have to play, just observe who looks Rich and get close enough to them to make small talk when they are around the dice table.

I mention dice tables because there is more interaction among people there. Roulette is good, too. I have a male client who is a professional gambler and he meets Rich women at the blackjack table. The key is to be in the most prestigious hotel casinos.

8. HAVE LUNCH IN A BUSINESS DISTRICT

Go to lunch at eleven-thirty in the morning. The Rich control their time, so they go to lunch early. They want good tables and they want food when it is freshly prepared. They accomplish all this by going thirty minutes before most people start their noon lunch hour.

9. FOLLOW A NICE CAR

Be selective about this. The car should be in a nice neighborhood and have someone in it you think you would like to meet. You just follow the car to see if the Rich passenger inside is, perhaps, going to a public restaurant or bar where you might be able to go, too. Once inside, you create a way to bump into the person.

10. CRASH PARTIES

The secret to crashing a party and getting away with it? Look and act as if you belong there. Dress the way the people are dressed who are at the party. Don't seem self-conscious.

The best party-crashing season is Christmas, but Halloween and New Year's Eve parties are also good. These should be parties held in large hotel ballrooms, so you have access to them.

Never crash an evening party before ten o'clock. As it gets later it is just easier to get in, and party-goers will be going in and out to the rest room or to make telephone calls. Observe a group of men or women as they return to the ballroom and, since you are dressed the way they are, just walk in with them past the gatekeeper. You may get caught, but if so, just say, "Oh, I thought this was the Jones party. Thank you so much."

11. SET UP AN INTERVIEW

You can pretend to be a freelance writer and set up an interview with someone you want to meet, since journalism is the best job of all for meeting the Rich. Ernest Hemingway was married when a magazine reporter came to Key West, Florida, to interview him. He fell in love with her and she became the third Mrs. Hemingway.

Many people have pretended to be freelance writers and succeeded, including lovely Georgette Mosbacher, and a woman in the Palm Desert area who set up a mock interview with a Rich widower (and married him). Two women in California told me they followed this advice and they landed dates with two celebrity basketball players.

12. STAKE OUT TO "CREATE FATE"

If there are particular women or men you want to meet, study their habits. Find out their hangouts. Learn the restaurants and times they go there. Then dress great and go.

Position yourself where they can see you. Interact in a pleasant way with others, even the server.

Make it seem like "fate." Try to arrive at the very same time. Smile and casually speak to someone else first and then to the Rich person you are interested in. Look terrific. Glance about and casually chat while you both wait to be seated.

If you are a man, hold off approaching the Rich woman, but make sure she sees you interacting with other women. I want you to establish desire in her to meet you. Then, when you see her again and make a move, she will be more receptive.

For a woman, let him think he discovered you. If he does nothing, it means he is not available to you right now. Don't go as often after that; but when you do, be sure to arrive at the same time again. See if he makes a move. If nothing takes, what of it? You have had a small adventure.

Also learn where the RM's office is and the times he or she goes to work. Then be in the same area and bump into them. If an RM keeps running into you, and you make it seem like an accident, the RM will eventually begin to think it is "meant to be." Create a little Fate.

Don't be a snoop, and do not become obsessed with anybody! No man or woman is worth the energy of obsession. You are just trying to manuever a meeting. If you do meet and the person is not interested, it's okay. You move on.

13. PUT YOUR TALENTS IN THE LIMELIGHT

People who put themselves where they can be seen by the right people—or who get in the public eye—very often romance the Rich.

I interviewed a beauty queen who was engaged to a boy from her small hometown until her state title brought her to the attention of a wealthy landholder. She began to see him, broke her engagement to the hometown boy, and married Mr. Big Bucks.

Likewise, a waiter in a small town got involved in a community theater production of *Bus Stop*. A Rich heiress, who was between marriages, supported the community theater. She saw him in the production, liked him, and got to know him at a party for the cast she gave in her mansion. The last I heard, they were still together.

If you like to sketch or paint, take this activity out in the sunshine where the Rich flock—say, in a business district at noon. Men and women will be curious and come over to watch what you are doing, often making comments on it and talking to you. You can also sketch events such as a golf tournament or a sailing regatta. You can even sketch a prosperous-looking woman or man you want to meet. Sign the sketch, put your number on it, and with a big smile, hand it to that person before you go.

I know one woman who used a 35mm camera as her "get to know you" technique with people. She would tell them she was taking practice shots for her photography class (she really took a class) and that she had snapped a great shot of them. Then, saying she would be glad to send them a free print, she gave her card.

I'm not sure she even had film in the camera all the time, but she met some interesting people and made long-lasting friendships.

14. TONE UP

Go to Rich neighborhoods and find the in spots to jog. Always check with your doctor before beginning an exercise program. If you are cleared for it, get out there!

Try jogging during the morning hours one week and the late afternoon hours the next week. Another week, try a different time. See which hours harvest the most people and which hours bring out the type of people you want to meet.

Don't wear headphones or you won't meet anybody. Headphones are isolation devices that say "Don't bother me. I'm more interested in what I am listening to than I am in meeting you."

15. UPSCALE HEALTH CLUBS

You can also join an upscale health club if you like. Try all the different peak periods—early morning, noon, late afternoon, evening—as well as pre-peak and between-peak workout periods, to see when the Rich are there.

16. ADVERTISE

One of my clients, who is an attorney, advertised and met a terrific man who had thirteen million dollars.

Well, why not? Personal ads can keep your dating life active, and you can meet some winners. Usually, though, you have to sort carefully through a lot of people who don't interest you— but just consider those dates as "practice."

And do be careful, always. Make safety your number one priority and stay safe by meeting a man or woman in expensive restaurants for coffee—and lots of people around. Gather information you can verify and *verify it*. Get a business card and telephone the company the person claims to work for and verify that the person is who he or she says and holds the position he or she claimed to.

Be honest about yourself in the ad and as specific as you can be for greatest success. Height, weight, hair color, eyes, coloring, and age range (late thirties, early forties) are the most important things to give. Have a sense of modesty in your description. The ads that read, "Tom Cruise look-alike wants to meet . . .' can be a turnoff. I doubt if even Tom Cruise would write one that way.

When you describe what you're looking for, state that money is important to you. Beyond that, stay open to physical appearance as much as possible. If you describe what you want right down to the centimeters, you have probably eliminated 99.9 percent of the really fascinating, really wonderful people. You want a real person you can hug, not some dream you can't even touch, much less find.

Respond to ten ads or responses a week. Anyone can fit in five minutes of phone chat or twenty minutes over coffee with two new, possibly Rich potential dates a day. And don't spend more than ten minutes on the telephone with someone you meet through personals (five minutes is better), or you may have nothing to say to each other when you meet. If the ads you answer require letters, never send detailed personal letters about your life to a stranger. Never.

17. TUNE UP

Metropolitan areas usually have local or regional opera companies. These companies need local people as "supers," which is short for supernumerary. Don't let the big word scare you. A super is the same thing as an extra in a Hollywood movie.

For example, an opera star may be a character being put to death by villagers for a wrongdoing. While the opera star belts out her dramatic aria to the villagers, you, as a super, are one of the villagers, fully costumed and looking menacing. Some supers may sing in the chorus or they may silently be part of the background crowd onstage.

This is fun stuff. Plus, you may meet a surgeon, a judge, or a Rich aficionado who loves hamming it up as a super during the production. You often meet famous men and women this way, too: opera stars, opera composers, librettists, conductors— and who knows, maybe one of them will go for you.

18. DANCE

I know an heir who loves to waltz. Every year he goes to Vienna, where the waltz was created for the compositions of Strauss. I would not mention this, except that I also know a wealthy businesswoman who goes to Vienna to waltz. Furthermore, when I was in Amarillo, Texas, once, I met a Rich couple who loved to waltz and who took trips to Vienna. All these unrelated people who crossed my path had two things in common: they had money and they went to Vienna to waltz.

Depending on what part of the country you live in, there are other dances that attract the Rich. For example, in Forth Worth, Texas, you could meet a millionaire by going country-western dancing.

If you like to dance, this could be a lot of fun. Plus, dancing is a great way to meet people because many come alone looking for dance partners.

19. GO ON-LINE

I know a number of women who swear by this as a great source of relationships.

My rule is that you utilize good sense about personal safety when meeting women or men in any method, including on-line. The on-line love interests can lie to you and sound convincing. They may be married. They may try to get your money.

If a person you meet on-line describes himself or herself as a knockout but will not supply a photograph, there is probably a very good reason. If you send a picture and there is no follow-through to meet you within two weeks, *stop communicating*.

In fact, make that your on-line guide, anyway. If someone in your area does not meet you within two weeks, forget that person. And if someone long distance does not meet you within a month, there is probably something fishy.

A recent Carnegie-Mellon study showed that the more time people spend on-line, the more depressed they are. You could be hooking up with someone depressed. Don't put on your ER uniform and try to rescue this person, or you are setting yourself up. Depression can get worse, until you could be dealing with someone dangerous.

And never give your address or your full name until you meet the person, find out some information, and verify it.

I also encourage you not to use the computer as your only method of interacting to find the Rich. And a virtual fantasy can never replace "touch and experience" relationships.

20. RICH NEIGHBORHOOD COFFEE HOUSES

Gourmet coffee houses, such as Starbucks, have replaced bars as casual hangouts for singles where romance can bloom. Always sit or stand facing the main action of the room.

You can ask a woman or man about a coffee they are trying that you haven't had yet. However, don't seem to hang onto anyone in particular.

Coffee houses that are part of bookstores can be a great way to get to know someone knowledgeable you have met in the bookstore. You can say, "Would you mind explaining my best use of this computer book over a cup of coffee? I am craving a decaf latte."

21. POSH HOTEL BARS

Five star restaurants and hotels have bars that local or traveling businesspeople frequent. These bars have a nicer ambience than most other bars.

I don't care what anyone says about going to bars; as long as the bars are very nice, it can be a poor woman's most direct access to Rich men. And you don't have to drink alcohol. Arrange to meet a friend, get there twenty minutes early, and order a club soda with lime. You may meet someone while waiting for your friend.

If you see someone at the bar that you'd like to meet, you can try one of the following:

• *Third party.* Any time you want to meet a Rich woman or man, just start a conversation with someone who is standing in close proximity to her or him. Then seem as if you are politely including the Rich person in your conversation.

• *Indirect approach.* Sit down next to the Rich woman or man you are interested in, but with your back to the person. Do not seem to notice the person at all. Quietly say something to other people on each side of you. Then slowly turn around as if casually looking for someone else. *Do not look at the RM yet.* See if she or he says something to you first. If not, smile and talk to someone else. Gradually include the Rich person in your eye contact, but not meaningfully. Then, ask her or him a question.

• *Bad girl.* A woman can talk to everybody around a Rich man, but ignore him. Force the RM to work for your attention. When he finally says something to you, causing you to look at him, keep your lips slightly parted and your eyes slightly haughty. Slowly warm to him. Very slowly.

22. UPSCALE SUPERMARKETS

Supermarkets in upscale neighborhoods—aware of their growing sex appeal—are adding gourmet food buffets, scrumptious desserts, and exotic coffees and teas. This way, couples who meet in aisle three can park their carts side by side while they get to know each other over cherry meringue pastry and mocha java coffee.

Dessert counters can give you the opportunity to say, "Excuse me. I would really like to have a serving of the chocolate fudge supreme cake, but I can't possibly eat all of it. Will you split it with me?"

23. HUMOR

If you are naturally funny, use it—but use it sparingly. Men and woman both will not be taken seriously for a romantic relationship if they use humor too often.

Too much humor puts you in the buddy category, or worse, comes across as silly, clownish, immature, or insecure. More than anything else, do not use self-negating humor. Remember, you are the ultimate authority on you; therefore, if you ridicule yourself, you give your listeners permission to ridicule you. And for Pete's sake, don't try to be funny if you are not naturally so. But if you are able to initiate contact with someone next to you by making a quiet, funny comment (only one), do it.

24. ASK MARRIED FRIENDS TO FIX YOU UP

Ask married friends if they know financially secure people you might enjoy dating. Do this with as many of your friends as you can. One of them will know somebody who might work out.

Don't tell them you want to get married or they may never fix you up; it is too serious a responsibility. Just say that you want to have fun and would like to meet as many single people as possible. If you are asking Rich friends, they probably know some RMs.

25. WAVE A FLAG

Get involved in your political party. There are lots of women and men who are active in political party volunteer work.

Working on a campaign is one of the most fun activities ever. When you get on committees, you meet more people than if you just do grunt work. However, do some grunt work, too, when needed.

Politics is exciting. You have a purpose in mind of bettering your world, and there are parties, barbecues, dances, fund-raising events galore! There will be a committee to fit any talent you have. Just ask what committees are available for you to work on.

The Rich you meet there tend to be either very, very diplomatic and charming, or very, very outspoken and charismatic. It's a nice choice. Take your pick.

You might even find yourself involved with a woman or man who has a strong political future. You might become famous yourself, either as a candidate, a first lady, or a tabloid "other woman" or "other man."

26. ATTEND

Exclusive singles organizations that require you to have a lot of money in order to join sound like a good deal, right?

Singles groups can be tricky, though. Some of them remind me of science-fiction movies where the aliens look like real people. At first glance, they look like real singles, men and women who are there for all the right reasons of wanting to meet people, develop relationships, date, get serious with one person, and get married.

But, in reality, a majority of them—the *regulars*—are really "professional singles." By that I mean they *think* they are looking for someone to marry, but the truth is that they are already married to the organization. A Rich man like this doesn't need a wife. The group fills that need. He and his "wife"—which is the group—meet mid-morning for breakfast on weekdays, and in the evening for cocktails that may go through dinner. They have parties every weekend. They celebrate all the holidays together. They are there for each other if an emergency happens. What does a man like this need a spouse for? He doesn't. And so the years pass and he stays happily married to the group, while telling himself and others that he is looking for the right one.

Oh, the men and women in the group have dates and relationships with one another. They seem serious at the time; but they rarely marry from the group. And male members discuss their dates with female members (and vice versa) quite casually, the way some dating service members do.

Occasionally, they have parties that let nonmembers visit one of their social events. Do go. But remember, you can waste a lot of time trying to corral a regular. Your best bet will be to meet the *newcomers*, who usually are really wanting to meet someone for a serious relationship. That is why they are there. Get them before they get entrenched in the group or they may never come out! You don't want to waste your time and you certainly don't want to become one of them. It's a substitute marriage.

27. DAY-TO-DAY ACTIVITIES

Go to areas where most of the people who are there are either Rich residents or Rich businesspeople. Then interact naturally with them in a nonthreatening manner.

Natural interactions are comments and small talk you could comfortably say to your best friend. Make a quiet, upbeat comment about something you have in common in the situation. You may not only attract the person you are interacting with, but you may also attract people who are observing your easygoing, natural personality.

28. GO TO A CELEBRITY SPORT'S CLINIC

What have you always wished you could play or do? Golf? Tennis? Snow skiing? Sailing? Horseback riding? Croquet?

Save your money and splurge on a vacation at an exclusive Golf Clinic or Tennis Clinic owned by a celebrity golfer or tennis champ. You'll meet Rich people who are there to perfect their golf or tennis games.

If you can't afford a clinic, take lessons from professionals at exclusive private clubs.

Go early to your lesson and wander around on the property. If you see a sign that says "Members Only Beyond This Point"— well, you did not see that sign. Keep walking and see who you meet. If anyone does mention that the area is for members only, just apologize, say you got lost, and get back to your lesson.

29. OBITS

I know, I know, it sounds awful, but people in New York City read the obituaries to find *apartments*. I can't help but think your desire to find love is more noble.

Be sure you are not crass. Wait a considerate amount of time before trying to meet the surviving spouse. But there is something you should know: men do not wait as long as women to begin dating again after they lose their spouses. Typically men start looking for another wife three months afterward. That is partly because men are absolutely lost and terrified without their spouse. But they also tend to accept the finality of death quicker than women do, and they move toward starting over as quickly as possible. Even if out of respect, they wait a year or two to actually marry again, they often have a woman in the wings until that day.

Women on the other hand may grieve one or two years. Rarely do they begin dating again in less time than that; but a few will begin relationships again after six months.

So be honorable and wait a decent period to pursue someone; but not so decent a period that the bereaved RM finds someone else first!

30. GIVE A BENEFIT

When I interviewed television talk show host Gary Collins for my book *How to WIN Pageants,* he told me that when he first saw his wife Mary Ann Mobley, who was Miss America at that time, he tried to figure out a way to get to know her. The idea he came up with was to ask her if she would help him host a benefit. A benefit is a fund-raising public entertainment to raise money for a charity.

This is right up the alley of a Miss America, and Mary Ann said yes. They worked on the benefit together, fell in love, and have been married every since.

You can do the same thing. Approach a charitable single millionaire you want to get to know and tell the RM you want to host a benefit for a specific cause. Not only will you be helping a worthy charity, you may develop a relationship with the RM of your dreams.

$\mathcal{T}$he Rich in Love

"Whoever loves true life, will love true love."

—*Elizabeth Barrett Browning*

The Rich tend to experience romance in one of the following patterns, which correlate to the effect money has on their lives. As you will see, Pedigrees tend to have the widest range of pattern possibilities.

- Traditional

- Controlling

- Frustrated perfectionist

- Challenge-seeking

- Organized

- Martyr

Every pattern has its upside and its downside. Do not seize on the downside and dismiss a contender. There are always mitigating factors in each individual that can offset downsides.

$\mathcal{T}$RADITIONAL

This Rich person would describe love as a feeling of the soul basking in the warm glow of the sun. Love is simple and pure, not overwhelming. Love simply adds a sparkle of joy to an already happy individual.

This love pattern will be characterized by absolute trust, loyalty, and easygoing interactions. There will be plenty of affection and hand-holding.

Usually intellectual, the RM of this type enjoys sharing books and long talks about them in front of the fireplace. The couple can take long walks in the country and never have to say a word because they understand each other perfectly. They think this love will last forever. And it might.

But then again, a Rich person with this love pattern is lulled into complacency, and his or her partner may get bored. There are no highs and lows in this relationship, no excitement. As years go by this may become a relationship of companionship with no passion.

This love pattern is most common with: Pedigrees, Practicals, and a few Status Rich.

$\mathcal{C}$ONTROLLING

Love is all-consuming in this pattern. This Rich mate in love is alternately overcome with passion, devotion, and jealousy. Sex is intense and frequent because every consummation is an act of reassurance.

This pattern is typically followed by a codependent personality with abandonment issues. The Rich person longs for love as his or her only panacea, but finds love painful due to the ever-present fear of losing the beloved. It is a fear that can only be alleviated by controlling every aspect of that person's life, which leads to volatile power struggles. (Fear also inspires suspicion and may lead to stalking.)

Generous gifts may be heaped upon the loved one in hopes of proving that no one else could ever love him or her like this. But when the beloved makes any attempt to be independent or move out from under the RM's control, punishment is the refusal of any help at all.

The insecurity that runs rampant in these individuals make this one of the most difficult relationship patterns.

This love pattern is most common with: Flamboyants and Celebrities, although any Rich profile could suffer abandonment issues and experience a codependency that can lead to this pattern.

FRUSTRATED PERFECTIONIST

The knight in shining armor or the beautiful damsel in distress—nothing less will do for the Rich with this pattern. They know exactly what they want in a mate, including what the mate will look like. They have their ideal mate defined (frequently in a lengthy list) right down to the gnat's you-know-what!

They often speak of "soul mates," and fall in love at first sight when they think they have found "the one." Instantly, these dear souls throw themselves wholeheartedly into the relationship, surrendering to love (and the heady, sensuous thrill of it).

Alas, time reveals flaws that their true soul mate could never possess and this Rich mate begins to question that this could be love. After all, flaws are a betrayal of what was expected.

Flaws in the beloved make this RM feel victimized. These Rich mates feel they have not been treated right. Betrayed by human flaws, they feel justified in having affairs. And the search is on again to find that elusive "true love."

In reality, their expectations were too high. The Rich mate with this pattern has never fully accepted his or her own flaws and, therefore, cannot accept flaws in others. After all, if the RM can get someone perfect to love him or her, then he or she, too, must be perfect.

The Rich with this pattern would deny that they expect perfection, but then they would sputter that a specific imperfection in their mate is intolerable.

As you can imagine the RM with this pattern also has a divorce pattern. He or she has usually been married and divorced more than three times.

Note: Rich men with this love pattern may have airbrushed centerfold beauties as their ideal. They may refuse to date anyone who does not fit the age and body shape of their ideal girl. A real candidate for a Stepford wife, this RM usually does not treat a centerfold beauty all that well, either. After all, if she loves him, there must be something wrong with her. It all goes back to not accepting flaws in himself.

This love pattern is most common with: Roller-Coasters and a few Pedigrees.

CHALLENGE-SEEKING

This person is not looking for perfection—only for a challenge! Love is to be desired, never attained. If a handsome man or a beautiful woman is easy to get, the Rich in this category lose interest. But a perfectly homely man or woman with a less-than-perfect physique who plays hard-to-get will be catnip to this fat cat.

And as long as the person keeps dangling in front of him or her like a carrot in front of a mule, the challenge-seeking RM will be head-over-heels. This RM will even marry someone just to "get" him or her, and will stay married as long as there is something about the person the RM cannot possess. After all, to this profile, love is a process of pursuit, not a static state-of-being. Full possession kills all pleasure.

However, the new spouse will never possess the RM, either, even in marriage. There will always be secret lovers for the Challenge-Seeking RM. After all, the thrill of getting away with something adds another kind of challenge to the pretended commitment of marriage.

This love pattern is most common with: Roller-Coasters and Flamboyants.

ORGANIZED

If love seems a little too streamlined and efficient with this Rich mate, it is only because love has to fit into a larger plan.

After all, "there is a place for everything and everything should be in its place."

It is not that love or passion is lacking in this Rich person's life. No, there is plenty of it when the time is right. In fact, the Rich with this love pattern may have more sex than others.

But passion has been relegated to its rightful place in their schedules. Unlike other love patterns, who have sex when the spirit moves them, the Organized Rich schedule it into their daily calendar along with everything else they do in their busy days. They have carefully calculated the most efficient time of day sex can serve their needs. In all likelihood, they have it every afternoon at three-thirty, right after a daily meeting with their stockbroker and just before going to a late board meeting.

If this person marries, she or he will probably stay married and carefully try to fulfill most obligations of marriage. Besides, a divorce would never be likely, since the choice of a marriage partner fit neatly into a plan. And the Rich with this pattern will never marry someone who does not fill the prescription they have for their well-organized lives.

This love pattern is most common with: Status Rich, Practical Rich, and Pedigrees.

MARTYR

The martyr lives to be needed. Sacrifice is not a dirty word to this Rich love pattern; it is proof of love. But it is even more than that to them. It is their very lifeblood.

Martyr Rich long to be the lifeblood to someone else. That, and that alone, gives them a feeling of importance. They seek the supporting roles: this Rich woman wants to be the wind beneath the wings of a man with a soaring career; the Rich male of this pattern wants to play Big Daddy to a lost and unfulfilled woman.

These RMs never love a person less because of flaws; they love him or her more *because of* the flaws. It makes the person more interesting to them. And the more they have to do to help the beloved, the more interested in the person they become.

They put up with a lot and they wear their suffering as a merit badge, as proof of their strength, of the depth of their passion, of their steadfast love. Their reasoning is that if they could not feel pain for someone, how could they possibly feel love for them?

They spend money lavishly on someone they love. And they will marry someone for love against the strongest opposition. The only time a martyr falls out of love is if the person heals and no longer needs them.

They may seem to be rewarding the person who hurts them, but then, what is a martyr for?

This love pattern is most common with: Roller-Coasters, Flamboyants, Celebrities, and even Pedigrees.

Don't let the flaws of each love pattern disturb you. After all, we all have flaws.

Every person is a mix of flaws and assets. How well we interact with others depends on how the flaws and assets of our personalities blend with theirs. Most of the time, our flaws and assets react benignly, and the result is harmony and goodwill. However, with some people, the combination of flaws and assets is explosive, causing unavoidable personality clashes, volatile relationships, or destructive behavior.

How can we know if we mix well with another person? How do we know if we can put up with his or her flaws?

Well, let's first take a look at a list of just a few qualities normally described as flaws or assets.

FLAWS	ASSETS
Controlling	Supportive
Angry	Always on your side
Drinks too much	Sober
Socially unpopular	Socially popular
Unemotional	Emotional
Financial problems	Pays bills on time
Sex problems	Great lover
Unreliable	Reliable
Lies	Honest
Can't keep a job	Ambitious
Cold	Affectionate

Realistically, your Rich mate can have *any one* of the flaws listed and still be wonderful, depending on:

- If he or she has three of more assets to every flaw
- The *degree* of the flaw
- How the flaw combines with yours

Three-to-One Counts Most

Your Rich mate can have several flaws as long as each flaw is countered by at least three assets. For example, the RM is controlling, but she is also always on your side, a great lover, and affectionate—all of which fulfills and satisfies you beyond belief.

Counting three to one, she has more assets than flaws. Her flaw does not overshadow her assets. This woman deserves your time and attention.

If she had three flaws to every one asset, it would have been another story. If she had been controlling, never on your side, and cold, then her great lover quality could not have saved her, if that were her only redeeming trait.

Degree of Flaw

If the RM is controlling, how controlling is he or she? Does this flaw immobilize your own goals in life? Does it flare up frequently but not daily? Does her effort to control you ease up when you call her on it or when you refuse to go along? Or can you not do anything because she counters every decision you make? Does she manipulate you in subtle ways that you realize only afterward? How often does it happen?

Yes, a flaw may surface from time to time, inconsiderately, but does it *dominate* the relationship? Does the flaw in any way keep you from achieving your goals or enjoying your life? Does your RM make sincere, consistent attempts to minimize the flaw? Do you *both* value your relationship more than anything else? Don't be a martyr, don't be a victim, and don't settle for anything less than a loving, respectful, safe relationship, but the flaw may be something you can live with.

𝓕LAW COMPATABILITY

In my study of long-lasting relationships, I have learned that it is not the compatible interests of a couple that make a relationship work. It is the "compatible flaws" that make a relationship work.

You have seen "Ken and Barbie" couples who have everything in common. They are both good-looking. They both ski. They both love the symphony. They look good together . . . The list goes on and on. Yet, for all their compatible interests, their flaws just can't get along—and the relationship ends.

You have seen other couples who make you think, "How did those two get together?" Perhaps he likes fishing and she doesn't and she likes opera and he despises it. They are so different from each other.

And yet, for all their differences, they celebrate anniversaries year after year, still in love. Why? Because, in spite of everything, they have *compatible flaws*.

Compatible flaws do not mean that a person's flaws won't bother you. They will. Anyone you are ever involved with will have flaws that will drive you straight up the wall—and your flaws will drive him or her straight up the wall (though you won't be able to understand why).

The difference between incompatible flaws and compatible flaws is that compatible flaws may put a terrible strain on a relationship from time to time, may upset you outrageously at times, even hurt both of you at times; but compatible flaws don't damage the relationship.

Incompatible flaws are those that damage the relationship—sometimes in major traumas or sometimes in slow, small, but irreparable ways.

If you have the same flaw as the man or woman you like, does that mean your flaws are compatible or that you're two of a kind and can never get along? Well, it depends. No two couples are alike. What mixes well for some may be like oil and water for others.

We have used the example of a woman having a flaw of being controlling. Let's take it a step further and say that you are also controlling.

You can be sure sparks are going to fly between you—and often—over every decision, from the simplest of what to order for dinner to more important career and family decisions. Still, those sparks may be just what keeps things interesting and exciting in your relationship.

I am thinking of a couple, married several years, who have this control issue. They find the constant sparring both aggravating and exhilarating. In fact, when an observer offered a solution to their heated exchange, they stopped mid-spar, both stared at the man, said, almost in unison, "This is the way we dialogue," and went back to sparring over whether or not to check their child's car seat as luggage at the airport.

Sure, their controlling tendencies make their life together an ongoing battle, but it has become almost a dance of interaction, which has become vital to their relationship. Without the control issue, they would both feel bored. Their relationship would be as flat as champagne left uncorked for a week.

Both partners are controlling, and that's just fine; it works for them. The control flaw is a compatible flaw in this relationship mix.

Now, this might not work for another couple. If you are controlling and cannot stand for anyone to argue with you, then, no matter how much your soul cries out for the other nourishing qualities your beloved possesses you would probably not tolerate a controlling trait in that person. You wouldn't consider constant sparring to be "dialogue." You would consider it a challenge to your judgment. You would not consider it an emotional "dance," but a constant state of frustration and aggravation. You would be miserable and seek escape. And that's fine, too. The control flaw is an incompatible flaw in this relationship mix.

What if you're not controlling at all? Could you be compatible with someone who has the controlling flaw? Your flaw may be that you are too agreeable and somewhat indecisive. You may be fairly laid-back, and not interested in controlling anything or anyone. However, you like to be around men with dynamism and direction. Your friends may complain that a man is trying to control you, but frankly, you prefer having someone else be in charge. Besides, he sticks up for you, and helps you get things done you have been putting off. The control flaw is a compatible flaw in this relationship mix.

You cannot simply define a man or a woman by a single flaw and dispose of the person. You must weigh a person's flaws in proportion with his or her assets and then evaluate *your* flaws and assets and determine the compatibility of your relationship mix.

𝒯HE ONE IMPOSSIBLE FLAW

There is only one flaw that makes a person an impossible mate and that is if the person has any priority ahead of the relationship with you.

If the priorities are right, you can make it no matter what the flaws are. If the person's priorities are not right—by that I mean if she or he puts a job, parents, children, friends, personal interests, addictions, playing around, money, religious views, or anything else ahead of the relationship with you—then you don't stand a chance together. I don't care how great the person is otherwise or how flawless he or she seems to be. If the person's priorities are in the right place—that the relationship with you is number one over everything else—and the person treats you as number one, then you can make it together, especially if your flaws are compatible.

thirty-one

20 Strategies for Romancing the Rich

"Be Big: Think Big. Act Big. Dream Big."

—Conrad Hilton

In the beginning . . .

1. HAVE A BELIEF SYSTEM THAT THE OPPOSITE SEX IS WONDERFUL

In 1994, *Cosmopolitan* magazine ran an article about the success of a woman in Houston who read *How to Marry the Rich* and then had twenty-seven dates with wealthy men.

In the article, this adorable lady also told about her private consultation with me and my teaching her to adjust her attitude toward men by saying these magic words: "Men are wonderful! I am wonderful! Sex is wonderful!"

I received letters from women all over North America who stated that just saying these "magic words" over and over produced remarkable results in the attention they got from men—Rich or not!

If you are a man and you believe women are jerks, or if you are a woman who believes men are jerks, I can assure you, here and now, that your love life will not improve. Everywhere you go, you will meet "jerks" coming out of the woodwork.

To attract the wonderful ones (and there are more wonderful women and men than there are any other kind), you have to get on the same wavelength with them. Tune your belief system into the mental frequency of wonderful people—and you'll find them everywhere you go.

2. NEVER TELL HOW BADLY A FORMER LOVER TREATED YOU

Never, ever tell an RM how badly another mate treated you in a previous relationship. So often relationship patterns are caused by telling a new person how the last person treated you. Very few people will treat you any better than the last relationship you describe.

Mark fell in love with Julie. That is why I was surprised to see him not treating her well. Finally, I asked him why he was so bad to her. He frowned and said, "It bothered me that Julie loved her ex-husband enough to put up with all he did to her. The only way I can know she loves me more than she loved him is if she puts up with more from me than she did from him."

When you tell how badly someone treated you, you are, in effect telling this new RM how little another person respected you. And you are also telling how little you respected yourself by putting up with it.

Very simply, don't talk badly about a past relationship—no matter how bad it was. Instead, when an RM asks you what happened in your last relationship, just say something benign.

Donald Trump does not trash his ex-wives. He says, "We grew apart."

Likewise, Cindy Crawford, when asked about Richard Gere, said, "We had different goals."

Always say, "I liked the person because overall they were so good to me. We just grew apart."

Don't trash your past. It will never reflect well on you.

3. DON'T TRASH YOUR PAST, BUT DON'T GO OVERBOARD WITH BS

I knew a woman who was crazy about a Rich man who never called back after one date with her. At her request, I asked him why.

"Well, Ginie . . ." He paused as if reluctant to tell me. "When I asked why she has never married, she gave some bullshit that she's had forty-five proposals of marriage and just never found the right one." He snorted a laugh. "Hell, anybody can do the math."

"What do you mean?" I asked, surprised that the woman had made such a silly claim.

"Well, she's about thirty-four now, so that is more marriage proposals than her age. And what kind of a woman keeps count, anyhow? Mathematically, it would take a marriage proposal every four months for eighteen years from the time she was sixteen. Do I look like a fool?"

Puzzled, I said, compassionately, "When people are lonely and want to see themselves a certain way, they sometimes need fantasies. She wants to see herself as that desirable—and she wants you to see her that way, too."

But he shook his head, unconvinced. "She hurts herself with such a claim, because a man knows that any woman who would be that hard to please has a serious problem."

4. DON'T PURSUE RMs WHO DON'T WANT YOU

Say these words, out loud, right now: "I have too much self-respect to want anyone who doesn't want me."

If you are obsessing over someone who doesn't want you, I urge you to run—not walk—to the nearest qualified shrink, because you have a problem that needs serious work *now*.

5. DISAGREE ON ONE TOPIC BEING DISCUSSED

When you first meet your RM, establish yourself as having a brain and a mind of your own by disagreeing with the RM on one topic that is discussed. One is enough or you will appear disagreeable.

6. Don't Stay Out All Night

Let your RM know you have plans early tomorrow and want to be home by midnight. If it is a weekend, two o'clock is okay.

7. Pace Your Availability

Keep in mind that if you are not reasonably accessible to a busy RM in the beginning, the RM will find someone who is. But, once you and an RM have had a really good date that clinches the RM's interest in you, insist they call you three days ahead. That is one of the rules of etiquette.

Once the relationship is intimate and daily, there will be informal, spur-of-the-moment events in addition to regular weekend dates; but always, always create a busy, full life for yourself apart from the RM that requires you to occasionally have to find a way to "fit in" your RM.

A man should always ask an RM for a date three days in advance.

If you are a woman and an RM asks you for a date at the last minute and you have no date, light up and say, "I'd love to; but can we make it Thursday instead of Wednesday?"

If the RM says no, then say, "Let me see what I can do about rescheduling a meeting." If you want to go, call back in a few minutes and say, "If we can make it at eight instead of seven, I can make it."

For a short notice date that you really want to attend, change either the date or the time—but change something that they have to acquiesce to—or don't go.

8. Never Have a Date with Your RM Late at Night

If an RM calls you late at night and wants to see you, hang up. In all likelihood he or she had an unhappy date and needs you to make him or her feel better. No way.

9. HAVE YOUR RM ASSOCIATE YOU WITH THE BEST

When asked if there is somewhere you would like to go, make sure you suggest the best places, so your RM knows you are not intimidated by fine places. And order what you please from items in each category on the menu, without considering price. All of this implants in your RM's mind the fact that you are equal to the best and deserve the best.

Throughout Dating . . .

10. TELEPHONE CALLS AND E-MAIL RATIOS

If you are always initiating contact, there is not enough mutual interest for a serious relationship. A male RM should call or e-mail a woman three times more than she calls or e-mails him.

It is okay for a man dating a female RM to call her up to two times more than she calls him.

11. DON'T COMPLAIN ABOUT THE RELATIONSHIP

The minute you complain to your RM about the way he or she is treating you, you have automatically defined yourself as the victim. Victims give power to the other person when they complain. And victims always lose.

That is why I am opposed to too many "Can we talk?" sessions. After you are married, working on communication is a given, because you are mutually committed through legal vows to work on a relationship.

But "working on the relationship" when you are dating? It is premature and takes all the fun out of the courtship. Courtship, by its own nature, is the fun period, where couples either find they click or they don't. Too many serious talks and complaints during courtship means one thing—the relationship is not working.

You may mention something you would like the RM to do, but only once. Then, you must accept the fact that this person is not going to change, and decide if you want to put up with it. If not, move on to a new relationship.

12. INCREASE YOUR DATING PORTFOLIO

The more people you date, the sooner you will meet the one you'll marry. It's that simple. Finding a mate—even a Rich mate—is just a numbers game. The more numbers you process, the sooner the person who will want you as much as you want her or him will surface. You can lose a lot of years by taking one relationship at a time, rather than dating a lot of people at once.

You may think you know what you want, but when you date a lot of people, you discover new aspects of yourself you never knew existed. And when you do marry, you know it is to the right person because you have checked out the others. Plus, you feel fulfilled from the rich, full social life you experienced before marriage.

13. POSTPONEMENT MEANS NO

What does it mean when an RM tells you he or she loves you but is just not ready to marry yet?

It means no.

What if an RM gives you a "reason" why he or she wants to delay the marriage for now?

Delay means one thing—no.

It's like parents who don't want to say no too much to their children, but they have no intention of doing something the children are asking them to do. The parents will say, "We'll see" or "Not now" or "We'll do it another time." It is a way of stalling long enough for the child to forget about it.

Postponement buys time for the RM—and steals your time—when there is absolutely no intention of follow-through. If you trust the false hope, you lose ground, lose time, and lose your RM, anyway.

It might be hard to hear, but I need to tell you: when an RM is stalling, it means the RM hasn't found the person he or she wants to marry yet. This RM doesn't want to marry you.

14. DON'T "PSYCHOLOGICALLY MARRY" YOUR RM

If you are not seeing other RMs, it means you are "psychologically married" to this one. Why should an RM marry you if you are already married to the RM psychologically?

Having sex before marriage has nothing to do with it, it is your RM having *commitment* from you before marriage that puts you in jeopardy. An RM must *earn* your commitment through the contract of marriage.

Single and committed are contradictions in terms. By definition, single means uncommitted. By definition, committed means not single. You cannot be both. If you are single, then enjoy the fruits of single life by experiencing many people of the opposite sex simultaneously. When you get married, you commit to one person—and not before then.

Should you tell the RM that you are seeing other people? Of course not. You are doing this for you. And you don't have to sleep with anyone if you don't want to. Just meet them for lunch, or at Happy Hour, or talk on the telephone—but keep in touch. And never tell one how you feel about the others.

However, if someone asks you, answer just like this: "When I decide to marry, that is the time to stop seeing other people." Make it your decision. Just knowing this about you can spur an RM to the altar.

15. ONCE LOVE HAS BEEN DECLARED, NEVER ACCUSE YOUR RM OF NOT LOVING YOU

This is one of the most destructive things you can do. Your self-pitying words can kill love.

A famous lawyer said, "Tell people what you want them to believe. Tell them again. Then tell them again. Tell them again and then tell them again—and eventually they will believe you."

Your RM will eventually believe you if you keep insisting she or he does not love you. You will convince them of it. That's loser talk. Be a winner.

16. STICK UP FOR YOURSELF IN THE RELATIONSHIP

I don't make a common practice of it, but occasionally I encounter a client who strikes me as a nice match for another client and I put them in touch with each other. And, of course, I never charge for doing that.

Well, James, a Rich owner of a string of television stations, had a consultation with me a few years ago.

As James talked, I thought of a lovely lady in the age range and with the type of looks he preferred. So I told him about her and he responded enthusiastically.

Several months later, he returned for a consultation, concerned about how to break off with her.

"I really liked her at first," he said dejectedly. "She was everything I ever wanted. But she was too nice."

I scowled at him after he gave several examples of how he took advantage of her. "Shame on you, James."

He looked me squarely in both eyes and said these exact words: "I would like to think I would never run over a woman; but the truth is, I want a woman who has the spunk to tell me 'I will not put up with that shit!' "

Many Rich men and Rich women feel this way—and they will treat you according to what you will put up with. Stick up for yourself! You'll only get the respect you demand.

17. DON'T DECLARE YOUR LOVE PREMATURELY

If your RM has given you no indication of how she or he feels, but you yearn to pledge your undying love and ask if your RM feels the same . . . *don't!*

If you feel the need to ask your RM about his or her feelings, let that be your clue that you would be premature. And revealing premature feelings will only result in both you and your RM feeling uncomfortable in the relationship.

As difficult as it may be, wait until you can feel a moment so pregnant with love between both of you that one of you will burst if you don't say it. Hear what I said: BOTH of you. And if you silently count to a hundred, your RM may confess love first—which is just what you wanted to hear.

18. DON'T OVERPLAY YOUR HAND

Conversely, don't play it so cool that the cycle of love peaks and levels off. A Johnny-come-lately can't take the relationship back to the magic days. It's a shame, but when the energy is gone out of a relationship, it's like trying to put dead leaves back on a tree—there is just no connection anymore.

One Rich woman said, "At one time, I would have loved knowing he cared, but he waited too long to tell me, and when he did, it was 'too little too late.' "

19. KNOW WHAT AN RM REALLY WANTS IN A MATE

An RM wants emotional excitement in a mate.

Perfect people are perfectly boring. If you are not emotionally exciting, your RM will take you for granted—and that is the kiss of death. And you will see it coming. He or she will begin to create distance from you in small, polite ways:

• Your RM will begin to be late for dates—apologetically calling in the beginning, but later not bothering to call.

• Your RM will have to leave early, or work late, or entertain family or guests.

• You will not get a call when your RM said he or she would call.

• When your RM shows up, there is something about him or her that causes you to feel your RM was somewhere other than where he or she said.

• Eventually, your RM stops calling, makes excuses to cut your calls fairly short, promises to call you back and doesn't.

These are all hints that your RM is bored and moving out of the relationship because it has lost the excitement for him or her.

When it gets to that point, don't waste time trying to save the relationship. You can stand on your head naked in the middle of the freeway and it won't faze your RM. It is too late.

Don't believe what an RM says she or he wants in a mate. Watch what the RM responds to. Emotional excitement binds a mate to you more than all the Girl Scout and Boy Scout traits ever will.

If you have a flaw that demands attention or nurturing or understanding, your RM has to invest him or herself in the relationship. A flaw will keep your RM intrigued with you for years—like working a fascinating crossword puzzle. This is especially true if the RM is always trying to "fix you."

I encourage you to embrace some of your flaws. Your flaws are the very magic of you, what keeps you unique and fascinating—and can keep an RM on his or her toes, and keep the relationship teeming with life.

So exhale with relief that you don't have to be perfect—in fact, if you are, you will definitely lose your RM. But be careful. These flaws can backfire. Find out through questioning what an RM has put up with before. Most of them have an M.O. (*modus operandi*, mode of operation) as to the flaws that attract them. You'll hear them complain about them often. But listen to their complaints. If there is a lot of emotion in their complaint, it is "unfinished business" and they will be drawn to it like honey.

Four flaws that work with some RMs are the following:

• *High-strung temper.* Many Rich men—especially quiet, self-possessed heirs—are charmed by women with a short fuse and complain with a smile about a woman's temper.

The president of a communications company was in an argument with his lover, who became so angry she picked up an ashtray and smashed it against the wall. Then she broke his desk lamp, overturned his desk, and practically destroyed his office before he could restrain her in his arms.

His secretaries were aghast when they came to work the next day and saw his wrecked office. And when they heard the story, they thought surely the relationship was over. But it wasn't. He married her.

An heiress fell for a man who literally kicked down her door. A bit boorish, I know, but she preferred it to her quiet, unemotional male peers. "At least I know he has a pulse," she quipped.

Note: NEVER use temper as a flaw if there is the slightest chance the RM has a violent temper or would hurt you. Be absolutely sure, before you use it.

• *Flirtatious*. My girlfriend dated a Rich man who complained continually about his flirtatious ex-wife.

"Never again," he swore vehemently. "I would never take her back—and never put up with a woman who flirts or cheats."

"There is too much emotion in his voice," I said to my girlfriend. "He is trying to convince himself, but I don't believe he is over her."

"He assures me he is over her," my girlfriend said, confidently, "and I believe him. Furthermore, I have told him he never has to worry about me; that I have unquestionable integrity. He knows when he marries me, I will be absolutely faithful."

Unfortunately, he did not marry my girlfriend. He remarried his ex-wife. Three years later, when she left him again for one of her lovers, he didn't even think of my girlfriend, who was excited by the news. No, indeed, true to his M.O., he married a woman who was a notorious flirt.

As much as he complained about it, that RM nevertheless found a faithless flirt more interesting than "unquestionable integrity"—even though he swore it was what he wanted.

• *Jealous and possessive*. This flaw can be murder on you because it sucks you into an RM's power and it is quite draining, so if it is not natural to you, forget it!

If it is natural to you, you may attract a Rich mate who tries to placate you. If so, this flaw can be endearing to your RM, who is flattered that you care so much.

One of my clients was devastated when a man she had dated for ten years suddenly married someone else. "I can't understand it," she moaned, "I was always understanding and let him do whatever he wanted to do. She is jealous and possessive of his every move."

My client had been trying to keep her RM happy. The other woman's jealousy kept him trying to keep her happy.

• *Withholds approval.* Who means more to you: a person you want to please or a person who wants to please you? That's easy. The person you want to please clearly means more to you, because you have to invest so much of yourself in the relationship. You try to please because you want that person's approval/ love.

It's no different with an RM. If he or she is trying to please you, you are in control. If you are trying to please the RM, that person is in control and has the upper hand.

Withheld approval can be unspoken, and sealed with a glance of disapproval when the person falls short. It can also take the form of mild to sharp criticism from time to time.

Most true love relationships have a balance in this area, but there is usually one person who more often withholds approval and keeps the other person hopping to please. But use withheld approval *sparingly.* We all need comforting recognition and will seek it elsewhere, eventually.

So study an RM's M.O., and don't utilize any of these flaws until you know for sure the RM responds well to it—or unless it is natural to you. And even then, don't unleash these flaws too often. Any more frequent than eight to twelve weeks apart, and your endearing flaws may turn into relationship breakers.

20. LET YOURSELF EXPERIENCE ROMANCE FULLY

Romance is the merging of two people on three levels: mind, body, and spirit. It may last forever or it may not. But always the joy of love is experienced when these three elements merge between a couple.

Sometimes, however, you may date an RM and only one or two connections occur. It will feel something like this:

• *Mind.* A connection of the mind can include compatible ethics, some interests in common, and sometimes a similar level of education.

You and a person can talk for hours about Kant or Descartes

or art. It is a wonderful connection, but the body and spirit are lacking, so you only feel friendship for the person.

• *Body*. Connections of the body include your first impression of each other—the way you dress, your body language, and sex.

You like what you see and feel attracted to the RM, but as you get to know the person, a mental rapport is missing, or there is not enough emotion in your spirit.

• *Spirit*. Connections of the spirit include an almost telepathic understanding of each other's moods. Connections of the spirit include a "knowing" of each other's needs, with full compassion and affection.

You feel drawn like a magnet to a person. It is almost as if your souls know each other. But there is no connection of the mind and no sexual spark.

When two connections occur, you can feel frustrated because it seems as if the relationship can work if only. . . . So you hang on, hoping things will get better. But they don't, because to feel true love you have to connect on all three levels.

When you do connect on all three levels, release all the pent-up emotions of love you have. Feel everything to the fullest and share it all. You are safe to feel all you feel, and safe to express all the emotions of your heart and soul, because you not only love, you are loved.

$\mathscr{R}$ich Sex ™

"Sex can be truly fulfilling only when it is accompanied by making love—by the sharing of hearts and feelings."

—Barbara de Angelis

Rich mates are typically very highly sexed individuals (wouldn't everybody be, if they didn't have to worry about making car and mortgage payments on time?).

RMs can be masterful lovers; but at the same time, they can be the most insecure about their sexual prowess. I think it is because sex is the one place where their money really cannot help them out.

Oh yes, they can pay participants for sex; but in the sex act, they are stripped, not only of their clothes, but also of the ability to buy control. They can't pay themselves to perform. Orgasms and erections are something a Rich mate cannot buy.

Another reason the Rich feel insecure in bed is their expectations. Since they can experience a superior lifestyle the ordinary John or Jane Doe cannot have, they want to believe they can experience a superior sex style the ordinary John or Jane cannot have.

The idea that their gardener, butler, or chauffeur experiences the same or better quality of sex life they experience can be irksome. They expect to experience more. They expect to experience better. So each sexual act is hampered by unrealistic expectations the RM may feel he or she cannot live up to.

A Rich Mate's Vulnerability

Your Rich mate is so used to being the top dog, the main authority, the one everyone else looks to for answers, that your RM never has a chance to be vulnerable, to have someone to look up to.

Everyone needs a space where he or she can be the weak one for a while and be taken care of. Everyone needs a place where he or she can be told what to do—even scolded—rather than always being the one issuing orders and reprimands.

You are not the Rich Mate's parent, but sex can be almost a parenting arena. A man may become fatherly to a Rich woman in bed. A woman often takes a motherly role—both with nurturing and discipline—to a Rich man.

Some of the Rich may feel guilty for any number of reasons, and seek a dominatrix to absolve them through sexual dominance. And sexual dominance does not necessarily involve whips and chains. It can be as simple as a role-reversal of control, so the Rich mate has a place to stop being in control and just relax.

To Do It or Not to Do It—That Is The Question

To perform sexually for an RM and to withhold sex from an RM are equally immature and futile manipulations—especially by a woman trying to make an RM marry her. Both tactics inevitably fail.

When you are pressured into performing sexual feats, you enter sexual servitude. This is especially true if you are led into kinky practices you don't feel comfortable about. Don't do it. When you do anything you don't want to do, you become a victim—and there's nothing sexy about that. Gimmicky sex may seem fun at first, but it eventually becomes impersonal. Then the pleasure is in the gimmick, and not in each other. At that point, the RM is not making love to you—anyone would do, so why should he marry you?

Withholding sex in hopes of marriage doesn't work either. Do you really think someone will marry you because he just has to have sex with you?

I'm not telling you to have sex with a man if that's not what you want to do. But don't use sex as a bargaining chip for marriage.

There are women who will tease a man with passionate kissing and foreplay, and then put the brakes on until a proposal comes. And proposals do come, but the men have no intention of following through.

One Rich man expressed it perfectly. "When a woman is acting hot and bothered, rubbing against me with heavy breathing, and I know she has no intention of following through unless I marry her, I always propose marriage with no intention of following through.

"After all, she's being dishonest with her body to manipulate me into marriage, so I am dishonest, too! I see if I can manipulate her into bed with a phony marriage proposal."

Not the nicest attitude to have, but if you play games, you have to be prepared to have someone play them with you.

Will a Rich man lose respect for a woman who has sex with him before marriage? Think about that question and what it implies. Then ask yourself if you would really *want* anybody who would think less of you for expressing yourself in sweet lovemaking with him.

Follow your heart, and let sex be the pleasurable expression of love it is supposed to be.

$\mathcal{V}$ALID REASONS TO WITHHOLD SEX

Whether you are a man or a women, there are some valid reasons to withhold sex with an RM you care about:

• To discern the sexual safety of your partner

• You don't want to have sex at the time

• For better treatment—physically, emotionally, and yes, that includes better financial treatment. Financial abuse is just as real as verbal abuse, physical abuse, or any other kind of abuse.

If you are sleeping with a Rich person you are in love with and who declares love for you—and if your means are significantly less wealthy than your Rich mate, the RM is being cruel if he or she does not pay your way on trips, or otherwise help ease your financial burdens (true love does that).

This is a person who thinks nothing of dropping hundreds of thousands of dollars into a charity coffer, but will not pay your light bill? Get real. . . .

The Only Reason to Have Sex

Whether you are a man or a woman, you should never go to bed with anyone unless you *want to*, even if you know you will never see that person again. When your own desire is your only motive, you will never be exploited—and you will always get what you wanted out of it.

How Soon to Have Sex

Sex usually begins soon with the Rich. That is because their lives move quickly. But, I repeat, you must have sex for you and not for anyone else. If you want sex with this person early, that is fine; if not, that is okay, too.

If you do decide to have sex, you *must* take every precaution.

Remember, AIDS and other sexually transmitted diseases make no exceptions for the Rich. So, if you love your sexuality— not to mention your life—protect yourself. It is not the responsibility of your RM to protect you sexually. That is nice, of course, but the bottom line is that it is *your* responsibility.

Both men and women should carry latex condoms at all times. Natural condoms do not protect against the spread of AIDS.

A Few Extra Guidelines

• *Don't try to please*. Nothing points out that you are not an equal to the Rich like trying to please—especially with a servitude mentality in bed. It is a no-win, degrading behavior.

If you do something in bed you don't really want to do, you end up feeling used (and you have been), exhausted, and hurt because your partner doesn't like you more. In fact your partner will probably like you less.

When you try to please demands of your Rich lover, it is begging for acceptance, and there is nothing attractive about a beggar. When you try too hard to please others, you are admitting you are in a losing position. Learn to say no sometimes. And learn to ask your Rich mate to do something for you. Don't try to displease, but don't try to please, either.

• *Don't put up with BS. Don't let the Rich get away with something you would not let anyone else get away with.* I do not care if the person you are dealing with is royalty, the person is no better than you. If the person is inconsiderate in any way, stick up for yourself!

• *Be true to yourself in bed and sex can be wonderful.*

1. Make it a simple, warm, loving experience.
2. The best way to impress your Rich mate with your sexuality is with sensual responses, not tricks.
3. Whatever the shape of your body, seem proud of it. Don't complain about faults.
4. Don't talk about lovemaking afterward with worry or regret.
5. Respond positively without gushing over it. Everybody is telling this Rich person the sex is the best he or she has ever had.
6. Be sure it is clear that sex is not a swap for money or gifts.

$\mathcal{G}$iving and Getting

"To thine own self be true and it must follow as the night the day, thou canst not then be false to any man."

—William Shakespeare

Jason is a young, virile, and handsome man who was the lover and constant companion of a wealthy woman in Los Angeles for two years.

He was well educated, but so smitten with his RM that he behaved like a lackey. He ran errands, picked up supplies for her, answered the door when she asked him to, drove her about, mixed drinks with the bartenders at her parties, and made sure guests were having a good time.

On weekends, they went to her second home in the mountains, and when she idly complained about the state of the yard, he set about cleaning it up.

Did all this endear him to her? Quite the contrary. Eventually, she took his self-appointed duties for granted and began reminding him it was time for him to clean the yard.

One weekend, while he labored in the yard of her mountain home, he looked up to see her car back out of the drive and pull away. It was odd, he thought, but he concluded she had driven to town for something, and he continued working until dark.

Later that evening, he received a call from her maid in Los Angeles telling him that his RM had gone away, indefinitely, and would he like to pick up his belongings.

Dumbfounded, Jason returned to Los Angeles and talked to some of her house workers. He learned that at one of her parties where he had busied himself mixing drinks and seeing to guests, his RM had engaged in conversation with an accountant and asked several questions about taxes.

The accountant had smiled slowly and replied, "My fee is two hundred dollars an hour. Call my secretary in the morning and she can schedule an appointment."

And she did schedule an appointment (to which Jason, her lover, had unknowingly driven her, and even waited in the car as she had told him to).

She soon learned that, unlike Jason, the accountant could not be used and would not perform menial chores for her. When she once asked him to answer her door, he shook his head, saying, "This is not my house."

When asked to mix drinks, he declined with "I would rather taste a drink made by you." And she mixed the drink for him.

Memorize this: an RM will not like you more for making his or her life easier. In fact, it is a dangerous practice. Appreciation fades into taking you for granted, which fades into boredom, and then the relationship itself fades.

Juliet organized a private estate auction for her Rich man when he mentioned giving some of his antiques to charity. He objected, but Juliet convinced him she could turn it into a handsome profit for him. He shrugged and she attacked the project with passion. And it was a great success.

But he never even thanked Juliet. Nor did he give her a percentage of the money she had earned for him. In fact, he left immediately afterward, taking another woman on a trip to the French Riviera.

I could literally fill a separate book with true stories like these of perfectly decent RMs who felt trapped by perfectly decent lovers who set themselves up to be used.

It is not the RM's job not to use you. It is your job not to let the RM use you. Don't do anything for the RM that he or she typically hires other people to do.

• Do not make the beds.

• Do not do laundry for your RM.

- Do not cook for him or her.

- Do not wash your RM's dishes.

For women, this is especially treacherous. It is so devastatingly domestic that it looks as if you are trying too hard to prove what a great little wife you would be.

The CEO of one of America's largest oil companies was on a date with a girlfriend of mine that I had introduced to him. I was dating his best friend, an independent and wealthy oil man himself, but not as Rich as the CEO. The four of us went out with another couple—a business associate of theirs and a beautiful widow he was engaged to marry.

During dinner, the conversation turned to the couple's impending marriage, and what constituted husband and wife material. The lovely widow said, "A man wants a woman who is a good cook and housekeeper. It's as simple as that."

And my girlfriend said, "Yes, I think that's true."

But I disagreed, saying, "I don't think a man marries a woman for how well she cooks or cleans house."

Instantly, all three men nodded and the CEO spoke first. "I agree with Ginie. I don't think a man even cares if a woman can cook at all, if he loves her."

The man who was engaged to the widow said, "I would never marry a woman because she is a good cook or housekeeper."

Then, to his credit, he took her hand and smiled at her, adding softly, "It is nice to come home to, honey, but I would marry you anyway."

Rich men do not marry for cooking and housecleaning any more than they marry strictly for sex. They marry for love.

Furthermore, a woman does not owe a Rich man dinner at her place because he has previously taken her to restaurants. Reciprocal dinners are for social alliances, not romantic dates. I never met a Rich man who expected me to supply dinner for him.

The only Rich men who expect a woman of limited means to cook dinner for them are either marginally wealthy, very stingy, users, or scorekeepers—e.g., "I did this for you, now you do that for me."

If you are a woman and you want to cook, do it for your own enjoyment, not because you owe it to him or to try to get him to the altar. And be careful that your own pleasure in cooking does not open the door for you to be used.

For some reason, it is sexy for a man to cook for his RM—if it is not done too often. I think it is because it was never an assigned role of domesticity for a man. So, men, if you'd like, don your aprons and serve up a scrumptious dinner for the Rich woman in your life, once in awhile.

THE EXCEPTIONS TO THIS RULE

Having said all that—and meaning it, fully—there are times when "tasks" can be part of the romantic action together, while deepening the relationship. And those times are only when the tasks are *performed together*.

A rustic weekend without domestic help on hand means beds have to be made. Cheerfully assign your RM tasks with you. "Let's make up the bed, Jim. You get on that side of the bed and I'll get on this side."

If your RM won't do it, you don't do it, either. Just leave it— no matter how much it bothers you.

Is this petty? No, it is essential. As the American Broadcasting System says: "This is a test. This is only a test." A test of whether or not you can refuse to be used.

When it is time to do the laundry, tell your RM to measure the soap and set the water temperature while you gather the wash. If she won't do that much, don't wash her things. Just wash yours. If she complains about it, tell her the facts of life with you: that you will do things with her, but not *for* her.

If, however, your RM pitches in—and most likely he or she will—the two of you will have fun making up the bed—perhaps having a pillow fight that ends up with tickling on the bed and possibly making love again. Even doing the laundry together can augment feeling closer to each other in the process.

And cooking occassionally is okay, too. Whether you are a certified gourmet cook or if you just love to experiment in the kitchen, put an apron on your RM and yourself while discussing what the two of you will cook up together in the kitchen (I'm talking about food).

Many RMs cultivate specialties of cuisine themselves as a hobby. In that case, you settle comfortably onto a stool at the counter and chat while your RM treats you. It might spoil his or her fun if you try to help, so leave it to the RM to ask you.

And of course, there are times when you and an RM are at your place and don't want to go out. For instance, after love-making on a rainy afternoon . . . or snuggling before a crackling fireplace on a snowy day . . . or sitting up in bed and talking until three-thirty in the morning and suddenly realizing you are hungry.

Don't break the mood by trying to bowl over your RM with lavish meals. Instead, keep the glow of intimacy high as you feed the body's hunger in an uncomplicated way. Here's a favorite easy recipe of mine:

Ginie Sayles' Eggs A L'Orange

1 can Pillsbury biscuits or croissants
Pam
1 container fat-free Egg-Beaters
4 fresh Oranges
1 box powdered sugar

Open the can of biscuits or croissants and follow instructions for baking.
Spray a skillet with fat-free buttery Pam.
Shake the container of fat-free Egg-Beaters, pour it into the pan, and cook on low.
Peel 3 fresh oranges, dice into large pieces, and mix them into the slow-cooking Egg-Beaters.
Put powdered confectioners' sugar in a bowl and squeeze juice from an orange into it until it makes a thin icing. Remove biscuits or croissants and drizzle with orange icing. Make espresso or cappuccino. (If your apartment kitchen is small, Black & Decker has a nifty and inexpensive microwave cappuccino maker that makes great espresso and cappuccinos. Although I have a large, expensive espresso/cappuccino maker, I prefer the Black & Decker Espresso Mio.)

> *Top your espresso with a twist of orange peel or sprinkle*
> *grated orange peel onto fat-free milk froth of cappuccino.*

This is ready in minutes, is low-fat, and very healthful. I like
to make it with different fruit as the theme—strawberries or raspberries, papaya, mango, nectarines—the variations are endless.
But keep one fruit as your theme. It's easy, delicious, and fast—
and it doesn't look as if you are trying too hard to impress anybody.

Your RM will be happier if you ask him or her to lend a hand;
peeling and dicing oranges or making the espresso or the frothy
fat-free milk topping are good helping tasks. And afterward have
your RM help load the dishwasher or dry dishes while you wash.
There are so few dishes with this treat.

For beautiful days outside, take advantage of the natural elements for romance with your RM:

Ginie's Sensuous Picnic

- *White picnic basket*
- *Sterling silver knives*
- *Wine opener*
- *White Linen napkins*
- *Two crystal wine glasses*
- *Two small bone china plates*
- *A bottle of Pinot Noir (the wine for lovers)*
- *Single cream Brie cheese*
- *Golden paté (a delicious goose liver meat) or a*
  vegetable paté
- *Hot loaf of bread (fragrant from your easy-to-use*
  breadmaker or neighborhood bakery)
- *Large fresh figs*
- *Two large, red pears*
- *Bright Red blanket*

Note: Make it fun. Carve initials in a tree if you are in a forest,
build sandcastles on the beach, swing in a park, fly kites on a
hilltop.

Although I can cook very complicated menus, I never did it
for a Rich man. When people tease me about my refusal to be a

cook for a man, I smile and truthfully say, "Nobody ever married me for my cooking."

Meals at your place should never be more than twice in a six-month period—or you are working too hard! One of the perks of romance with the Rich is having unimaginably expensive dinners in the best five-star restaurants in the world. And, for heaven's sake, why compete with a five-star chef?

$\mathcal{G}$ IFT GIVING

Of course you buy or make a gift for your RM for major holidays, such as Christmas, Valentine's Day, and your RM's birthday. If you are a woman, be sure the RM has a holiday gift for you before you give anything—or it will embarrass both of you. And make sure the gift is appropriate for the relationship. Go overboard and you not only break the bank, you probably will feel humiliated.

Dating One Month

It can be very tempting in the tingly high excitement of new love to let your heart open your pocketbook—but *don't* do it!

Even if you are seeing each other every day, even if you are already sexually involved with each other, and even if you have both declared love for each other, keep your gifts impersonal.

Appropriate gifts for one month of dating range from $1 to not more than $25 ($1–$10 is better):

- A cute or funny card

- A small, inexpensive box of liqueur candy or liqueur cake

- A small plant

- A hard-bound book (especially if you get it on sale)

If you are sexually involved, it is okay to give a cute, sexy gift, such as a gold lamé G-string or sexy nightie.

If you write anything on a card, keep it very light, cute, and teasing. If your RM surprises you with a greater gift, do not feel badly about yours and do not apologize for it—ever. You have been appropriate.

Dating Three-to-Six-Months

Let's say you are more madly in love with your RM than ever at this point and you are sexually involved.

If you are seeing each other only once a week—or less, or if you don't know *for sure* that your relationship is exclusive, or if for *any* reason you have ever felt insecure in the relationship, the only appropriate gifts are still those in the category above.

However, if you are seeing each other virtually every day— to the point that it would be unlikely for anyone else to be in the picture, plus mutual declarations of love have been made, plus you feel secure in the relationship, then you can give gifts that have a little more meaning.

Still, keep a $50 limit on the gift itself—and do make it a gift that brings a smile, rather than one that overwhelms.

- Personalized writing paper
- A handsome pencil/pen set (not Mont Blanc or Cartier)
- A pretty sweater/cardigan (L. L. Bean)
- A fairly exotic plant (if it will be taken care of)
- Tickets to a single event (*not* season tickets)
- A tie (not Hermés)
- Massage oils
- A name-brand fragrance
- A paperweight
- A creative gift

It is very important during this time period that your creative gifts do not give the impression that you knocked yourself out to impress your RM with your creativity. And at this point, do not monogram anything other than writing paper. Monograms are too personal.

After Six Months

If you have been with your RM for more than six months and things are going strong, it is okay to give more expensive and personal gifts. By now, you should know your RM well enough to get a gift that will really mean something. The only coveat: don't spend more than you can in an attempt to impress or compete. You'll never succeed. Instead, let your gift come from the heart.

WHAT TO DO IF AN RM FORGETS A VALENTINE OR BIRTHDAY

There is an unfortunate double standard, here.

Most female RMs are pretty good about remembering birthdays and other special days. Women are teethed on such things. So it does not bode well for you if she does not give you a gift. Usually it is not because she forgot (although it is possible). It probably has more to do with her not being pleased about your behavior in the relationship or because she is hinting she wants out.

If she does not give you a gift, find out if it is because she is angry at you. Did you forgot a special occasion and she is getting even? Whatever the reason, no gift from your Rich lady is usually a bad sign.

Rich men, on the other hand, may flood your apartment with gifts for no reason except that they are thinking of you—and then completely forget your birthday.

Jim is a wealthy attorney in Canada who is very good to women in relationships. "But I'm not so good about things like valentines and birthdays," he muttered, shamefaced. "I can even write it in my datebook and then get so busy I forget it. And women get so mad!"

Never dump a good RM who shows he truly loves you in most other ways just because he has a mental block about special days. Some of them were brought up with self-sacrificing mothers who taught them they didn't have to spend money on such things and that birthdays are trivial. Those are the men you train, if the relationship is satisfying in other ways.

ℋOW TO TRAIN AN **RM** FOR SPECIAL DAY GIFTS

Let's say it is Valentine's Day and your Rich man arrives sans gift. Do not let him know you have a gift for him, if you do. Instead, tell him this is Valentine's Day and the two of you are going shopping for gifts for each other before dinner. If dinner reservations will interfere, cancel them.

Now make a fun event out of it. Each of you will write a list of five things you would like and then go to the best mall or upscale shopping area together.

Check your watches, and tell him you will meet him at the Crepe Shoppe in one hour. You will each bring back:

- One gift on the list for each other

- One surprise gift you think of yourselves

- A beautiful card.

At the end of the hour you will meet each other, faces flushed with excitement, ready to unwrap presents and open cards over dinner. It will be a very happy Valentine's Day, indeed.

With the Rich man who is good to you in all other respects, turn his forgetfulness into a fun project—to help him save face and feel successful, and to keep your blood pressure down.

$\mathcal{A}$ Marriage-Prone Relationship

> *"The Rich have to marry somebody, why not you?"*
>
> —*Ginie Sayles*

Your time is valuable and you don't want to waste it in a relationship that does not stand a chance of ending in marriage. For that reason, you need to be able to evaluate the status of your relationships at any given time and know whether or not it is marriage-prone.

I have received tremendous appreciation from people all over the United States and Canada for the following method of determining, instantly, whether or not a relationship they are in is likely to lead to marriage.

A marriage-prone relationship has two striking features:

- High-frequency dating
- Same level of interest

$\mathcal{H}$IGH-FREQUENCY DATING

One of the biggest clues to the seriousness of a relationship is the frequency of dating between a man and a woman.

A person sometimes comes to me complaining that a relationship has not moved into marriage. I ask how often they date each other. If the answer is "once a week but we talk on the telephone daily," I have the unhappy task of telling this person that the dating pattern is not marriage-prone dating. If a Rich mate is dating you only once a week, you are *casually dating*. Out of thirty days in a month, you are seeing each other four or five days. You see your postman more often than that! Your RM is spending more time *without you* than with you. What is he or she doing the other twenty-five or twenty-six days each month?

When a man or woman is serious about you, he or she wants to be *with* you and often! The more serious the RM is, the more activities he or she wants you involved in together. Marriage is an everyday relationship, not a once-a-week dinner-and-sex date. There are happy once-a-week dating scenarios, especially among much older couples. This works out fine if it is simply companionship and sex between two people who like each other but who do not have a desire to marry.

Yes, a relationship that starts out this way could end in marriage but only if the level of interest changes from four or five dates a month to a much higher frequency. You will know a Rich mate is getting more serious if the RM sees you more than he or she doesn't see you.

What is an acceptable frequency of dating for the probability of marriage? A minimum of three days a week—and preferably more!

Same Level of Interest

If the Rich person you are dating is much, much crazier about you than you are about him or her, you do not have a marriage-prone relationship, unless you simply decide to go ahead and get married.

If you are much, much crazier about the Rich person you are dating than the Rich person is about you, you do not have a marriage-prone relationship. Period.

I tell you these things, not to hurt you, my friend, but because I want you to find fulfillment—not frustration—with your Rich mate. I want you to keep your ability to love healthy. The way you do that is to vow, daily, that you have too much self-respect to love anyone who does not love you.

If you have to face that your relationship is not marriage-prone, I know you will have some pain to deal with, but you will overcome it and move on. Best of all, you will have made the steps that honor your own heart and bring you closer to what you really deserve—true love.

Remember, love does not hurt. If it hurts, it is not love. And furthermore, if the RM doesn't think the relationship is good, then the relationship is not good for you.

However, you may have just realized that you do have a marriage-prone relationship. And if you do, heed this message: marry while it is good. If you marry when love is on the downside, it never lasts. Even on the good side, it could fail—but it is not as likely to do so.

𝒯IMING YOUR RELATIONSHIP FOR MARRIAGE

Many people could have married someone they loved, if they had been aware of the all-important key of timing. Timing is everything!

A marriage-prone relationship has three phases: In Phase One, it shoots up quickly; it plateaus in Phase Two; and it either goes on up or goes down in Phase Three. Timing marriage—which is an emotional investment—is every bit like timing when to make a financial investment in a stock.

Phase One

Once a couple's interest heats up to frequent dating, the relationship shoots up like a rocket with passion, intensity, excitement in being together—which is known as falling in love.

This period lasts an average of three to seven months, sometimes longer. It can be the easiest time frame in the course of a relationship for getting married. You are both in love and you know it. You want to please each other and you want to be together.

Most people who marry know they want to marry each other very soon in their relationship. It clicks. It fits, the way a shirt either does or doesn't fit and you know it. You don't have to figure out whether or not the shirt fits. You know it as soon as you try it on. It does not take a long time, certainly not *years*.

My husband and I married less than five months after we met and we are in our fourteenth year of marriage.

Phase Two

If marriage does not happen during the first phase, the relationship enters a second phase, which I call the plateau phase. The relationship will level off emotionally and become fairly static. But the plateau phase is good overall. The madly-in-love phase is past, but your relationship is deepening and growing.

On the average, the plateau period lasts from six months to eighteen months, but I have seen a plateau phase last as long as twenty-eight months.

Phase Two is also a good time to get married, because your love for each other is real and deep.

Phase Three

If marriage does not occur during Phase Two, the relationship will likely enter a third phase of very, very gradual descent. It can be hardly noticeable at first. There may be some moments of magic again occasionally, but those become fewer.

Conflict increases until there is more unhappiness than overall happiness in the relationship. Eventually, the relationship degenerates to the point that it ends.

If marriage occurs during this phase of a relationship, it is not going to work. At this point, couples marry for one of two reasons:

- As a Band-Aid for the relationship
- Obligation

Band-Aid Marriage. A man may say to himself, "We are fighting so much now. Suzy has always wanted us to get married. Maybe if we marry that will make her happy. Maybe getting married will solve the problem and things will settle down and get back to normal."

Band-Aid marriages seem to improve for a while, but the problems resurface because they went too far and marriage is used as a cover-up.

Obligation Marriages. A woman may say to herself, "I don't really feel in love anymore, but Joe stood by me when my father died. All our friends consider us a couple. I would look like a cad if I didn't marry him now." A man may say, "I have lived with Cindy this long. I owe it to her to marry her."

Obligation marriages do not fare well. Obligation creates too heavy a toll on the one who felt obligated; resentment, then rebellion are sure to follow

The extreme up-and-down pattern of Phase Three is a signal that a relationship has almost run its course and is ending. This is sad, of course, if you want it to last, because the instability of this phase makes it unlikely. Temporary reprieves get shorter; hurt gets longer. The lesson to be learned for the next serious relationship is to be aware of timing and marry during phase one or two.

*B*RING UP MARRIAGE LIKE A WINNER

Men: When you feel a woman loves you, she probably does. And if she loves you, she is receptive to the idea of marrying you. First, you have to tell her you love her and then simply say the words, "I thought we might get married over the holidays"—or whenever you have in mind.

Women: After three months have fully elapsed, if the subject of love or marriage has not been introduced, you need to find out if the RM even loves you. Don't ask. That makes you sound needy. Instead, casually mention the possibility of a date with another and watch for your RM's reaction. Is he jealous? Alarmed that he might lose you? Just that possibility might prompt him to declare his love and his desire to date you exclusively. If he has no response or wishes you a good time, you might have to accept the fact that you should just be friends and look for love elsewhere.

If you and your RM have already shared your feelings of love, it is perfectly acceptable to simply say, "Darling, I love you so! It's only two weeks until summer. Let's get married in Atlantic City (or Las Vegas, or whatever)—just the two of us. We can surprise everybody when we get back!"

Even if the RM refuses, you have proposed with strength. It is far better than a half-whined "Are we ever going to get married?" or an overly serious expression that looks as if you have drawn your sword and expect battle to begin.

If you simply cannot propose, ladies, the next two scenarios may be best for you. Read them to get the general idea and then use it as is or tailor it to fit your needs.

$\mathcal{A}$N OUT-OF-TOWN JOB OFFER SCENARIO

Announce to the RM that you have been offered a job in another state and since it means more money, you could be moving as soon as three weeks. Say that you will leave first and have a moving company pack you and follow to the address you locate.

Study the RM's reaction. If at the end of three weeks—and on your supposed "last date"—your RM does not propose marriage or express enough grief about your leaving that you can suggest marriage, you have your answer.

One woman who followed this through to the "last date" got out of the RM's car when he opened the door and just as she turned away, he caught her arm and turned her to him.

"Do you think I could possibly let you go?" He asked, stumbling sadly over the words, then he pulled a diamond ring from his coat pocket. "We can have this sized, if I got it wrong . . . but I want you to give up that job in California and marry me."

$\mathcal{A}$ PAST LOVER RETURNS ON THE SCENE—SCENARIO

During the sixth month, if your RM has not mentioned marriage, and if you think you cannot bring up the subject, it is time to introduce a competitor.

But don't just fake it. Really do see other people. In fact, I urge you to date, date, date. Stay busy. And when your RM is surprised that you cannot go out, say it is because an old friend is in town and you are obligated to entertain.

There may be a few questions about the "old friend," to which you simply say (with a touch of happiness and excitement in your voice), "Well, it was a couple of years ago, but it was a fairly serious relationship. I just wasn't ready for the next step of commitment at that time. Of course, we are just friends, now. I really didn't expect this visit. It was sort of out of the blue." (Something like that, only in your own words).

Before the RM can say anything, instantly say, "Listen, I have to go. I'll call later."

Then don't call.

Are you trying to make your RM jealous? Let me put it this way: you are trying to help your RM confront his or her feelings about you and your future together.

And if your RM does not call back or calls later and still does not talk about marriage, you have your answer. Change the relationship into friendship and move on, as painful as it may be. Just don't hang on. If your desire is to get married, why waste your time with this guy, when your future husband is out there somewhere waiting for you?

$\mathscr{P}$renuptial Agreements

*"Your value is determined by the mold
you, yourself, make."*

—Conrad Hilton

You may feel insulted by a prenuptial agreement, but if you want to marry an RM, you may have to sign one. Resist at first, if you want to, but don't let it keep you from a marriage you may benefit from. I know several men and women who refused and left the RM in a huff of pride—and they only deprived themselves.

One woman had three small children from a previous marriage when she met a Rich man and fell in love with him. He was generous with her and with her children, and when he asked her to marry him, she couldn't believe her good fortune. But when he took her to his lawyer to have her sign a prenuptial agreement, she was crushed, then indignant.

She left the attorney's office, took her children and boarded a train to another city. The only job she was qualified for paid poorly and her ex-husband was irregular with child support payments. She found herself begging from relatives and finally called long distance collect to the RM to ask for money. He sent it and called regularly to see how she was, but when she still held out for marriage without a prenuptial agreement (insisting that if he really loved her, he would not require one), he gave up.

After two years of only talking on the telephone long distance and sending small amounts of money to keep her and her children from starvation, he finally married another woman who signed his prenuptial agreement—and he is still married to her.

The woman who could have married him has lived a sad, lonely, desperately poor life. She and her children could have enjoyed years of abundance, opportunity, and fine living, if she had signed a prenuptial agreement (after having another attorney look at it and work with his attorney on the terms, if necessary).

And even if the marriage had ended, she and her children would have had a better life than they wound up having. Besides she could always seek legal recourse against the prenuptial agreement, if it came to that. Best of all, she would have had friends on a social level who could introduce her to other Rich men to date and possibly marry. After all, if you marry one RM, you can marry others.

If you are going to sign a prenuptial agreement, I insist you see a separate attorney—paid for by your RM. Simply tear out several deposit slips for your bank account and hand them to your RM, saying, in a reasonable tone, "I will let you know how much money you can deposit into my account, so I can pay my attorney with my checks." And don't give checks to an attorney until your RM puts the necessary funds into your account.

If this person will not pay your legal expense, you may be getting a raw deal. But you should not just sign whatever your RM's attorney draws up. After all, the RM's attorney is looking out for the best interest of the RM, not yours.

If your RM will not pay your legal fees and you desperately want to marry the person, do the best you can: perhaps through free legal aid services; or through law school intern programs, where soon-to-graduate law students can help you. You'd be surprised what eager beavers these students can be on your behalf.

When you meet with your attorney, ask yourself this question: *If this marriage fails, will my life be substantially better off for having married this RM?* This is the most sensible way to approach it, because now you can shove aside extraneous hurt or punitive feelings about it and get down to protecting yourself in a mature and loving way for both of you in the terms of a prenuptial agreement.

TERMS OF A PRENUPTIAL AGREEMENT

1. *Have money promises spelled out in the prenuptial agreement with no "back door" exceptions.*

If you are told you will receive a million dollars if there is a divorce, after three years of marriage, be sure there are no "exception" clauses that nullify that promise. After all, three years of your life is three years of your life. Any paragraph on this matter should strictly maintain that it is mutually agreed upon compensation for your time—which is, without exception, irreplaceable.

2. *Have money promises collateralized in escrow.*

Collateral is something of value (property or cash) that is set aside as a guarantee to fufill an obligation. Escrow is a third party custodian (a bank, usually) who protects the collateral until conditions are fulfilled.

That means if your RM promises you a million dollars upon divorce anytime after three years of marriage, then you want to make sure that the Prenuptial Agreement states at the time of signing, that one million dollars (or its equivalent in property or securities) has been turned over to the custodial care of a bank, who will release it to you if divorce occurs after you have fulfilled three years of marriage.

This is very important. One of my clients signed a prenuptial agreement that said if he stayed married to the RM for a period of three years, he would receive three million dollars in the event of a divorce. This sounded pretty good until the three years ran out and he filed for divorce, only to find that the RM had all her money tied up in loans so there was nothing to give the divorcing husband. This is an RM whom I suspect stays deliberately "debt rich" as a protection from lawsuits and ex-husbands.

So be sure you have the financial promises collateralized in escrow before signing.

3. *Be sure there is a paragraph that irrevocably prevents extensions.*

A prenuptial agreement may say that if you divorce the RM before five years, you will be entitled to nothing, but that after five years, you are entitled to increased financial privileges as a spouse, even in the event of a divorce.

One woman had such a prenuptial agreement, but before it expired her RM told her to sign an extension on it for another five years or he would divorce her. At the end of another five years, he did it again. So for fifteen years, she was virtually blackmailed into a losing position in a marriage to her RM.

4. *Be sure your prenuptial agreement specifies percentages or periods of times for upgrading your position in the benefits of the prenuptial agreement*.

If you signed a prenuptial agreement agreeing to virtually nothing when you were young, and twenty years later you have not only had children with the RM but you have also helped the RM increase his or her fortunes, you should be entitled to more. But if your position has not been upgraded (like a raise) in the prenuptial agreement, you are losing out significantly.

5. *Try to get as generous a settlement as possible, but at least try to get the basics*.

Certainly, in the event of a divorce, you want a fair settlement, but sometimes settling for less can mean having more than you have now (or more than you are likely to have years from now if you do not marry your RM).

The basics include a cash settlement or savings account; a two- or three-bedroom condominium in a respectable part of town (possibly defined in a prenuptial agreement by price range—with a percentage adjustment for inflation); furnishings; a new car (defined in a price range or style, type, model); health, home, and life insurance of a certain value; computer; clothing; and jewelry you have received. Retirement benefits, such as IRAs, Keoghs, and such should also be included, if possible

𝒯AKING A PRENUPTIAL AGREEMENT TO COURT

Prenuptial Agreements can be nullified in cases of:

• *Duress*. Which means you were put under pressure to sign during the last few minutes before a wedding. The embarrassment of having your RM walk out on you is undue stress (duress) that courts have sometimes ruled to be unfair.

• *Unfairness*. One person is getting disproportionately more than the other.

• *Misrepresentation*. One mate did not fully reveal assets and financial standing.

• *Fraud*. One mate has attempted to defraud the other.

$\mathcal{E}$NTER MARRIAGE WITH HAPPINESS

Let the two lawyers thrash out the terms. You should deal closely with your attorney, as I'm sure the RM will certainly do, but avoid dragging the legal fights of the lawyers into your love life. It may not be fully possible, but try.

You may not get everything you want, but once the terms are fairly reasonable, sign the agreement and get married, expecting the best. After all, this is a person you would want to marry even if money were no consideration, therefore, don't let it destroy your love and happiness, now.

thirty-six

17 Most Asked Questions

> *"When the student is ready, the teacher appears."*
>
> —*Eastern proverb*

1. HOW MANY MILLIONAIRES ARE THERE IN THE USA?

As of this writing, *Profit* magazine says there are more than 4.8 millionaire households in the United states—up 80% in the last eight years. According to the magazine, only a few of these millionaires inherited their money it; most earned it, "either in traditional ways as executives or entrepreneurs in manufacturing, distribution, and service businesses, or as pioneers in new technologies such as the burgeoning computer industry."

Wealth is on the rise, with a new millionaire, worldwide, every four minutes. All of this means you have an increased chance of marrying the Rich. Sure, many of them are already married, but face it, they keep getting recycled.

2. WHY SHOULD ANYONE CONSIDER MARRYING THE RICH?

Only 30.79 percent of income-producing men make over $35,000 in this country. Only 11.99% of income-producing women make over $35,000 a year.

It is practical to consider making your life better when you think of getting married. By marrying a Rich person, you are hoping to make your life better, not only emotionally, but also financially.

3. Isn't it primarily women who are interested in marrying the Rich?

In their report on what men and women find attractive about each other, the television magazine *American Journal* showed that men are more interested in money in a woman than women are in a man. A woman's wealth has an importance of 6% to men, whereas a man's wealth rates only 1% to women.

I do not know what the age range of their poll was, but I imagine it was a fairly young single set. Even so, I find it relevant that young men find the wealth of a woman important in her attractiveness.

In my twelve years of *How to Marry the Rich* seminars, I have watched male attendance rise to an average of 35% of the audience.

4. How important is age in marrying the Rich?

It is not important at all. A person's value, lovableness, and marriagability are not determined by how many times the earth goes around the sun.

A few years ago, a divorced woman who was about to turn sixty came to me for a consultation because she thought love would be over for her on her birthday.

I explained to her that age is just an excuse to hide behind, and pointed out all the assets she brought into a relationship at her age, plus how lovable she was whatever her age. I encouraged her—as I encourage you—to date as many people as possible; this elevates lovability, attractiveness, youthfulness.

In less than nine months, she met one of the wealthiest men in her part of the country. He was sixty-six years old and had just come out of a thirty-year marriage. He took her to Europe and the Orient, then bought her a new Lincoln Town Car. He settled her debts and paid off her house. A year and half later, they married—and she was sixty-two.

5. WHAT ABOUT LOVE? ISN'T IT IMPORTANT FOR MY MARRIAGE TO SOMEONE, EVEN IF THAT PERSON IS RICH?

My husband and I are completely in love with each other and happy together, so I believe that love is the ultimate gift. And it is the premise of this book that you are seeking love with a Rich mate.

At the same time, I believe there are many justifiable reasons to marry apart from love. Many older couples marry for companionship, which is not the love they felt for their deceased spouses, but is appropriate for their needs. Many younger couples marry to have children. Certainly, marrying to have children is nature's original purpose for marriage—procreation. It is also the purpose for most religious sanctions "to go forth and multiply." According to certain old texts, marriage originated as a property arrangement. It was a way to bind Rich families together and to increase or to protect property. Royal families have required bloodline and titles for marriages in order to keep countries unified.

If a 50-percent divorce rate is testament to the success of marriages for passionate love, perhaps we should look into the future with a more open mind about people who marry for other, justifiable reasons.

Basically, I think the following is necessary for a happy marriage to the Rich:

1. You must truly like the person.

2. You must respect the person.

3. The person must be kind.

4. The person must be generous-hearted.

5. Sex must be something you look forward to.

6. SHOULD I TAKE A RISK ON A PERSON WHO HAS BEEN RICH BEFORE BUT WHO NOW HAS NO MONEY?

Study the profile of Tip Roller. Usually, a person who has had the know-how to make money the first time can make it the second time. The question is, Can you stay with this person and not regret it, if money is not made?

7. WHAT IF A PERSON IS NOT RICH BUT HAS WEALTH POTENTIAL?

I think wealth potential is fine for a marriage mate. Potential is exciting, and the prospect of success together is part of the intimacy you enjoy.

Dreams are the lifeblood of a high achiever, and dreams keep romance alive in a marriage for years. But give yourself the following reality check, and if it all checks out, go for it!

1. What action is the person doing now to move toward the goals being espoused?

2. What qualifications does this person have for the career under discussion?

3. How many hours per day and per week does this person work toward achieving the goals?

4. How much television does the person watch?

5. How consumed by the goal is this person?

6. What else does the person talk about?

7. How intense is the person while working?

8. How much does the person drink/do drugs?

8. How can I know if the person is really Rich?

You can't. Things have changed a lot in the last ten years. You see, in spite of fears that no one has privacy anymore, the Rich are able to keep their true wealth secret in many ways.

They may use a license address that is not the address of where they live. They may not give home telephone numbers to anyone but family. And their money may be in foreign bank accounts so that you would think they have no money, when they have a great deal. An IRS Return may truthfully report very little personal income; yet valuable assets may be producing income for a separate corporation or corporations that are reported and paid to the IRS, but that you will never know about.

Peeping Tom background and credit checks do not tell you the full story about someone. Believe me, if the Rich don't want you to know how much they have, you won't know.

I think you should ask yourself, How generous is this person? Because it won't make any difference whether or not the person has any money if you don't get any of it.

Is the person generous with you? Is he or she reliable? Does the person keep his or her word? Is the person kind?

I would rather have a mate who is less Rich and more generous than one who is extraordinarily Rich and stingy.

9. I am well educated and recently met a Rich man who never finished junior high. I am attracted to him, but worry that it would be a mismatch.

Sometimes these differences are magic. One of the most magnetic couples I know is a female attorney who married an asphalt giant who never finished high school. They balance each other. She has the education he lacks; he has the money she lacks.

But it depends on what you want. If you want to be on the A-list of high society, this man may not make the grade—although with your education and if you have social savvy, that could happen.

If you don't care a hoot about the social A-list—you just want the freedom that comes from money—enjoy this man. Money is money.

10. WHAT IS THE DIFFERENCE IN THE MARRIAGABILITY OF A SELF-MADE MAN AND A RICH HEIR?

The self-made man marries faster than any man on the planet, of any economic level. He marries faster than poor men, middle-income men, and faster than heirs.

He may propose marriage on the first date, second date, or third date. I have dozens of stories of first-date marriage proposals from self-made men.

One woman, applying for a job, had just completed her interview with a Rich man when he said, "I have a better idea. Why don't you just marry me?" She did and they are still married after six years.

Interestingly enough, the longer a self-made man dates a woman, the less likely he is to marry her. I know a woman who lived with a Rich man for five years, thinking they were going to get married someday. While on a trip, he met another woman and married her in less than five days.

Marriage is important to a self-made man. He does not like the on-again/off-again instability of dating. It causes too many distractions from his moneymaking goals.

And that brings me to a drawback to most self-made men: they are high-absentee husbands, and it has nothing to do with you. They are so focused on making money, that they spend an incredible amount of time working. If you don't mind going to the opera alone or with women friends, this is the man for you.

11. WHAT DO YOU THINK ABOUT MIXED-RACE MARRIAGES?

I think it is the only true solution to racism. When we are all blood-related through children, we will see how foolish racism is.

12. HOW IMPORTANT IS WEIGHT FOR DATING A MILLIONAIRE?

Millionaires come in all sizes and shapes, too. A few of them will not be concerned with weight—their own or yours—although many of them will be.

I was invited to the wedding of a Rich widower who was marrying a woman who was considerably overweight. He was so thrilled that she was twenty-two years younger than he, that weight meant nothing to him.

Rich women are sometimes more picky on this subject than Rich men. They want their man to look good in his clothes (and out of his clothes). However, if a man has a lot of accomplishments or prestige, that will often compensate for a little heft.

Weight should not be a struggle between you and a mate; if it is, it may signal an unhealthy relationship.

Georgia lives with a wealthy man and suffers trying to please him with her weight. Every other month, she spends three weeks at a health spa losing weight. She goes back home to him and spends the next two months gaining weight. Then, back to the spa for three weeks. This seesaw cannot be good for her—and their relationship mirrors this tug-of-war. Believe me, the problem is deeper than her dress size.

13. I AM TERRIBLY ATTRACTED TO A WOMAN WHO IS FUN AND SEXY, BUT SHE HAS NO MONEY. MY FATHER WANTS ME TO MARRY A RICH WOMAN, BUT THE ONES I MEET BORE ME.

Money is not your hot button—and that's just fine. Marrying the Rich is only for those people whose hot button is money. Your hot button is fun and sexy.

Your father will not have to live with the person you marry, you will. Forget marrying the Rich. Go with your hot button.

14. WHAT SHOULD I DO IF THE RICH PERSON I MARRY GOES BROKE?

I consider this my strongest ethic: *I hope you will never abandon a mate who has defended you with his or her dollar or his or her name.*

If the relationship itself was over before the financial crisis occurs, I still urge you to see the person through the crisis. This is a person who loved you when you had nothing. Surely you can be a beacon of encouragement during the crisis, rather than just another rat leaving the sinking ship.

Once the crisis is past, you can move out of that person's life as discreetly as possible and try to do it in a spirit of friendship, if possible. If that is not possible, well, you have done your best, and you have seen that person through the crisis, like a champion.

If the relationship is good, but the thought of being without money frightens you, face the fact that business cycles can change the fortunes of anyone, including the Rich. Sometimes it has nothing to do with the person you marry.

During our fourteen years of marriage, Reed and I—like many people in the oil and gas industry—have experienced financial ups and downs, but I love Reed and could never leave him because of money losses.

However, don't stand by your mate if you think it will make him or her love you more, because it won't.

Napoleon Bonaparte, when exiled to Melba, was surprised to see one of his former wives (not Josephine) arrive, declaring her loyalty as she unpacked to live out exile with him. He called her a fool and told her he would never think more of her for doing it and would be disgusted that she thought so little of herself as to price her life so cheaply.

There are scores of men and women going through hard times who would never be that honest. They would be glad to have someone to comfort them as they suffer through their loses. But just as often, some of these people have reclaimed their fortunes and left behind the very person who stood beside them.

Don't feel angry just thinking of the unfairness of it. After all, if you stay with someone, you should do it because you want to and not to try to obligate the person to stay with you.

Accept responsibility for your decision. It is your choice to stay.

15. SHOULD I CHANGE MY RELIGION IN ORDER TO MARRY MY RM?

Wars have been fought over religion from the beginning of time, and they are still fought over religion—not only in undeveloped countries, but sometimes in the homes and marriages of educated, Rich people.

Be sure you and a mate can respect each other's faith differences if you decide to marry and not change faiths. And just as important, be sure you can live happily with a change of faith, before you do it.

One man in a mixed-religion marriage found that his Rich wife's adult children openly ridiculed the holy days of his religion even when his mother died and was being buried according to the laws of his faith. Worse yet, his wife laughed with them.

The disparity of faith does not seem as important during the "love can solve anything" phase of a relationship. But the longer two people are married, the more important that fundamental difference can become.

A person with deep spiritual beliefs who converts to another faith simply to get married may find guilt surfacing when the marriage runs into trouble, and may think God is punishing him or her. People who reach this point either have to convert back to their original beliefs to alleviate their pain, or divorce the spouse if that is not acceptable.

16. SHOULD I SPLIT THE COST OF A DATE WITH AN RM?

The most important reason for having an RM pay for the date is that it requires a conscious investment in you and in your time. A person needs to build equity into the relationship—and he or she will think twice before letting it go, just as with any other investment.

17. ISN'T IT BETTER IF I EARN MONEY MYSELF?

You can still earn it yourself—and probably faster. Marriage to the Rich does not prevent your being able to earn riches yourself, unless you marry someone who is opposed to it.

I refused to marry a Rich man whom I loved because he wanted me to abandon my own ambitions. These are his words: "If you want to help your daughter reach her goals, you'll have all my resources at your disposal; but as my wife, I want you to enter my social circle and shine. That is the only job you should have. And you'll never have to worry about money again."

My own parents were upset with me when I didn't marry him (in fact, I can't repeat what my dad said). And I would definitely have married him if he had not been afraid to compete with my goals. I also would have married him if he had come along at a different point in my life, when personal goals were not as important.

One of the reasons I am so happy with Reed is that he not only enjoys the variety of goals I have, but he does everything he can to help me achieve them.

$\mathcal{U}$ltimate Riches for Business, Friendship, or Romance

Wealth can change your life for the better or for the worse, depending on how anchored you are within yourself. If you have false ideas of what money can do for you, then attaining millions of dollars can be like giving a child a handgun to play with.

False ideas are usually based on low self-esteem. We all suffer bouts of it, sure; but, I am talking about the false notion that if you earn wealth, or if you become accepted in high society, or if you marry someone Rich that you will somehow become more worthy.

False ideas can also mean that you believe money will entitle you to do anything you want to without consequences.

In all my years of interacting with the Rich, I have noticed that those who are the happiest are those whose identities are not swept away by wealth. They have an anchor within themselves that cannot be influenced by the behavior of others with money. Typically this anchor contains the following:

• A spiritual faith in an all-abiding good that is greater than themselves

• A desire to live up to the moral code of their spiritual faith

• An unwillingness to participate in behavior that requires them to abandon the morality of their faith

Money can come and go in the tide of time, but if you have a spiritual anchor you will never be swept away by having Riches or by losing them. With a strong spiritual anchor, you will enjoy Riches when you have them and you will survive when you don't have them.

A spiritual anchor gives you ultimate Riches—for you will never lose you—and you are a special, unique gift to this world. Indeed, you will find that it really does not matter how Rich you become in business, or how many Rich friends you acquire, or how wonderful a person your Rich mate is.

All that really matters—with or without money—is the kind of person *you* are.